Scattered Africans Keep Coming:

A Case Study of Diaspora Missiology on Ghanaian Diaspora and Congregations in the USA

Yaw Attah Edu-Bekoe & Enoch Wan

Institute of Diaspora Studies – U.S.
Copyright © 2013 by Yaw Attah Edu-bekoe and IDS-USA @ Western Seminary

All rights reserved. No part of this work may be reproduced or transmitted in any form or by any means, electronics or mechanical, including photocopying and recording, without the prior permission of the publisher. The only exceptions are brief quotations in printed reviews.

This book is the second in a series on Diaspora Studies.

Published by the Institute of Diaspora Studies – USA
Western Seminary
5511 SE Hawthorne Blvd., Portland, OR 97215, USA

Scattered Africans Keep Coming:
A Case Study of Diaspora Missiology on Ghanaian Diaspora
and Congregations in the USA

Yaw Attah Edu-Bekoe & Enoch Wan

ISBN: 978-1484006184

For more information on IDS-U.S. at Western Seminary or Enoch Wan, please visit the following sites:

- www.Westernseminary.edu/diaspora
- www.enochwan.com
- www.GlobalMissiology.org

ACKNOWLEDGEMENT

FROM BOTH AUTHORS:
We are grateful for the kind assistance of two staff members of Western Seminary in format checking: Ms. Karen J. Arvin (the technical services librarian) and Mrs. Karen Hedinger (the Administrative Assistant of the Doctoral of Missiology Program).

FROM YAW ATTAH EDU-BEKOE
I want to express my appreciations to members of the PCG in the USA: Ms. Adwoa Debra-Dwamena (Atty.), Rev. Dr. Gyang-Duah (the USA PCG OMF chairperson) and his wife Gladys.

I am grateful to Stella Boye-Doe and her son Billy of Houston, TX, PCG for assistance during my field research in Houston and Ms. Boye-Doe for hosting me when I worked on the draft of this book. I am thankful to the following individuals for assistance of various kinds: Osei Yaw, Joe Stevenson's family, Very Rev. Kwaku Owusu of GEMC, Pastor Ato Pratt of VBC-I, Pastor Ntiamoah Sakah of CoP-I, Pastor Kofi Nelson-Owusu of PIC, Georgina and Edith of PCGNY, Paul Asiama and his wife of Chicago Bethel PCG, Opanyin Ofosu of GEMC, Ebenezer PCG, Bronx, NY, New Jersey PCG, Irvington, NJ, Bethel PCG, Chicago, IL, Cincinnati PCG, Cincinnati, OH, and Houston PCG, Houston, TX, and GEMC, Newark, NJ.

I want to acknowledge the leaders and the entire membership of all the USA GPC congregations, societies, and assemblies for being supportive of this study. I am also grateful to Casper Saupen (Librarian) and Catherine Cook Davis (Director of Students Relations and Senior Placement) of PTS who providentially helped me networking with Drs. Terry Burns, Enoch Wan, and Ken Epp at Western Seminary, Portland, OR.

Last but not least, I am grateful to my wife Tina, children and grand children for their support during my research for this book.

ABBREVIATIONS

BEMS:	Basel Evangelical Missionary Society
BPRC:	Bethel Presbyterian Reformed Church
CAC:	Christ Apostolic Church
CGPCNA	Conference of Ghanaian Presbyterian Churches in North America
CKPC:	Christ the King Presbyterian Church
CMS:	Children's Ministry Service
CMST:	Children's Ministry Service Teacher
CS:	Children's Service
CoP-I:	Church of Pentecost International
CP:	Church Planting
CPM:	Church Planting Movement
DO:	District Organizer
DVLP:	Diversity Visa Lottery Program.
EA:	Ethnic Association
EBKGC:	Embassy of the Blessed Kingdom of God Church
EMS:	Evangelical Missiological Society
ERP:	Economic Recovery Program
GA:	General Assembly
GEMC:	Ghana Emmanuel Methodist Church
GNA:	Ghana News Agency
GNC:	Ghana National Council
GPCs:	Ghanaian Protestant Churches
IDS:	Institute of Diaspora Studies.
IMF:	International Monetary Fund
JY:	Junior Youth
JYMS:	Junior Youth Ministry Service

KICC:	Kingsway International Christian Church
LBG:	Local Born Ghanaian
LCWE:	Lausanne Committee for World Evangelism
LDLT:	Lausanne Diaspora Leadership Team
LOP:	Lausanne Occasional Paper
ME-1:	Mission-Evangelism-1
ME-2:	Mission-Evangleism-2
ME-3:	Mission-Evangleism-3
NAMLC:	North American Mission Leaders' Conference
NCOGA:	National Council of Ghanaian Associations
OBG:	Overseas Born Ghanaian.
OMF:	Overseas Mission Field.
PAMSCAD	Program at Mitigating the Social Cost and Development
PCC:	Presbyterian Church of Canada
PCG:	Presbyterian Church of Ghana
PCGNY:	Presbyterian Church of Ghana in New York
PCUSA:	Presbyterian Church of United States of America
PIC:	Portland International Church
PNDC:	Provisional National Defense Council
PTS:	Princeton Theological Seminary
SAP:	Structural Adjustment Program
SUPFC:	Scottish United Presbyterian Free Church
TTS:	Trinity Theological Seminary
UGCC:	United Ghanaian Community Church
USA:	United States of America
WBRD:	World Bank for Reconstruction and Development
WMMM	World Migrant Mission Map
WWI:	World War I
VBC-I:	Victory Bible Church International
YAF:	Young Adults Fellowship
YMCA:	Young Men's Christian Association
YPG:	Young Peoples' Guild

TABLE OF CONTENTS

Part I — General Survey of African Diaspora and Ghanaian Diaspora in the Usa 1

Chapter 1 – Introduction 3

Chapter 2 – African Diaspora and Ghanaian Diaspora in the U.S. ... 9

Part II — "Diaspora Missiology" in Action: Ghanaian Diaspora in the U.S 44

Chapter 3 – Ghanaian Congregations in the Usa 45

Chapter 4 – Diversity, Identity and Receptivity of Ghanaian Diaspora in the USA 83

Chapter 5 – Leadership and Discipleship in USGPCS 113

Part III — Case Studies 147

Chapter 6 – Case Studies in Europe and the Usa 149

Chapter 7 – Conclusion and Recommendation 169

Appendices 189

Bibliography 205

Part I

GENERAL SURVEY OF AFRICAN DIASPORA AND GHANAIAN DIASPORA IN THE USA

"He did not say this on his own, but as the high priest that year he prophesied that Jesus would die for the Jewish nation, and not only for that nation but also for the scattered children of God, to bring them together and make them one" (John 11: 51-53).

Part One consists of the introduction which is made up of two chapters. They include the background, research methodology in chapter 1, and African and Ghananian diaspora in the USA in chpater 2.

Chapter 1
INTRODUCTION

BACKGROUND OF THIS BOOK

Diaspora—meaning scattered—is rooted in the Greek words dia and speiro. As Robin Cohen suggested, "The word 'diaspora' is derived from the Greek verb speiro (to sow) and the preposition dia (over). When applied to human beings the Greeks thought of diaspora as migration and colonization" (Cohen 2001: 1). Narry Santos separated the noun "diaspora" from the verb "diaspeiro." In a narrow sense, the noun diaspora "generally refers to the Jews living outside Palestine" (Santos 2004; Luis Pantoja et al. 2004: 53). In a broader sense, nonetheless, "the applicability of the use of diaspora has been widened to any religious or racial minority living within the territory of another religious or political society" (Santos 2004; Pantoja et al. 2004: 53).

Contemporarily, three major reasons have given rise to the study of diaspora missiology. First, diaspora mission is a viable and significant strategy for today's church in general. This is due to the fact that global migration has gone on from time immemorial, creating diaspora communities. Second, "traditional Protestant mission strategies appear land-locked with internal geographical focus. The global Protestant church needs to understand that the world has become borderless" (Enoch Wan, Western Seminary 2010 DIS 751K - lecture notes). Owing to easy travel and information technology, globalization has created a "global village" with missiological implications. Third, the global church needs strategies that will effectively reach millions who are traversing the globe (Enoch Wan, Western Seminary 2010 DIS 751K - lecture notes).

Ghanaian diaspora has contributed its quota through the Protestant churches in the United States of America (USA). Two Ghanaian scholars express the motives of diaspora Ghanaian evangelical Christians that are cited later. For Tom Marfo, God is gathering diaspora Ghanaians as Africans for His purpose of church planting (CP). Discussing Ghanaian churches in North

America, Wisdom Tettey also suggested that the church is mandated in obedience to practice and propagate what our Lord Jesus Christ has commanded. Tettey was describing the primary purpose of the Ghanaian Church of Pentecost International (COP-I). In effect, some diaspora Ghanaians consider themselves to have the obligation of carrying the gospel to all people around the world.

The USA Ghanaian Protestant Churches (GPCs) are responsive to the requirements of their congregants as they use the church as "soothing balm of Gilead" for their stressful physiological, psychological, and spiritual needs. This book seeks to uncover the connections between the biblical diaspora characteristics and the characteristics associated with the African diaspora, with two cases of African diaspora congregations in Europe and five Ghanaian diaspora churches planted in the USA.

Purpose of the Book

The purpose of this book is to provide an ethnographic description of Ghanaian Diaspora and Protestant congregations in the USA. This book on African diaspora is a "case study" of diaspora missiology in action. Two African diaspora congregations in Europe and five Ghanaian Presbyterian congregations in the USA are highlighted to showcase how "diaspora missiology" is strategically supplementary to the "traditional mission paradigm" in the new demographic reality of the 21st century.

Readership of the Book

This book is written for both general practitioners in Christian mission and researchers in diaspora missiology. There are "questions for discussion" at the end of each chapter for those who are looking for helpful guidelines in actual ministry to diaspora groups in other contexts outside of the USA. There are also resourceful material in the bibliography and appendixes for seminarians and researchers in diaspora missiology.

Organization of the Book

This book is organized in three parts. "Part One" is a general survey of Ghanaian Diaspora in the USA. "Part Two" is an in-depth study of "diaspora missiology" in action as illustrated in the Ghanaian diaspora and Presbyterian congregations in the USA. "Part Three" includes seven case studies: two African diaspora congregations in Europe and five Presbyterian Ghanaian congregations in the USA.

Two major considerations compose this African diaspora survey. The first consideration is an academic ethnographic description with regard to the distinctive markers of diversity, identity, and receptivity of the gospel in the multi-cultural USA society. The second consideration involves a practical missiological understanding of the formation, development, and mobilization for mission of the USA Ghanaian Protestant Churches. The research for this book was done in fourteen congregations of Presbyterian Church of Ghana (PCG), two Ghana Methodist (MCG), two Church of Pentecost (CoP), one Victory Bible (VBC-I), and one Portland International (PIC) churches. However, the five selected case studies include PCGNY, NY; Ghana Emmanuel Methodist; Church of Pentecost, Philadelphia, PA; Victory Bible (VBC-I); and Portland International (PIC) church.

The outcome is a survey made up of a three-part interdisciplinary approach: the content of the research, an ethnographic composition, and a practical missiological understanding in light of the formation, development, and mobilization for mission of the Ghanaian Protestant Churches (GPCs) in the USA.

RESEARCH METHODOLOGY AND DATA COLLECTION/INTERPRETATION

First, the research for this book considers how the Ghanaian diaspora has attempted to acquire and improve their language facility, cultural sensitivity, and relational competency in the multi-ethnic USA for missions.

Second, the research also seeks to find out how the Ghanaian diaspora has been motivated to engage in diaspora missions. This is with regard to inter-cultural and cross-cultural gospel communication and evangelization by networking to proclaim and develop activities for reaching the unreached in the USA and elsewhere. This is a slow and long process that began at the time of the inception of PIC.

Ethnographic Interview

The methodology of ethnographic research of this volume had been informed by two earlier publications: *The Ethnographic Interview* by James Spradley and *Writing Ethnographic Fieldnotes* by Robert Emerson, et al. Spradley suggested that "ethnographic interviewing involves two distinct but complementary processes: developing rapport and eliciting information" (1979:78). Field notes were taken during the time of participant observation and ethnographic interviews. Following the three basic essentials proposed by Emerson, et al. in *Writing Ethnographic Fieldnotes* (1995: 144), field notes were processed in the following order:

Reading Field Notes, Coding Field Notes, Initial Coding, Focus Coding, Memos of Field Notes, Initial Memos, and Integrative Memos

Sampling

Sampling is the choice of collecting workable data from a large population. As Thomas Schwandt stated, "Sampling are of three types—simple random sampling, more complex stratified sampling, and cluster sampling...A convenience sample may also be used—that is, a case is chosen simply because one was allowed access to that case" (2007: 271). The choice of samples is done as judiciously and carefully as possible in order to achieve an objective and authentic analysis from the four methods used. Figure 1.1 shows the representatives of the various identified groups being sampled.

Figure 1.1: Number of Indentified Groups Interviewed.

Identified Group	Number Interviewed	Number Sampled
Clergy (OBGs)	9	9
Caretakers (Untrained Leader OBGs)	5	5
Presbyters (Founding Leader OBGs)	15	8
Other OBGs	21	8
Youth: 1.5 2nd Generation OBGs	24	8
Youth: LBGs	12	7
Total	86	45

Convenience sampling of each identified group of interviewees was helpful for transcription and analysis. Since sampling was done on more than 50% of the total population, it was more than a fair representation.

Coding

Coding is the segmentation of a group of data to arrive at meaningful interpretation. Data gathered were coded and analyzed according to the six recurring themes: diversity, identity, receptivity of the gospel, and formation, development, and mobilization for mission. "Coding is the process of organizing the material into chunks or segments of text in order to develop a general meaning of each segment" (Creswell 2009:227). Thomas Schwandt also stated, "To begin the process of analyzing the large volume of data generated...Coding is a procedure that disaggregates the data, breaks them down into manageable segments, and identifies or names those segments" (2007: 32). Interviews were organized into clusters of six thematic markers as shown in Figure 1.1 above by using codes.

Reporting with Quotes

In *The Cultural Experience* by David McCurdy, et al., it is recommended for research students of ethnography to include three types of quotes of respondents in reports: opinion, explanation, and story quotes. Opinion quotes are opinions from respondents. Not all opinion quotes are relevant. However, "some opinions reflect cultural themes…and these can be used to support a point about the existence of the theme in an ethnographic report" (McCurdy, et al. 2005: 91, 92). Explanation quotes are those used to explain the themes as understood by the interviewees. Most of the explanations are interpreted after transcribing the recorded interviews. Sometimes, self-explanations are better than those of interviewees.

Since ethnographic research is descriptive, stories are informative and can go well with quotes. In this book, the respondents tell their own stories in a telling way, as articulated well in the quote below:

> "Stories are the best way we know of to illustrate points. Stories give an 'inside' feel to your ethnography and can often include contextual information that you don't have room to include in any other way" (McCurdy, et al. 2005: 92).

Six themes emerged from data collected and extensive use of quotes from informants had been included in the written report were included in various chapters of this book.

Validation

To validate the accuracy of the research findings, data collected were processed through the six-fold analyses including: Raw data, Organizing and preparing the data, Reading through all the data, Coding the data into themes, Description of interrelating themes and Descriptive interpretation of the meaning of the themes (Creswell 2009:185).

Themes gradually emerged in the process of data analysis to provide a framework for ethnographic description, with a focus on diaspora missiology.

SUMMARY

In this introductory chapter, matters related to the purpose, readership and organization, data gathering and data analysis of the book are succinctly presented, laying the foundation of basic understanding for the book.

QUESTIONS FOR DISCUSSION

1. How is this book on African diaspora acting as a "case study" of diaspora missiology in action?
2. How many African diaspora congregations in Europe and how many Ghanaian Presbyterian congregations in the USA are included in this study?
3. How many themes eventually had emerged that were presented in Chapter Two?
4. Can you keep in mind that many insights and operational principles are relevant to other diaspora communities in the USA?

Chapter 2
AFRICAN DIASPORA AND GHANAIAN DIASPORA IN THE U.S.

INTRODUCTION

This chapter will begin with an overview of global migration and the demographics of African diaspora in the USA, followed by a historical review of "when," "why and "how" Ghanaian diaspora left their homeland for the USA. A demographic survey will include matters of "where" and "how many" Ghanaian diaspora are found in the major cities in the USA.

This chapter will conclude with an ethnographic description of the various aspects of cultural legacy of Ghanaian diaspora. Included in this chapter are presentation of the gospel and culture encounter and engagement, characteristics of the Ghanaian diaspora, and the Ghanaian culture and the Christian faith.

THE UNITED STATES OF AMERICA AND GLOBAL MIGRATION

Owing to easy travel and information technology, globalization has converted the world into a "global village" with missiological implications. In 2010, the United Nations Population Agency (UNPA) estimated the world's population to be 6,908,688,000. However, by October 2011, the global human population had reached 7 billion. Demographers have rightly discovered a connection between the world's diaspora peoples and the general growth of populations. In addition, they have established a positive relationship between increase in global populations and migration.

Demographics of Global Migration

The 2008 World Migrant Mission Map (WMMM) informs scholars that the world's total migrant people had reached 200 million with 115 million out of this figure as migrant workers. In 2010, the world's migrant population was estimated by the U.N. to be 213,943,812. Out of this international migrant population, 7.6% representing 16,345,740 were global refugees. Figure 2.1 is an overview of the world's immigrant distribution.

Figure 2.1: 2008 World's Immigrant Distribution Chart

Continent	Immigrant Population
Europe	56,100,000
Asia	49,900,000
North America	41,858,500
Africa	16,300,000
Latin America	5,900,000
Oceania	5,413,500
Total	185,472,000

The highest recipient of immigrants is Europe (WMMM, 2008). While the Euro-Americas (the North or the West) continue to draw immigrants, the Southern continents (Asia, Africa, and Latin America) also keep supplying immigrant populations. Figure 2.2 reflects the global net immigrant populations by the highest ten countries.

Figure 2.2: Net Immigrant Populations of Some Major Nations (2005-2010)

Increase in Migration (+) More Immigrants than Emigrants (Immigrants>Emigrants)		Decrease in Migration (-) More Emigrant than Immigrants (Emigrants>Immigrants)	
Nation	Net Increase	Nation	Net Decrease
U.S.A.	4,955,000	India	-3,000,000
U.A.E.	3,077,000	Bangladesh	-2,908,000
Spain	2,250,000	Pakistan	-2,000,000
Italy	1,999,000	China	-1,884,000
Russian Federation	1,136,000	Mexico	-1,805,000
Australia	1,125,000	Indonesia	-1,293,000
Canada	1,098,000	Philippines	-1,233,000
Saudi Arabia	1,056,000	Zimbabwe	-900,000
United Kingdom	1,020,000	Peru	-725,000
Qatar	857,000	Morocco	-675,000

The African immigrant population outside the continent had reached 16.3 million in 2008. Interestingly the information indicates that while South Africa is the only African nation that received more immigrants than emigrants, Zimbabwe and Morocco had more people leaving than the immigrants they received. It also indicates that the USA is the highest recipient of immigrants.

The United States and Global Migration

The 2008 WMMM estimated the total population of the USA as 298,444,200 (Birgit Herppich 2011). Out of this, the number of immigrant people was 36,410,186; the number of migrant workers—persons who migrate into the USA from neighboring nations such as Mexico to work and go back—was 21,985,200. Among these numbers are 52% Protestants, 24% Roman Catholics, 2% Mormons, 1% Jewish, 1% Muslim, 10% other religious adherents, and 10% non-believers. By the estimations of the United Nations Population Department (UNPD), the number of international immigrants in the USA is 42,813,000 out of its population of 308,745,538 in 2010 (UNDESAPD 2011). This represents 13.8% of the USA total population. Meanwhile, the total estimated number of the world's global immigrant population is 213,944,000. Accordingly, about 20% of all diaspora peoples live in the USA. The trend over the last decade indicates that the foreign-born component of the USA population has kept increasing over the years. A 1996 study titled "The New Immigrant Survey" reveals that "as most of the source countries of immigrants in America are predominantly Christian, the numbers of Christians who arrive in America would only have increased. Figure 2.3 illustrates the estimated overseas-born (foreign-born) residents in the USA.

Figure 2.3: Estimated Foreign-Born Residents of the USA (2000-2010)

Agency	Foreign-Born	Total Population	% Population
2000 U.S. Census	28.4 million	281 million	10.4%
2009 ACS	38.5 million	307 million	12.5%
2010 UNPD (est.)	42.8 million	310 million	13.5%
2010 ACS	39,955,854 million (c. 40 m)	308,745,538	12.94%

Almost 65% of the "foreign-born" are Christians—Catholic 41.9% and Protestant 18.8 %" (Herppich, 2011). These figures include Africans.

SCATTERED AFRICANS KEEP COMING TO THE USA

Contemporary diaspora mission is a viable and significant strategy for today's church in general. This is due to the fact that global migration has gone on from time immemorial, creating diaspora communities (UNDESPD, 2011). Moreover, "traditional Protestant mission strategies appear land-locked with internal geographical focus. The global Protestant church needs to understand that the world has become borderless. Further, the global church needs strategies that will effectively reach millions who are traversing the globe" (Enoch Wan, 2011). Though African peoples have had long time connections with the USA since the 18th century trans-Atlantic slave trade, voluntary dispersion of Africans became significant during the 1980s. The eras of the 1970s and 1980s were epochal to many Africans. These were the periods for political instability, military coups, civil wars, socio-economic disruptions, and political refugees. With such "push" factors for migration, many Africans had no options but to move out, intensifying African global dispersion.

African Foreign-Born Diaspora by Region of Birth in the USA

Records through the USA census bureau reflect much on the African foreign-born in the USA. The demographic distribution indicates that African immigrants are progressively growing in the USA in the last twenty years. "From 1980 t0 2009 the African-born population in the USA grew from just under 200, 000 to almost 1.5 million. Today, Africans make up a small (3.9%) but growing share of the country's 38.5 million immigrants" (Kristin McCabe, 2011) <http/:www.migrationinformation.org> (May 22, 2012). Figure 2.4 is an illustration of this fact.

Figure 2.4: Estimates of African-Born Population in the USA

Year	1990	2000	2009	2010
Number	36,3819	881,300	1,502,163	1,606,914
% of Foreign-Born Population	1.84 %	2.80 %	3.90 %	4.02 %

The overall foreign-born estimate, out of the over 300 million Americans by the American Community Survey (ACS), is 39.96 million. Out of this figure, 1.62 million representing 4.02% is from Africa (Grieco and Trevelyan 2009; ACS 2010). Careful study of the figures indicates that most of these African immigrants come from West Africa. These estimates are used further to establish that West African immigrants are a progressively increasing percentage of African foreign-born in the USA (Herppich 2011;

<www.factfinder2. census.gov> (October 11, 2011). Figure 2.5 illustrates the regional estimates from Africa.

Figure 2.5: Estimates of Regional African Overseas-Born Immigrants in the USA

Year	Northern Africa	Southern Africa	Central Africa	Eastern Africa	Western Africa
1980	25,000	10,000	2,000	20,000	50,000
1990	10,000	15,000	5,000	50,000	100,000
2000	25,000	25,000	10,000	195,000	315,000

Another study of the demographics indicates that majority of the African diaspora in the USA was from Eastern and Western Africa. "In 2009, about two-thirds (64.7% or 965,330) of African immigrants in the USA were born in Western or Eastern Africa" (McCabe 2011). Over the years, this has been the trend. Figure 2.6 is an indication (McCabe 2011).

Figure 2.6: 1960–2009 African Immigrants in the USA by Region of Birth

Region	Number of Immigrants	% of African Immigrants
West Africa	542,023	36.3
East Africa	423,298	28.4
Northern Africa	264,536	17.7
Middle Africa	65,457	4.4
Other Areas	112,317	7.5

Records for individual national African demographic estimates are scanty in the USA census. The statistics in Figure 2.7 are some of the top nations of origin for African immigrants in the USA (McCabe 2011).

Figure 2.7: 2009 Top Nations of Origin for African Immigrants in the USA

Nation	Number of Immigrants	% of African Immigrants
Nigeria	209,908	14.1
Ethiopia	148,221	9.9
Egypt	138,194	9.3
Ghana	108,647	7.3
Kenya	87,267	5.8
South Africa	82,339	5.5
Liberia	72,111	4.8
Morocco	58,283	3.9
Sudan	35,821	2.4
Cape Verde	32, 885	2.2
Sierra Leone	32,467	2.2
Cameroon	30,726	2.1
Eritrea	23,840	1.6

In 2009, the top nations of origin for African immigrants included Nigeria, Ethiopia, Egypt, Ghana, and Kenya. Over the years these nationals have kept coming.

Size and Distribution of African Foreign-Born in the USA

Where are the Africns in the USA? Over one-third of all African immigrants resided in New York, California, Texas, and Maryland. McCabe stated,

> The first five states collectively accounted for 37.1% of all African immigrants. As of 2009, 47.7% of the 1.5 million African immigrants in the USA entered the nation in 2000 or later, and 28.8% entered between 1990 and 1999. Thus, more than three-fourths of the African born arrived in the USA in the last two decades. In terms of earlier arrivals, 13.7% entered between 1980 and 1989, 6.5% between 1970 and 1979, and just 3.2 prior to 1970. (2011)

Figure 2.8 illustrates where Africans usually move in America. It indicates the destinations or residences of the overseas-born African immigrants in the USA.

Figure 2.8: Some 2009 Resident Destinations of USA African Immigrants

State	Number of Immigrants	% of African-Born Population
New York	168,426	11.3
California	143,314	9.6
Texas	124,691	8.4
Maryland	117,315	7.9
New Jersey	79,420	5.3
Massachusetts	76,832	5.1
Georgia	75,692	5.1
Virginia	69,941	4.7
Minnesota	63,982	4.3

"Classes of admission for African immigrants who gained lawful permanent residence in 2010 were also diverse" (McCabe 2011; USA Census Bureau; 2009 ACS; 2000 Decimal Census; Department of Homeland Security's Office of Immigration Statistics). Figure 2.9 is representative of the lawful permanent resident Africans in the USA.

Figure 2.9: Lawful Permanent Resident Africans in the USA (2010)

Cause of Residence	Percentage
Family Relationships	48
Diversity Visa Lottery Program (DVLP)	24
Refugees and Asylum Seekers	22
Employment	5
Other Means	1
Total	**100**

As McCabe stated, "Compared to the foreign born overall, African immigrants reported higher levels of English proficiency and educational attainment in 2009, and were more likely to be of working age and to participate in the labor force. Yet, African immigrants were also more likely to be recent arrivals to the USA and to live in households with an annual income below the poverty line" (2011). Relatively, Africans represent a small part of all foreign-born immigrants. However, over the years the demographics indicate that the number of African-born immigrants has increased substantially over the past 50 years. "Though African immigrants represent only 0.4% of all the foreign born in 1960, this share grew to 1.4% in 1980, to 1.8% in 1990, and to 2.8% in 2000" (McCabe 2011).

HISTORY AND DEMOGRAPHICS OF GHANAIAN DIASPORA IN THE USA

Ghana has an estimated population of about 24.2 million according to the 2010 provisional population and housing census. The influx of Ghanaian immigrants to the USA since the 1960s has continued due to two major factors. The first are "push" factors in Ghana causing large-scale emigration for decades. The second are the "pull" factors in the USA with flourishing perceived opportunities that attract and pull Ghanaians.

Ghanaian Neo-Diaspora: Historical Perspectives of Coming to America

The trans-Atlantic slave trade that reached its zenith in the eighteenth century and the partitioning of Africa, both by Europeans, disrupted the socio-economic development of the African continent. For example, the slave trade forcibly transported almost 12 million Africans to foreign lands between 1450 and 1850. Micah Bump stated, "Of the 12 million approximately, 6.3 million slaves were West Africans and about 4.5 million of them were shipped to North and South America between 1701 and 1810. Estimates indicate that 5,000 a year were shipped for the Gold Coast (now Ghana) (2011;

<http//:www.immigrationinformation.org> May 22, 2012). Ghana's diaspora history in the USA can be divided into three major epochs: the pre-1980s, 1980-1990, and post-1990.

Pre-1980s Era: During the 1960s and 1970s, the number of Ghanaians who travelled to the USA trickled in lesser numbers. These were mostly students—people who travelled to America to take advantage of educational opportunities. Another group of the Ghanaian immigrants were people who travelled to join their spouses and relatives. These were smaller numbers.

1980–1990 Era: Ghana's migration history reached its zenith and a crisis in the 1980s epoch. "Beginning from the mid-1980s Ghanaians have constituted themselves into communities in Europe and North America, mainly in…large cities such as London, Amsterdam, Hamburg, Toronto, and New York" (Moses Biney 2011:13). In 1983, Nigerians expelled undocumented immigrants through an expulsion order reminiscent of the Ghanaian Alien Compliance Order of Ghana in 1970. The U.N. reported that approximately, 1.2 million Ghanaians were forced to return to their homeland under very traumatic circumstances., "A rapid result of this expulsion of non-indigenes of Nigeria was the changing of the migration order of West Africans and the expansion of the migratory view of Ghanaians to include other African regions, Europe, and North America" (Micah Bump 2011). The demographics indicated that "skilled workers and professionals dominated early flows from Ghana, but, by the 1980s, many semiskilled and unskilled workers chose to leave as well" (Micah Bump 2011).

Post–1990 Era: During this era, majority of Ghanaians emigrated in search of a higher social mobility. "Formal education has enabled Ghanaians to speak good English and has thus equipped them with an international language both for social and emigrational mobility while social education has furthered their ability to… adapt to new environments" (Gerrie Ter Haar 1998:136). Economic development and the labor market never matched educational development. The result is that massive unemployment continues to cause young people to look for employment outside Ghana. "The vast majority of these have emigrated in search of a higher standard of living. In many cases their immediate goal is to acquire the funds necessary to build a house back home in Ghana, to buy a car for export to Ghana, or to set up a private business which will then permit a sustained income" (Ter Haar 1998:132).

Demographics of Ghanaian Diaspora in the USA

Quoted below is a description of foreign-born Americans provided by the USA Census Bureau:

The term foreign-born to be people residing in the USA on census day who were not USA citizens at birth. The foreign-born population includes immigrants, legal nonimmigrants (e.g. refugees and persons on student or work visas), and persons illegally residing in the USA. By comparison, the term native refers to people residing in the USA who were USA citizens in one of three categories: (1) People born in of the 50 states and the District of Colombia; (2) People born in USA Insular Areas such as Puerto Rico or Guam; or (3) People who were born abroad to at least one parent who was a USA citizen (Bump 201; USA Census Bureau, Census 2000 Summary File 3; Migration Policy Institute (MPI) Data Hub. Migration Facts, Statistics, and Maps; <http//:www.migrationinformation.org>).

By the mid 1990s, it was estimated that between 2 and 4 million Ghanaians or 10 to 20 percent of Ghana's approximately 20 million people, were living abroad" (2011); <http//:www.migrationinformation.org> (May 22, 2012). Figure 2.10 is an illustration.

Figure 2.10: 2001 Main Countries of Residence for Ghanaian Immigrants

Nation	% of Ghanaian Immigrants
United States of America	17
Germany	14
Nigeria	10
Italy	9
United Kingdom	9
Other European Union Nations	10
Other Non-European Union Nations	31
Total	100

In Figure 2.10 (Micah Bump 2011), the main countries of destination and residence for Ghanaians are shown. Although Ghanaians continued to immigrate to other West African nations, greater numbers left the region than in the past. The Ghanaian population in the USA has "grown rapidly over the last decade and a half, particularly between 1990 and 2000, when the population jumped from 20,889 to 65,570 or 210%. Family reunification, refugee resettlement, and the strong American economy in the 1990s are the factors driving this increase…the foreign born from Ghana represented 0.2% of the USA' total foreign born population of 31.1%" (Micah Bump 2011). It is an open secret that the figures of Ghanaians in the USA are grossly underestimated. This issue comes up because of the question of un-documentation. "Many believe these figures to be undercounts and unofficial estimates reach as high as 300,000" (Bump 2011).

It is not surprising that majority of Ghanaian diaspora in the USA is from the working class. "As is characteristic of migrant populations, the majority of the Ghanaian population in the USA is of working age, and Ghanaian males slightly outnumbered their female counterparts in 2000" (Bump 2011). Figure

2.11 reflects on the age and sex distribution for Ghanaian-born population in the USA (Bump 2011; USA Census, Census 2000 Special Tabulation STP-159. Figure FBF-1 to 3: Profile of Selected Demographic and Social Characteristics: 2000 – Ghana); <http//:www.migrationinformation.org>.

Figure 2.11: 2000 Age and Sex Distribution of Ghanaian-Born in the USA

Age and Sex	Number	% of Ghanaian-Born
Total Population	65,570	100
Male	36,985	56.41
Female	28,585	43.59
Under 5 years	660	1.01
5 – 9 years	1,250	1.91
10 – 14 years	2,265	3.45
15 – 19 years	3,270	4.99
20 - 24 years	4,885	7.45
25 – 34 years	16,680	25.44
35 – 44 years	19,765	30.14
45 – 54 years	12,100	18.45
55 – 59 years	2,330	3.55
60 – 64 years	1,340	2.04
65 – 74 years	740	1.13
75 – 84 years	220	0.34
85 years and over	75	0.11

It is obvious from Figure 2.11 that the age groups that contributed the bulk of Ghanaians in the USA were between 25 and 54 years. They formed 74.03% of the Ghanaian population in the 2000 census. "Of the 281.4 million people in the USA, the foreign-born from Ghana accounted for less than 0.1% of the total population. The five states with the largest populations of foreign born from Ghana were New York, New Jersey, Maryland, Virginia, and Illinois. Combined, these five states constituted 60.7% of the total Ghanaian foreign born in the USA" (Micah Bump 2011). Figure 2.12 gives the information for the ten states with the largest Ghanaian foreign-born population in the USA in 2000 (Bump 2011; <http//:www.migrationinformation.org>).

Figure 2.12: Ten States with the Largest USA Ghanaian Foreign-Born

States	Number	% of Ghanaian Population
New York	16,813	25.6
New Jersey	7,079	10.8
Maryland	6,550	10.0
Virginia	5,956	9.1
Illinois	3,380	5.2
California	3,103	4.7
Texas	2,993	4.6
Massachusetts	2,985	4.6
Georgia	2,671	4.1
Ohio	1,602	2.4
Total	65,572	100

"Push" and "Pull" Factors of Ghanaian Diaspora

Seemingly favorable immigration conditions have contributed to the relatively massive exodus of Ghanaian diaspora. Both "push" and "pull" situations have had traumatic influences based on the diaspora Ghanaians' forced or voluntary ejection from their homeland. In certain situations, both of these factors operate at the same time. For instance, the Ghanaian medical field depicts a clear dynamic tension between the two factors. "The factors contributing to the flight of trained medical personnel from Ghana include low salary and remuneration, poor long-term career prospects, the low respect/value placed in health workers by the Ghana medical system...At the same time demand for doctors and nurses has increased in countries that do not produce enough of their own medical professionals" (Micah Bump 2011). Figure 2.13 summarizes the "push" and "pull" factors that compel Ghanaians to immigrate.

Figure 2.13: "Push" and "Pull" Factors of Ghanaian Diaspora

"Push" Factors	"Pull" Factors
Political Instability: Military interventions; political dictators, and political refugees	The "Bright Western Life" Syndrome: Modern "civilized" Euro-American world
The "Gloomy Home Life": Socio-economic difficulties; poverty, hunger, squalor	Globalization: The universal emphasis of movement of people
Human Resource Development: Greater quality education; Ghanaians speak the best English in Africa. Communication is not difficult for them in the USA, for instance	Attractive USA Immigration Policies: Diversity Visa Lottery Program (DVLP) In recent years this has been the major "pull" factor
The Search for "Greener Pastures": The adventurous immigrate, searching for "greener pastures"	The "Burger" Syndrome: The quest to be like the others

One major "pull" factor is attractive USA immigration policies. This was the opening up of the "floodgates" through the Diversity Visa Lottery Program (DVLP). Moses Biney stated, "Since the passing of the Immigration Act of 1990, which created the Diversity Visa Program, a larger number of Ghanaians have been admitted as legal permanent residents into the United States. Between 1991 and 2001, for instance, 30,669 Ghanaian immigrants were admitted legally into the country" (2011:12). There has been a categorical USA official attempt to attract Ghanaians into the American economy since the 1990s. A reference in a Ghana News Agency (GNA) report stated,

> "Chief of the Consular Section…explained that the D Visa Lottery programme was instituted by the U.S. government to give opportunity to non-Americans…to become American citizens by choice and in Ghana about 7,000 winners were declared in the previous entry, which indicated a lead in the winning race worldwide (GNA 2009).

Yet, in another instance Operation World 2010 records the 2010 Diversity Visa allotment for Ghanaians as 8,752 (Operation World 2010).

Rick Calenberg observed, "There is a serious misconception about life in the USA which makes it appear to be 'heaven on earth'…for diaspora Africans coming to America, major cultural, familial, and spiritual problems lurk…there are Africans who lament having 'won the lottery' and long for the simplicity of life at home in Africa" (2010: 1). Most Ghanaian immigrants do become disillusioned due to the harsh socio-economic conditions they face in the USA upon arrival. On their arrival at their destinations in America, apart from the stressful documentation, settlement, and job securing issues, the Ghanaian diaspora is faced with diversity, identity, and receptivity of the gospel challenges.

Immigration Process for Diaspora Ghanaian Christians

Ghanaians are perceived as the most travelled in the West African sub-region, spread all over the globe. Gerrie ter Haar confirmed, "Of all West Africans, Ghanaians constitute by far the largest migrant community in Europe…In 1997, unofficial sources often suggested that as much as a quarter of the total sixteen million…may have emigrated" (1998:132). With regard to ultimate results Margaret Peil also posited that "Ghana is only one of the economies in the world which depend on the earnings of emigrants. The Ghanaian housing industry in particular is believed to be largely dependent on overseas remittances" (2007: 359). In 2008, the President of Ghana reiterated this point by stating that the diaspora remittances into the Ghanaian economy had reached about $4 billion in 2007 (<www.ghanaweb.com > March 5, 2011). The former brain drain situation has been turned into current brain gain.

Jacqueline Hagan and Helen Ebaugh provided a schema for the process of immigration suggesting that Ghanaians use religion at all stages (Hagan and Ebaugh 2003:1145-1162). As a comparison with Wisdom Tettey's summation (2007; Olupona and Gemignani 2007:132), the schema for immigration is generic in time and space. Ghanaians go through them like most diaspora Africans, to immigrate to the USA. *Operation World* 2010 estimated, "Some 47% of Ghana's educated citizens live abroad. United States is the primary destination. From 1996 to 2001 Ghanaian immigrants in the USA quadrupled to from 24,000 to 97,000...Most of these Ghanaian immigrants are in the major metropolitan areas in America" (*Operation World* 2010). In agreement with other scholars, Birgit Herppich stated, "African immigrants in America are a growing minority of missiological significance...More than 75% arrived after 1990 [almost half after 2000]...Better proficiency in English, education and employment than others. They originate from countries with rapidly growing vibrant Christianity. They have already planted numerous churches in the U.S." (Herppich 2011).

Diaspora Ghanaians travel with their religion. A majority of these immigrants are Christians who move with their type of African Christianity into Euro-America. Because the "African is notoriously religious" (John Mbiti 1969:1), diaspora OBGs carry their religion "on them like their skins" (Peter Sarpong 2008) or their passports and visas everywhere. A majority of these immigrants are Christians who move with their type of African Christianity into Europe and America. Consequently, they wish to be identified both as true Christians as well as true Africans. Figure 2.14 provides the stages of the process of immigration for Ghanaians.

Figure 2.14: Stages of Immigration Process of Ghanaians into the Diaspora

Stages	Jacqueline Hagan & Helen Ebaugh	Wisdom Tettey
1	Making the decision to migrate	Contact of priest for prayer about journey
2	Preparing to travel	Formal congregational prayer for spiritual needs
3	Making the journey	Interregnum between departure and arrival: Migrants relying on spiritual support of their religious leaders of home communities
4	Arriving at the destination	Migrants make contact with their home pastor from destination
5	Joining an ethnic church	Joining ethnic church with an established congregation
6	Developing transnational linkages	Transnational linkages between migrant and ethnic church and worship communities in home nation

ETHNOGRAPHIC DESCRIPTION OF GHANAIAN DIASPORA IN THE USA

Ghana is composed of several ethnicities that have had diaspora experiences. They include the *Akan, Guan, Mole-Dagomba, Ewe, Nzema,* and *Ga-Adangme,* among others with the various cultures. The choice of the *Akan* for this book is informed by its prominence. In the Ghanaian diaspora, the various generations are inherently developed differently.

Ethnographic Description of Ghanaian (*Akan*) Cultural Legacy

Out of all creation only humanity experiences culture. The only generation which is sometimes fully connected with its traditional culture is the OBGs. They generally exhibit the cultural values that they carry to the diaspora. Adapted from Wan's theology of Asian cultures, Figure 2.15 is representative of the cultural and moral values of the OBGs in the USA.

Figure 2.15: The Cultural and Morality Values of the OBGs

Category	Description
Cognition and Emotional	Humility: Ghanaians are gentle; modestly aggressive; peaceful. Honor: Proud in morality and integrity Shame: Guilt manifested when wrong; frown on sin; evil Overtly show no pain—glad to make sacrifices
Interpersonal Relationships	Community: Tribal and extended family first, before self. Sharing: Everything belongs to others; e.g. mother-earth is for all Respect; Honor: for elderly—do not criticize elders Acceptance: Good from all others but despise evil; chastise the bad Children: Gift from God; shared with others
Religion	Religion is supreme and relevant, transcends every aspect of life Medicines should be from natural herbs, as gifts from God & earth
Learning	Learning through legends: Past great stories remembered – source of knowledge; wisdom Mother-tongue aspirations: Cherish own language; speak it whenever possible *Sankofa*: Return to traditional ways; values—old ways; values are best; have been proven. (See symbol three in chapter 5)
Socio-Cultural	Land is precious: orient self to land Diligence: live with hands—hard work is sacred Leave things natural

What Is the Culture of a People Group?

Culture is simply the totality of the way of life of a people group. Culture is both intrinsic and extrinsic. Intrinsically, culture involves the cognitive expression of attitudes, values, norms, beliefs, and worldview of a people group such as the *Akan*. The extrinsic nature of culture involves the clothing styles, kinds of food and drink, material artifacts created, and some external traits such as handshake. Edward Tylor stated that culture is "that complex whole which includes knowledge, belief...and any other capabilities and habits acquired by man as a member of society" (1871: 1). Culture, "therefore, provides the models of reality that govern our perception, although we are likely to be unaware of the influence of these models on us" (Charles Kraft 1979: 37-39). For Lingenfelter and Mayers, "Culture is the conceptual design...by which people order their lives, interpret their experiences, and evaluate others...rules, and values are specific to each socially defined context" (2003: 18).

These descriptions indicate that culture and cultural anthropology involve complexities which are most important in a missiological study. Studying culture in missiology should be tested to see whether it is scripturally founded and theologically sound. Here, biblical absolutism and ethno-theology become relevant. Basically, biblical absolutism should be considered supreme in the field of mission because a connection should always be found between Scripture and culture. Cultural relativism "proposes that as people in another society are studied [their] moral and aesthetic ideas must not be evaluated by the norms of the observer's own culture, but must instead be understood and appreciated in their cultural context" (Norman Allison 1996: 36). In missiological study, cultural relativism should complement biblical absolutism for an obvious balance in objectivity. In the discussion of Ghanaian diaspora, it is useful as a reminder that the African is inherently and "notoriously religious" (John Mbiti 1969: 1).

Akan Culture: The Worldview and African Traditional Religion (ATR)

Robin Horton developed a model (i.e. "intellectualist" or "cognitive") for interpreting religious change in modern Africa. According to his theory, there is a two- tier pattern of African cosmology (Horton 1971: 91-112). Level one is microcosmic, where devotion to divinities exists. Activities of adherents who often lack formal education are underpinned by localized events and processes. Level two is macrocosmic. Adherents support the idea of the Supreme Being whose relationship with humanity is underpinned by universal events and processes. With these two levels, a center-periphery analysis was developed.

On one hand, at the first microcosmic level, the deities are prominent and are shifted into the center of adherence. The Supreme Being is relegated to the periphery. Ancestral, deity, and natural spirits occupying marine bodies, rocks, trees, and forests operate at this level. On the other hand, at the second macrocosmic level, knowledge and adherence to the Supreme Being is moved to the center while the deities are shifted to the periphery. Adherents include the educated, the socio-economically well-to-do, and urbanized people.

COMPOSITION OF THE *AKAN* COSMOLOGY

Five distinctive markers of ATR compose the *Akan* cosmology: God, ancestors, deities, myriad spirits, and land. A basic human explanation can illustrate the *Akan* cosmology and worldview in Figure 2.16.

The idea of the Figure 2.16 has been adapted to critique Paul Hiebert, et al., when they stated that Africans worship high God and low God. From an emic perspective, there are a few caveats with this figure. For instance, their use of the designation high God and low God—all with the capital "G" is problematic (Hiebert et al. 1999: 81; Wan and Edu-Bekoe 2011; Moreau and Snodderly 2011: 38).

Using Horton's intellectualist analysis the *Akan* traditional cosmology can generally be placed in a hierarchical order. Offering of libation illustrates the *Akan* cosmology. *Akans* use the offering of libation as traditional prayer. The composition of such prayer includes invocation, petition, and doxology. Its invocation and doxology are provided here:

Otumfuo Onyankopon Kwame, nsa;	Saturday born Almighty God, a drink;
Asaase Yaa Obeatan, nsa;	Thursday born mother earth, a drink;
Yen Nenanom nsamanfo, nsa;	our ancestors, a drink;
Abosom ahorow, nsa; etc…	various deities, a drink; etc…
Ye dome obiara a ompe yen	anyone who wills this
Abusua yi ye. Ye fre nananom	family ill is cursed. We call on you
Nsamanfo, yen abosom, ne	ancestral elders, our gods, and
Ahonhom se womfa apranaa	spirits to strike such a person
nkum no.	with thunder.

Akan Christians have caveats with such a traditional prayer. First, after the invocation of the Almighty, Creator, and Providential God, there is no need to call on the others in the pantheon. Second, the doxology is too vindictive. Christians are called to love their enemies and pray for them. In addition, forgiveness is a virtuous and valuable cornerstone in the Christian faith. To call for the killing of one's enemies with thunder is untenable. This may be found in parts of the Old Testament, though. However, with Christ, forgiveness is a new and different covenant dispensation for the Christian faith.

Figure 2.16: The Ghanaian (Akan) Cosmology and Worldview

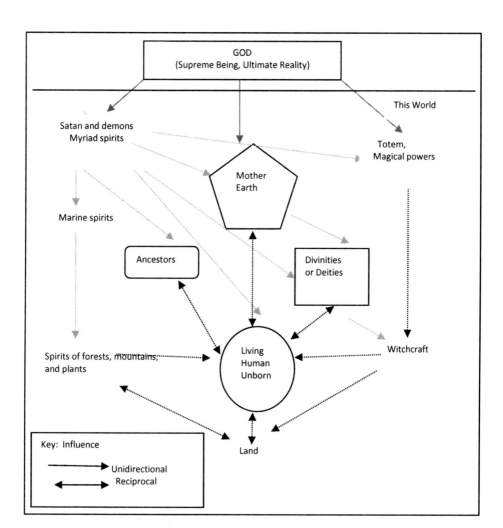

COMPOSITION OF THE AKAN COSMOLOGY

The composition of Akan cosmology is constituted by five distinctive markers of ATR: God, ancestors, deities, myriad spirits, and land. Some scholars include human beings but the separation of the human being is convenient for discussion.

God—Ultimate Reality

For the Akan, there is no high and low God as posited about African religion by Paul Hiebert, et al. God is God and the Ultimate Reality, the incomparable Supreme Being. God's elevation is appropriate because of His attributes. God's attributes include

Otumfoo Nyame (Omnipotent God),
Owo Baabiara Nyame (Omnipresent God),
Onimde Nyame (Omniscient God). Others are:
Tetekwaforamoa Nyame (An Ancient to Ancient God),
Ototrobonsu; oboo asu boo awia Nyame (Creator God who created rain and sun),
Ahumobo Nyame (Compassionate God), and
Abawmubuafre Nyame (God upon whom one calls in one's experience of distress—the Dependable God).

These attributes are exclusive to God. The evil, capricious and vengeful others in the cosmology do not share these attributes with God. The Akan concept of the attributes of God is similar to those of Christians. However, the Christian doctrine separates the essential attributes of God which are not shared from the moral attributes which are shared by humanity.

Ancestors—the Living-Dead

The most important link between the world of the spirits and the living Akan is the ancestral cult. Akan life is cyclical, making ancestors keep their eyes on whatever happens in the physical world. Do the Akan worship the ancestors—"the living-dead"? Two schools of thought exist about this issue. Some scholars, mostly from the etic missionary perspective, contend that adherents of ATR worship the ancestors. Akan ancestral cultic secrecy is factual. Community or family leaders do perform secret rituals during festivals and other occasions. These rituals are performed to appease the ancestors. The secret cultic rituals usually culminate in slaughtering animals for blood purification, "feeding" dead ancestors, offering libations, and cleansing stools. A stool is the authoritative throne of office of the king or chief. It is a carved wooden seat on which the ruler sits. For the ancestral cult, each dead ruler has a stool that is stored for remembrance and inheritance. Stool names are chosen through the selection of the stool of a former ruler. Some of these rituals are done in stool rooms where the majority of the people are not participants. Thus, the perception of these scholars is that festivals are anniversaries for Akan ancestral worship. This is the foundation for the speculation of ancestral worship.

Conversely, some other scholars from the emic perspective contend against the notion of ancestral worship. Their contention is that the "worship" argument has been presented mostly by non-African or Western scholars over the years. First, only God, the Ultimate Reality is worshipped. Thus, at best, the description of the relationship between the living and the "living-dead" is that of ancestral veneration, not worship. Second, ancestral belief is universal. The point is that since the main issue is associated with veneration, the question of how to factor the ancestors into African Christianity is the challenge.

Divinities

The divinities or deities include idols, totems, amulets, and magical powers. Linguistically, the deities or lesser gods are no gods at all. They are called abosom. Etymologically, abo means stones and som means worship. Thus, those involved with them are worshiping stones, woods, and carvings not Onyankopon—Almighty God. The Akan traditionalists consider these deities personified as "children of God" or "linguists" through whom humanity can communicate with God. Traditionally, just as members of the community communicate to kings and chiefs indirectly through akyeame—linguists—deities serve as "linguists" of Almighty God. The liaison between the deities and humanity is the okomfo (diviner or traditional priest).

Definitely, only God deserves human worship. This Akan idea about the divinities as idols is reminiscent of Hezekiah's prophetic prayer "You are God, You alone…and have cast their gods into the fire; for they are not gods, but work of men's hands—wood and stone…Save us…that all the kingdoms of the earth may know that you are the Lord God, You alone" (2 Kings 19:15-19).

Myriad Spirits

In their diagram Hiebert and colleagues put animal, plants, and the land together, suggesting that they belong to one category in the pantheon (1999: 81). This lumping of animals, plants, and land in the pantheon might be problematic for some Akan scholars. They are animate and inanimate objects created by God to be respected, tilled, and used. Plants and animals are God's (mother earth's or natural) provisions for food and medicines.

For the Akan, the spirits which possess or indwell these creations of God are considered as part of the pantheon, not the physical animals and plants. Kofi Asare Opoku described these natural spirits as "totemism, extra-sensory spirits, and protective objects…Some African societies…regard animals and plants as emblems of hereditary relationship. That is …totemism…Among them are agents of witchcraft, magic, and sorcery…There are charms, amulets and talismans which the Akans of Ghana call suman" (1978: 10). Opoku further suggested that they are used for both defensive (protective) and offensive purposes. Operating through these myriad spirits to influence all others within the pantheon are Satan and his demons. Thus, in this physical world they operate as marine, mountain, forest, animal, and plant spirits, ghosts, witches, and wizards.

Land

The land in its created earthly form is next to God as asaase Yaa (Thursday-born mother earth). Land is used for production of food for humanity. Land is personified as providential "mother earth" who feeds her children. It also serves as the hiding place for dead human bodies. The Akan believe that there is life hereafter. The Akan dead is "hidden" in the community land (graveyard) for life after death. The Akan term for cemetery or graveyard is amusiei. Etymologically, amu means dead body and siei means hiding place. Therefore, amusei means hiding place for dead bodies.

For both the individual and community the above composition of the cosmology influences the religiosity and worldview of the people. Cultural relativity culminates in recognizing the different worldviews of the tribes in Ghana, though their worldviews might have similarities. Likewise, the worldview of the Ghanaian diaspora is different from the worldview of Euro-Americans.

HUMAN BEINGS, FAMILY, AND KINSHIP SYSTEMS

The human is specially created. For the enjoyment of God's handiwork, both the human being and culture were created. Therefore, only humanity experiences culture. Within the Akan cosmology, the separation of human being for an ethnographic description is useful because the human being is a living being influenced by the others.

The Person

For the Akan, the person is a combination of onipa honam (human body), okra (soul), and honhom (spirit). The person is dead whenever the soul and spirit are separated from the body. Since the soul and spirit are not tangible, understanding their separation from the body is difficult. Depending on a person's good life and morality, the soul and spirit join the communion of ancestors or ancestral "hall of fame." "The Akan believe that the composite parts of the human person are the okra (soul) and sunsum (spirit), which are immaterial or spiritual, and honam or nnipadua (body), which are material or physical" (Biney 2011: 60).

As Fig 5.1 indicated, the living human being is caught up in the middle of all the events in the Akan cosmology. The spiritual, physiological, cognitive, and religious orientations of the Akan person are impacted by the entire composition of the cosmology. Such orientations have had a strong impact on the worldview including that of diaspora Ghanaians.

The Family System

For the Akan, each individual belongs to a family made up of the living, the living-dead, and the yet unborn. The family is both nuclear and extended. The extended family is close-knit and empathy is very endemic. For example, when there is a problem, family members meet together to assess the situation in order to find a solution. John Waliggo discussed "prominent family qualities of the Buganda of Uganda" (Waliggo 1977; Mugambi ed., 1977: 122-124) which are similar to that of the Akan. For instance, unity is the foremost concern of the family. The sense of belonging and togetherness extends from the clan down to the family. Family unity is promoted through participating in various common activities: sharing talents, giving material gifts to each other, and showing respect for everyone. Joys and sorrows are jointly shared by all family members. Building relationships is another important qualitative characteristic in the family. Members strive to know each other. Relatives exhibit neighborliness and friendship. In moments of joy and sadness relatives or family members and neighbors are usually the first to hear.

There is greater fellowship in the Akan family system. No human individual is an island unto himself/herself. Thus, everyone is supposed to be one another's keeper and one-otherness is the cynosure of cohesive society. Biblically, the symbol of the family is not farfetched. "The 'family' is a biblical metaphor (Hos.1:1-3; Gal. 4:5). This emerges from the basic vision of the community of faith. There are enough 'kinship' shared values among themselves in actual practice" (Robert Kysar 1999: 39). Kysar's suggestion is helpful because it reflects on the connection and resonance of Scripture and Akan family values.

The Akan family inheritance system is matrilineal. Such a family is traced through a matriarch whose line runs through the female members. A child belongs to the family of the mother. In this system, the eldest maternal uncle is responsible for the child's upkeep and nurture. A network of cousins is, therefore, important. An Akan proverb states abofra se n'agya nanso owo abusua. To wit, despite the resemblance of a child of its father, it is for the family.

The Kinship System

Within the Akan kinship and clan relationships are particular associations of the extended family. "Kinship is more than a network of biological relationships; it is also a network of social relationships. It establishes social ties, patterns of behavior, obligations and responsibilities, and patterns of authority. In short, it is a, 'road map' or structure of interpersonal relationships" (Grunlan and Mayers 1988: 162). Grunlan and Mayers suggested the basis of kinship and identified three types of kinship relationships:

- Affinal Ties—kinship relationships tied together by marital bonds.

- Consanguine Ties—kinship relationships tied together by biological relationships, that is, by 'blood.'

- Fictive Ties—kinship relationship in which a person is legally, ceremonially, or religiously tied to the kinship network. It is a 'socio-legal' relationship such as that of adoption (1988: 162).

The role of kinship includes understanding of the clan system, relationships built through marriage, socialization, social security, decent regulations, social control, and inheritance systems. Awareness of this Akan family and kinship systems helps to develop Ghanaian diaspora discourse in missiology. Every member of the Ghanaian diaspora in the USA continues to be influenced and strongly impacted by such a family and kinship systems. For example, while members of the Ghanaian diaspora struggle with their immediate families, other members of their extended families in Ghana call them to make both practicable and impracticable material demands.

AKAN RITES OF PASSAGE

The major signposts for human physiological development are universally similar. However, the rites of passage associated with these signposts are different in various cultures. The Akan have various rites for birth, marriage, and death, three of these signposts. Though the Akan is used as an example, all the other African and Ghanaian tribes celebrate these rites of passage and others that are not celebrated by the Akan. While puberty rites are defunct with the Akan—where they have been replaced by the Christian confirmation—they are performed by some other tribes. For instance, the Krobos of the Ga-Adangme perform the dipo as puberty rite for girls.

Celebration of Life—Rite for Birth

The foremost rite of passage is associated with birth. While fertility is of utmost importance, infertility is abominable. The arrival of a newborn baby is a joyous occasion. A person's name perpetuates ancestral continuation. Cyril Okorocha stated, "A name is supreme for the continuation of one's ancestry….Thus, continuation of one's good name is close to the heart…the desire for continuity is manifested in…desire to be like others anchored in God's gift of children" (1987: 205). Similar sentiments are shared by the Akan. Obadinto (naming ceremony) is, thus, very important.

The Akan believe that human development starts from giving a name to the child during its outdooring. Noel Smith described, "The outdooring ceremony…follows the pattern described…Libation is sometimes poured and prayers are sometimes addressed to the forefathers even though some Christians think the prayer should go to God instead of the ancestors" (1966: 250). "Outdooring" is the first trip outdoors by the newly nursing mother and her baby on the eighth day after its birth for the naming ceremony. With the reality of diversity in the USA, obadinto, or "outdooring" is a strange culture. However, one significant cultural heritage performed by all diaspora Ghanaians is "outdooring." Adaptations from the USA host culture in addition to this naming ceremony are "baby shower" prior to the baby's birth and "godfather and godmother" system after birth.

Celebration of Relationship—Rite for Marriage

In adulthood, the second important signpost is marriage and rites associated with it. Right from the beginning of marriage of two persons a different relationship is built. Unlike the USA, Ghanaian marriage rite is partially a celebration of a relationship between two families contracted through a matured male and female. No same-sex marriage exists in the Akan culture. The Akan allow traditional polygamous marriages. The foregoing description is the traditional marriage without which, incidentally, no Christian marriage can be contracted. For Christians, after this customary marriage, a wedding is organized later for God's blessings in the church.

Since one cannot marry from one's own clan, the coming together of two lovers cements a close bond between two families where a matrimonial relationship is built. "Marriage is a social institution, that is, a pattern of norms and customs that define and control the relationship between a man and a woman and the relationship between them and the rest of society" (Grulan and Mayers 1988: 147). Mercy Oduyoye contended, "The marriage ritual is one of bonding—the physical bonding of two individuals as sexual partners and the covenant bonding of two families" (2004: 81). At the ceremony of marriage agreement at an appointed time, negotiations ensue, the bride price is paid, and the husband is allowed to take his wife home to start a new nuclear family. For some feminist Akan scholars, "Marriage simply transfers the Akan woman from one suzerain (her uncle) to another (her husband)…she provides children to the one (her matrilineal family)" (Oduyoye 1995: 134, 135). The positive thing is that USA Ghanaians (Africans) in the diaspora keep performing these marital rites both home and abroad. Family members are then informed about these "foreign" marriages.

Celebration of Death—Rite for Funeral

The final rite of passage for the Akan is associated with the funeral. Death is inevitable to human life. If a befitting funeral is denied a dead relative it exhibits a manifestation of an unacceptable behavior of the Akan living relatives. Every person deserves a decent burial at which the living bid the dead a fitting final farewell. This is in order to avoid ancestral curses. Rather, ancestral blessing on the living is the focus. Until a possible future encounter, the living should have their peace while the dead have their blissful rest.

Akan communal life demands that the whole society be involved with a funeral. To join one's ancestors, every Akan dead body should be buried in one's hometown. The rites associated with death are performed by the Ghanaian diaspora in America. Customarily, activities are done by representatives in the absence of biological parents and their families. Reports are then sent to the families back home in Ghana.

CULTURAL SYMBOLISM

A relevant Akan cultural legacy is symbolism, the use of pictorial signs, emblems, and symbols to depict hidden meanings and to facilitate easy learning. "Christian symbolism is the use of signs and emblems to teach and present religious truths. Words often fail where symbolism succeeds… Christian symbolism…adds a certain beauty and mysticism to religion, speaking as it does of an unseen world and supernatural faith" (Clifton Clarke 2006: 58). Ablade Glover depicts examples of some of the good symbols in the Adinkra and linguist staff. Glover provided the history behind the Adinkra by stating, "Tradition has it that Adinkra, a famous king of Gyaman (now Ivory Coast), angered the Asantehene…by trying to copy the Golden Stool. Adinkra was defeated and slain in an ensuing war...the art of Adinkra came from Gyaman...Adinkra means farewell or good bye...on funeral occasions (ayie), to say goodbye to the departed" (Glover 1992).

Three of these Akan symbols are selected for illustration.

Gye Nyame (Except God)

God is sovereign. An Akan proverb says, "Wonsan kokroboti ho mmo pow;" to wit, the thumb is essential in making a knot. Christ told believers that without Him we can do nothing. To the Akan so is God. God is indispensable.

Nsa Kura Nkesua (A Hand Holds an Egg)

The meaning is that "power is like an egg. A successful ruler should be both firm and sympathetic" (Glover 1992). Leadership—traditional, political, or ecclesiastical—can learn from this meaningful wise and powerful saying. Power is so delicate. If it is held too tightly it might break. If it is held loosely and falls it will still break. Power should, accordingly, be handled with care just like the delicate egg.

Sankofa (A Bird Signifying Returning to Take)

An Akan proverb can explain this symbol. "Se wo were fi ade na wo san kofa a wonkyi." To wit, it is "no taboo to return to fetch something that is forgotten. You can always correct your mistakes" (Glover 1992). This can teach some diaspora Ghanaians who seem to lose their identity, culture, and moral values to look back in search for them.

Symbolism reveals rich Akan cultural values. Other examples of the numerous symbols of the Adinkra and linguist staff include Bribi Wo Soro; enti Onyame ma me nsa nka—something is in heaven; so God give it to me and Nyame Nwu na Mawu—God never dies for me to die, among others. These symbols can help teach the attributes of God and the appropriation of wisdom found in them to practice morality.

CHARACTERISTICS OF GHANAIAN DIASPORA IN THE USA

Ted Rubesh discusses seven distinctive characteristics for the Jewish diaspora experience in Egypt and two additional ones in Babylon (Rubesh 2011: 39-72). The assumptions for Rubesh's discussion include the assumption that the Old Testament is not only a valuable theological document but is also historically reliable. In addition, it is assumed that the biblical record of Israel's experience in both Egypt and Babylon is credible (Rubesh 2011: 39-72). Scripture is the authoritative Word of God inspired by the Holy Spirit. For Jehu Hanciles, theologically, the whole Bible consists of diaspora experiences. He stated, "The biblical record—from the expulsion of Adam...in Genesis (3:23) to the magnificent vision of...John...in Revelation (1:9)—reveals a profound interconnection between human mobility or dispersion and unfolding salvation" <http://www.lausanneworldpulse.com/themedarticle>, 1. (March 5, 2010). Robin Cohen identified some characteristics that apply to most diaspora peoples. They include "dispersal from the original homeland, expansion for a homeland in search of work...and lack of acceptance in the host society"

(Cohen 1997: 177-196), and the like. Understanding diaspora mission concerning Ghanaians is strongly related to the characteristics of Ghanaian diaspora. Four of Cohen's characteristics apply here.

Scattered from the Homeland: Political Instability and Globalization

Cohen described the diaspora peoples as often traumatically scattered from the homeland. This characteristic applies to the factor of African political instability because of its traumatic nature. Historically, Ghana was one of the leading nations of political instability in Africa. For example, the military regime between the 1980s and 1990s caused a massive exodus of Ghanaians. "Political instability led to a military takeover…in 1981, at a time when Ghana was also hit by a severe drought…when about a million people returned from Nigeria in 1983" (Ter Haar 1998: 133). Enos Ohene, 60, an OBG retired soldier in NY said about his immigration to the USA, "For me, the socio-economic destruction of Ghana was caused by pure selfishness. Our political leaders during the 1980s were plain selfish and dealing with them was our difficulty. After retirement from the military I had to leave Ghana for political and economic survival" (Interview, November 19, 2010). Another OBG, Paul Asiama, 63, said,

I was a teacher and the civilian "commandant" of the national school children's parades…during the military rule. When the government changed in 2000, the outgoing government offered an opportunity for me and my family to emigrate from Ghana. I took the chance and came to America. Honestly, though I wouldn't have left Ghana my motherland, I saw it as an opportunity to educate my children (Interview, October 18, 2010).

Political instability had pushed many Ghanaians outside their homeland. Perceived as political enemies, some opponents were branded dissidents who were exiled.

Expansion for a Homeland in Search of Work and in Pursuit of Trade

A combination of a "gloomy home life" and the "the search for greener pastures" can be compared with Cohen's Jewish "expansion for a homeland in search of work, in pursuit of trade, or to further colonial ambitions" (Cohen 1997: 177-196). During the same political era, the International Monetary Fund (IMF) and the World Bank for Reconstruction and Development (WBRD) introduced programs such as the Economic Recovery Program (ERP),

Structural Adjustment Program (SAP), and Programs Aimed at Mitigating the Social Cost and Development (PAMSCAD).

The ERP, SAP, and PAMSCAD ushered in serious and disastrous economic conditions that forced the emigration of Ghanaians globally, especially to Europe and America. Paul Gifford stated, "By the late 1990s there was widespread poverty with 70% of the population earning under USA $1.00…50% of Ghanaian doctors leave the country…and 80% within the first five years of graduation…Education collapsed" (2004: 2-5). The resultant "brain drain" was drastic. Professionals such as doctors, nurses, bankers, and teachers, among others, emigrated for greener pastures. On the average, those who left included the relatively young labor force of all areas of a developing economy with serious repercussions. Micah Bump stated, "Skilled workers and professionals dominated early flows from Ghana, but, by the 1980s, many semiskilled and unskilled workers chose to leave as well" (2011). Therefore, one major characteristic of many immigrant populations, including Ghanaians, is the working class who emigrate for work opportunities in foreign lands.

"Good Old Days" Memory and the "Home-Sweet-Home" Syndrome

Cohen suggested that the Jewish diaspora had "a collective memory and myth about the homeland, including its location, history, and achievements" (Cohen 1997: 177-196). Another of Cohen's characteristics was "an idealization of the putative ancestral home and a collective commitment to its maintenance, restoration, safety, and prosperity, even to its creation" (Cohen 1997: 177-196). A combination of these two characteristics within the Ghanaian diaspora exists. First generation OBGs have shared memories of their ancestral homeland. They call it the "good old days" or "home sweet home." Most of the OBGs in the USA are homesick as they repeatedly make reference to the "good old days."

Edith, 50, stated, "Nothing can compare with the job I had back home in Ghana. I was the boss in the computer programming department of Social Security Bank (SSB). Now I take instructions from others. Having obtained my documentation in 2009, I feel homesick. Sometimes I wish to return home" (Interview, December 2, 2010). This is her response to the question about the opportunities she has had since her arrival in the USA in 1992.

GHANAIAN CULTURE WITHIN CHRISTIANITY

Meaningful application and practice of the Christian faith should be relevant to every people group. Traditional OBGs have a deep-rooted spiritual background which makes the practice of their Christian faith within their rich cultural categories inevitable. Thus, a contextual application within the *Akan* culture is more relevant than any meaningless abstract applications. Ghanaian Diaspora and Some Reformed Theological Connections. Two groups of scholars have had relevant reformed theological discussions on mission. John Terry, et al., eds. and Scott A.Moreau, et al., discussed theology of mission, missions, and missiology. Similarly, Luis Pantoja Jr., et al. as well as Enoch Wan and Sadiri Joy Tira discussed theology of mission, missiology, and diaspora missiology. Wan and Tira recognized the formulation of the "theology of global diaspora" with Tereso Casino (Wan and Tira eds. 2009: 38). Casino stated, "Theology…developed…through the lens of the missionary intentions of God…The mobility of God's people…help to cement the complementary characteristics of both theology and diaspora missiology; missiology is inherently theological as theology is indispensably missions-oriented" (Casino 2009; Wan and Tira eds. 2009: 38). Two major insights, among others, connect theology to Ghanaian Christian beliefs about God and salvation. The theology of Incarnation (Christ-Event) is relevant for the theory of culture. Sherwood Lingenfelter and Marvin Mayers analyzed incarnation in light of the theology of cross-cultural missiology in their volume *Ministering Cross-Culturally*, which is reminiscent of the Incarnation. In diaspora missiology, this analysis is valuable.

Individual and Shared Culture

Culture is contextual; each cultural way of life has deeper contents, meanings, and cues. "A cultural cue is a specific signal or sign that people use to communicate the meaning of their behavior" (Lingenfelter and Mayers 2003: 18). Such cultural cues might not be observable to the cross-cultural missionary. An expedient and insightful suggestion is to dichotomize between individual and corporate or societal culture. Lingenfelter and Mayers designated these as personal and shared culture within cultural particularity.

Each individual develops a personal lifestyle and a set of standards and values by which to order and organize his or her life. Building of individual identity is done through the choices made. However the process of making these choices is done within a particular society called socialization. Culture is acquired and shared with others within a context. "People perceive and respond to one another in a culturally conditioned way" Lingenfleter and Mayers 2003: 22). This is the process of sharing culture.

Incarnation Model Relevant for Cross-Cultural Mission

Scripture fully exhibits the theology of Incarnation (John 1:14). Christ is fully God and fully man. As God, He incarnated by taking human flesh and pitching among humanity. What is the application of Christ's Incarnation by the diaspora peoples? Thousands of cultural cues should necessarily be grasped for diaspora cross-cultural mission because "a failure to grasp the meaning of such cues" (Lingenfleter and Mayers 2003:18) might culminate in unfortunate mission failure. The most effective pattern of mission practice is to imitate Christ's Incarnation with cultural incarnation (Philippians 2:5-6). The principle of cultural incarnation could be explained with a mathematical analysis. "Jesus Christ is 200% God-Man—100% God and 100% man. Each person is 100% human. In the diaspora missions and ministries the practitioner should strive to be 150%" (Lingenfelter and Mayers 2003: 22). This means in the cultural incarnation model, the diaspora mission practitioners should learn to add 50% of the existing culture in context to their unchanging culture and worldview. For instance, Ghanaian diaspora in the USA should add 50% of the positive American culture to operate effectively.

Absolute Sovereignty of the Ultimate Reality

The Ultimate Reality is all-powerful—almighty. God alone is absolutely sovereign. Most African cultures recognize the sovereignty of God. For instance, the *Akan* believe in the sovereign attribute of God as omnipotent. Most members of the Ghanaian diaspora share this belief. With regard to the Ghanaian diaspora Christians, in reality, "God's sovereignty establishes the framework for the missionary expansion of Christianity" (Santos 2004: 59) and, for that matter, diaspora missiology.

During the opening devotion of the PCG OMF council meeting on March 27, 2010 in Irvington, NJ, caretaker Dwomo Sarpong reflected, "When we told our relatives that we were travelling to America, none of us had conceived the idea of forming a church. We all immigrated for greener pastures. But I believe almighty God has purposefully gathered us here as the church" (Devotion, March 27, 2010). Charles Gyang-Duah in support also said, "When you immigrated, nobody had plans to form a church. But even at creation, almighty God knew that He was going to use you to form His congregation in America" (OMF Quarterly Meeting March 27, 2010). These statements indicate the African belief in God's sovereignty.

Akan Concept of Salvation

The *Akan* concept of salvation is understood as a package for the enjoyment of *nkwa*—life. *Nkwagye* (salvation), therefore, means an embodiment of *nkwa tenten* (longevity), *apow mu den* (good health), *and ahonya* (prosperity or material wealth), among others—a whole totality of wholeness and abundant life (Larbi 2002: 4; 2008 <http:// www.pctii/cybererj10/lrabi.html> (February 28, 2008). Others include: *Onyamesom/anyamesom ho nkabom* (harmony with the

Deity/deities), asomdwoei (individual/community peace), *nhyira* (blessings), *nkoso* (development), *banbo* (security), *tumi* (power), *nkunimdi* (victory), and *asaase/mmoa/nnipa awo* (land/animal/human fecundity). For the Christian *Akan*, however, all the above are good for life but none can wash human sin away. Only the Blood of Jesus Christ can. The Christ-Event—the Incarnation—epitomizes the love of God for humanity (John 3:16, 10:10, and Romans 5:8). This is the divinity, kingship, lordship and the salvific authority of the Lord Jesus Christ. For that reason, Christological salvation is the basis of the Christian faith. The research for this manuscript established that some diaspora Ghanaian receptivity of the gospel is derived from the quest for salvation in Christ Jesus.

Another related development among diaspora Christians has concentrated on end-times doctrine recently. The upsurge of evil and institutionalization of immorality in all cultures globally has given impetus to end times' doctrine. Wan and Tira posited, "The future eternal Kingdom is already present today...One day, all the scattered people of God will gather before the throne of the Lamb (Rev. 7:9-10) and with the New Jerusalem where they will dwell with God (Rev. 21:1-3)" (Wan and Tira 2009: 42). Struggling to enter God's kingdom is one of the greatest challenges of the Ghanaian diaspora believers in the Protestant Churches in the USA.

African Christology of Ancestors

One of the unique scholarly understandings of contextualization is the theology of Christology of ancestors. On this African Christian doctrine, two *Akan* contentions prevail. One contention is that *Akan* ancestry is based on clan lineage. Thus, African Christology of ancestors is challenging (Bediako 2004: 23). Christology in ancestral veneration studies is unique but open to debate. King Addow Dankwa III (Paramount chief of the Akuapem traditional area of Ghana) debated on this issue. His contention in some of his scholarly presentations is that for an ancestor to be an authentic ancestor there should be blood lineage relationship, as Bediako asked Pobee. Therefore, Christology in ancestral veneration is problematic to some African scholars. Christ has no African lineage. Thus, it is difficult to understand why Jesus is the Greatest Ancestor as posited by scholars such as Pobee.

For the late Kwame Bediako, "Ancestors are essentially clan or lineage ancestors. So they have to do with the community or society in which their progeny relate to one another and without a system of religion as such" (1990: 23). He asked, "Why should an *Akan* relate to Jesus of Nazareth who does not belong to his clan, family, tribe and nation?" (Bediako 1990: 23). Bediako posed the question as a critique of John Pobee. Conversely, Pobee responded, "We look on Jesus as the Great and Greatest Ancestor, since in *Akan* society the Supreme Being and the ancestors provide the sanctions for the good life, and the ancestors hold that authority as ministers of the Supreme Being" (1996: 94). Such scholars of African Christology contend that Christ has shed His blood for believers as senior Brother because of his Son-ship and believers' son-ship to God (Romans 8:29). Since Christ is ahead of believers, then He is the Greatest Ancestor in the family of God—the new Israel. Moreover, should believers recognize the "communion of the saints" in the book of Hebrews, the biblical "hall of fame," then theologizing about Christology of ancestors in Africa should not be difficult. Nevertheless, it is factual that Pobee, Bediako, and the like had opened a platform for further research and debate.

These views have much impact with regard to contextualization of the Christian faith in relationship with the *Akan* unchangeable worldview. They explain the resilience of African spirituality when an African converts to Christianity. No group of Africans can totally cut themselves from their cultural roots and remain African in whatever religion. Any religion that does not offer answers to the challenges of the African worldview will result in its rejection. The people will then leave, seeking answers that are relevant to their worldview. In the encounter between gospel and culture, Christianity offers answers to the deep issues within African culture. Conversely, Christianity challenges some tenets of the African worldview. Converting to Christianity may not denote the total cultural conversion of the African. This framework of contextualization applies to diaspora Ghanaians in the USA as well.

Rich *Akan* Indigenous Knowledge Connections with Biblical Worldview

Mission does not exist in a vacuum. Neither does worldview. Theological connections have to be found for missiology and cultural/worldview studies. Common biblical and *Akan* worldviews include respect for God's creation, ancestral veneration, subsistence agriculture, community life, strong family ties, and strong moral norms, values, and beliefs that influence behavior. In ministry, there is the need to develop connections between biblical worldviews, theology, and indigenous knowledge. For Ghanaian diaspora, there is a close connection between African and biblical worldviews. The quest for the connectivity between biblical and *Akan* worldviews should culminate in Scriptural absolutism with an expression of cross-cultural perspective. "Most Christian anthropologists would agree that the cultural forms in Scripture must be understood in the context of their own culture, and it is their meanings that are sacred, absolute, and authoritative" (Allison 1996: 38).

Apart from language, some other rich *Akan* indigenous knowledge exists. "The oral literature of the African people is their unwritten Bible. This religious wisdom is found in African idioms, wise sayings, legends, myths, stories, proverbs and oral history...it so much resembled familiar wisdom literature, with all its 'aphorisms, epigrams and similes'" (Philip Jenkins 2006: 59-61).

Proverbs, for instance, are very important in African societies. This explains the relevance of such indigenous knowledge about the generic African Christianity. Hannah Kinoti writes about the importance of proverbs in the African cultural context. She emphasizes that proverbs are important because of their spiritual values and stated, "From a religious perspective, proverbs constitutes a form of worship" (Kinoti 1998; Mary Getui, ed., 1998: 2).

Worshiping as authentic Akan Christians, categories that can be used to minister are stories, wise sayings, proverbs, anecdotes, and symbolism. A story and a proverb are used to illustrate:

> "Once, a furious bushfire swept through a village…The only thing a mother-hen could do was to gather all its little chicks under her wings while the raging fire drew closer…All the grass and the mother-hen were totally burnt but the little ones were safe because of their mother's wings that covered them" (E.L. Asamoah 1987: 1; Wan and Edu-Bekoe 2011; Moraeu and Snodderly 2011: 35-62).

This story illustrates Christ's vicarious death (Romans 5:8). No Pauline scholarly theology of Christ's death in place of sinful humanity can be explained better to simple Akan people than this story. An Akan proverb also states, *Abe pe nkwa tenten nti, ode ne ho kowuraa odum yam; na ama wanwu da.* Literally, this proverb means it is because of longevity that the palm tree embedded itself in the belly of the oak tree so that it will never die. "In the African tropical rain forest, the oak tree, considered as a forest god by the Akan, can stand for two hundred years if not felled. Periodically farmers and hunters find an oak tree where a palm tree grows in its roots. As a parasite it is believed that the life of such a palm tree depends on the life of the oak tree" (Wan and Edu-Bekoe 2011; Moreau and Snodderly 2011: 35-62). The above proverb also illustrates Paul's difficult in-grafting as part of Christian life (Romans 11:11-24) and it also explains John's concept of having Christ for eternal life (1 John 5:11-13).

Most diaspora OBGs have simple backgrounds. They like and understand such stories and proverbs more. The GPCs can take advantage of indigenous knowledge to reach out to the unreached within the general Ghanaian diaspora. The fundamental grounding of such a worldview is the basis for the strong cultural and moral values of the Ghanaian diaspora, which have cognitively created a mindset for the OBG in their diaspora context. In the practice of the Christian faith, Jean-Claude Loba-Mkole posited, "True inculturation is the one which crucifies all the sins of a culture that encounters the Christ and allows him to change the culture into a new creation" (2004; Wendland and Loba-Mkole, eds., 2004: 37-58). The emphasis is that every people group's culture is a creation of God and contextualization of the faith is useful.

Cosmological Warfare

African Christology of constant warfare is indicative of one serious doctrine in diaspora missions that resonates well with the majority of diaspora Ghanaians as Africans. For most Ghanaians (Africans), since there is no separation between the sacred and the mundane, most negative occurrences in human life are attributed to one's perceived and/or real enemies. God is sovereign, eternal, merciful, compassionate, and providential. Conversely, Satan and his demons are devious, capricious, and malignant. Constant warfare between the two forces is a reality. The human being is caught up in this conflict and struggle. Activities of witches and wizards, diviners, occultists, charmers, and malignant ancestors are all directed against Christians to prevent them from enjoying an abundant life or fulfilling their destiny.

For majority of Ghanaian (African) Christians, the greatest fighter in this struggle is Christ, God's Son. Christ is the greatest *Osagyefo*, the Supreme Commander-in-Chief who fights to win this constant struggle for a victorious Christian life. Here, *osa* means war and *gyefo* means redeemer, savior, or conqueror. *Osagyefo*, therefore, means redeemer or conqueror in war. Some activities of the GPCs in the USA related to the constant warfare include revivals, prayer, fasting, healing, and deliverance services. "Doctrines of loosing the captives, casting out demons, healing and deliverance, liberating the oppressed and defeating poverty take place against the backdrop of constant spiritual warfare between the Triune God and Satan with his demons" (Jenkins 2007: 149-151). Christ has already won this battle for Christians on the cross with the power of His resurrection. Accordingly, preventive deliverance through discipleship essentials should relatively be preferred to curative deliverance.

SUMMARY

Chapter Three consisted of five ethnographic descriptions. The chapter started with the scattered Africans who keep coming to the USA. It then looked at the history and demographics of Ghanaian diaspora in the USA. There was the ethnographic description of the Ghanaian (Akan) cultural legacies such as the worldview, religion, humanity, family, and kinship systems, rites of passage, and cultural symbolism. The chapter continued with the theoretical description of the characteristics of the Ghanaian diaspora. The final section consisted of an analysis of the practice of the Ghanaian (Akan) culture within the Christian faith. The formation of GPCs is taken up in the following Chapter 4 in Part Two.

QUESTIONS FOR DISCUSSION

1. How is the net immigration of USA in comparison to other nations?
2. What is the decade-long (2000-2012) trend of immigration to the USA?
3. Which state in the USA has the largest Ghanaian Foreign-born?
4. What are the six themes of Ghanaian diaspora in the USA that emerged from ethnographic data collected and interpreted?
5. Do you think those six themes are uniquely appropriate for Ghanaian diaspora in the USA? Are there parallel elements in other diaspora communities in the USA?

Part II

"DIASPORA MISSIOLOGY" IN ACTION: GHANAIAN DIASPORA IN THE U.S.

"Those who have been scattered preached the word wherever they went" (Acts 8:4).

Part two consists of three chapters. Chapter three is a description of the formation of Ghanaian congregations in the USA. Chapter four is an ethnographic description of the distinctive markers of the Ghanaian diaspora—diversity, identity and its formulation, and both socio-cultural and gospel receptivity. Chapter five is a description of the leadership and discipleship in the USA GPCs.

Chapter 3
GHANAIAN CONGREGATIONS IN THE USA

INTRODUCTION

Socio-cultural diversity provides an enabling context in which mission practice in the diaspora enhances planting of community GPCs. Chapter 4 reflects on the missiological understanding on the practice of mission by diaspora Ghanaians (Edu-Bekoe and Wan 2011; Wan ed., 2011: 211-230). The chapter is made up of four sections. The first section is "missions and ministering to the diaspora" in light of the formation of GPCs in the USA. Added to this section are topics such as church planting movements (CPMs) and the planting of viable USA GPCs with relevant research insights on their formation. The second section consists of another discussion of "missions and ministering to the diaspora" Ghanaians with regard to the theological development—the internal spirituality of members. The third section explores yet another "missions and ministering to the diaspora" related to the organizational development. The final section discusses mobilization for "glocal" mission which looks into both "missions and ministering through the diaspora" and "missions by and beyond the diaspora" of the USA GPCs.

FORMATION OF THE USA GPCs ("MISSIONS AND MINISTERING TO DIASPORA")

The gathering of a group of believers, the Body of Christ, is the formation of a church. In the NT, a church can be a believing household or gathering of any size, a cluster of such households and gatherings, or all such clusters and gatherings viewed collectively. The church evolved out of the gospel—the good news of the Christ-Event. In other words the gospel creates the church, not an entrepreneurial practice. The Christian story is essential to summarize who Jesus Christ is and why He is special in the proclamation of the Reign of God. Christian mission is God's—the mission of Christ. Believers are mere participants in partnership with Christ in His mission. In "mission and ministering to the diaspora," the USA GPCs are providing the necessary space for worship opportunities for diaspora Ghanaians.

Biblical and Theological Basis of Church Planting

Some scholars have posited scriptural and theological foundations of church planting (CP). "Church planting is not an end in itself, but one aspect of the mission of God in which churches are privileged to participate" (Stuart Murray 1998: 30). Aubrey Malphurs contended, "I would argue strongly that church starters seek biblical-theological training because church planting is a deeply theological enterprise" (2009: 7). One would strongly agree with Malphurs for stressing that church planting is serious and needs deep biblical-theological training. However, one would at the same time disagree with Malphurs for describing church planting as enterprise. This is the usual linear Euro-American mindset of seeing the church as a business or enterprise. God's dealing with humanity is spiritual. Accordingly, as a missionary God, God's CP is a deeply theological vocation, not enterprise. Four necessities for planting churches among any people groups are suggested. "These requirements are…sowers…seed…soil…and Spirit. Paul and his team represented the sowers. The gospel is the seed sowed in the hearts, or soil, of the Thessalonians. The Spirit is the Holy Spirit, who opens hearts to the gospel and brings about the birth of his churches" (1 Thessalonians 1:2-10) (Charles Brock 1994: 30; Payne 2009: 13). The multi-cultural USA and its resultant diversity create an enabling environment for the formation of diaspora Ghanaian churches. The importance of CP has culminated in church planting movements (CPMs).

Multi-cultural Context and Formation of Diaspora Churches

Methods and strategies for CP are complementary for the missiology meeting point. Enoch Wan suggested the type and process of diaspora CP in Figure 3.1

Wan then stated,

It is natural and logical, and even expedient for ethnic… to form a monolingual and homogeneous church as in example (4) in figure #7.1.

This is a common practice of OBE (OBG)...Christians....The opposite alternative is to form a multilingual, heterogeneous, and multi-congregational church (i.e., 1 in figure # 7.1). The operation of a multilingual and multi-cultural church (2a of figure # 7.1) would usually require a lot of mutual respect, careful coordination and Christian love to ensure the health and well-being of such heterogeneous church (1995:167, 168).

Figure 3.1: Congregation Type and Church Planter's Option Scale

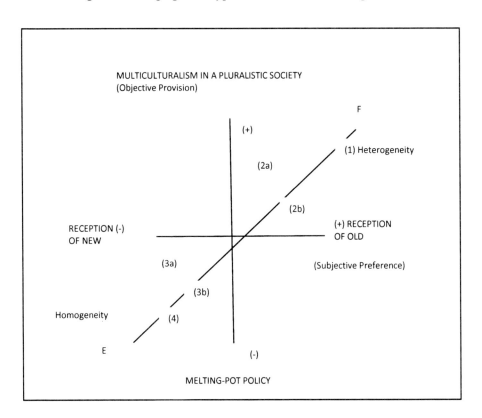

With the following, Wan explained the figure:
Notes:
1. heterogeneous & multi-congregation church.
2a. multilingual & multi-cultural church
2b. bilingual & bicultural church
3a. monolingual & monocultural church, ethnic but open (OBG + LBG + etc)
3b. monolingual & bicultural church, ethnic but conservative (OBG dominant)
4. monolingual & homogeneous church (only OBG or LBG)
5. The E-F line in the figure is the linear Church planters' option scale. (Wan 1995: 167).

Jarvis D. Payne saw CP as both method and strategy. He suggested,

> The best way to fulfill this mandate…is through the planting of contextualized churches…For it is in the process of evangelizing, baptizing, and teaching that local churches are planted…Scripture should always be the source of guidance for doctrine and practice…As a method, church planting tells how to make disciples…As a strategy, church planting offers a paradigm for reaching villages, urban enclaves, and entire cities with the gospel (Payne 2009: 4, 5).

DEVELOPMENT OF USA GPCS: CHURCH PLANTING MOVEMENTS AND THE PLANTING OF VIABLE CHURCHES

The passion for CP among the GPCs depends on the mobilization, motivation, and engagement of the members for mission by the leaders of the church. CP is the ultimate basis of the formation of viable churches. Such viable churches reflect an enabling environment of transformational discipleship among the members who are developed, encouraged, and mobilized for mission.

Church Planting Movements (CPMs)

CPMs are actions through which God is transforming human lives in our generation throughout the world. God is extraordinarily drawing the unreached to Himself through the CPMs in the diaspora churches. Offering worship space for Ghanaian believers to practice their faith, the empowered church of Christ is to quantitatively and qualitatively reproduce, multiply, and develop internally and externally. In the USA, such church growth happens in the complexity of a diverse context. In doing this, David Garrison proposes reverse engineering to tackle the complex phenomenon as CP. Garrison contends that CPMs are the means to easily see God at work transforming hundreds of lives. He stated,

> It seeks to understand these movements by beginning at the end, with an actual Church Planting Movement. Then it reverse engineers the movement, dismantling its component parts, analyzing how it was constructed and how it works. Done properly, reverse engineering can reveal volumes about the creator's designs, desires, and method of operation (Garrison 2004:11).

Clusters of churches receive, share, and send apostles, prophets, pastors, evangelists, shepherds, and teachers. Christ is present in the midst of those who obey His commands. A viable church is "the minimum church which is able to evangelize its own ethnic group without any external assistance" (James Heimbeger, 2003: 17); <http://www.comimex.org> (June 21, 2010).

Cross-Cultural Church Planting and the USA Ghanaian Diaspora

The formation of GPCs in the USA has depended significantly on the tripartite relationship among home groups, church planting, and growth. Donald McGavran stated,

> Church growth follows where the lost are not merely found but restored in the normal life in the fold…The multiplication of the churches nourished in the Bible and full of the Holy Spirit is a sine qua non in carrying out the purpose of God" (1990: 6, 7).

In addition, McGavran suggested three basic types of mission and evangelization relevant for all diaspora peoples: ME-1, ME-2, and ME-3. Figure 3.2 is an overview. In Figure 3.2, ME-1 is the practice of mission to own people group. ME-2 is the practice of mission by crossing a cultural and geographical barrier and ME-3 having a corps of specially training missionaries for cross-cultural foreign mission practice.

Figure 3.2: Basic Methods of Mission and Evangelization

Mission and Evangelization Types	Method of Evangelization
ME-1: Mission-Evangelism 1	Reaching out to own kind of people group; Ghanaian wins other Ghanaians and establishes them in a church
ME-2: Mission-Evangelism 2	Crossing some kind of barrier to go, usually physical, such as going into a new community; ethnic Ghanaian wins other ethnic groups for Christ
ME-3: Mission-Evangelism 3	The church must have a corps of missionaries with special training; cross-cultural foreign mission of Ghanaians

Using the above evangelistic types in Figure 3.2, David Hesselgrave suggested two types of immigrant CP—nucleus and pioneer. Figure 3.3 represents the nucleus CP (Hesselgrave 2000: 27; Edu-Bekoe and Wan 2011; Wan ed. 2011: 216).

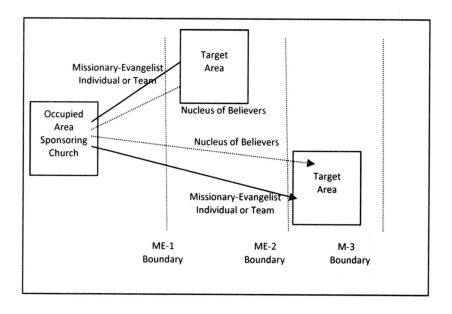

Figure 3.3: Nucleus Church Planting

On one hand, Hesselgrave stated, "Basically, the existing church (and its leadership) has two possible courses of action. First, guided by the Holy Spirit, it can plan to start another church on its own…The former option usually involves ME-1 or ME-2 programs…can be called nucleus church planting" (2000: 27, 28; Edu-Bekoe and Wan 2011; Wan ed. 2011: 215). Ghanaian diaspora perception of the receptivity of the gospel was informed by activities with their own Ghanaian ethnic groups in the USA. For example, the PCG used this method in "missions to the diaspora" Ghanaian communities in the USA (ME-1 and ME-2 in Figure 3.3). Invariably, a nucleus of believers who reside in the target area gathers together to fellowship. It could be a home, school, or community cell fellowship. PCGNY was formed this way. On the other hand, rather than doing it alone, a church can cooperate with others to plant new congregations. Hesselgrave refers to this as pioneer CP. Figure 3.4 is representative of pioneer church planting (Hesselgrave 2000: 78; Edu-Bekoe and Wan 2011; Wan ed. 2011: 216).

Figure 3.4: Pioneer Church Planting

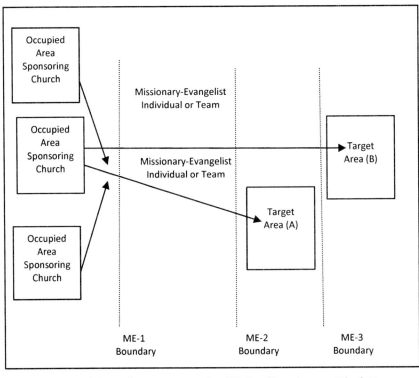

Here, A and B are the target areas for CP. For Hesselgrave, "the latter option usually involves ME-2 and ME-3 programs" (Hesselgrave 2000: 78; Edu-Bekoe and Wan 2011; Wan ed. 2011: 218). Figures 3.3 and 3.4 are adapted figures with few changes.

Sadiri Joy Tira also posited four steps necessary before forming a diaspora congregation, using the biological birthing of a kangaroo. The steps include

Step 1: Intentional Prayer

Step 2: Identify a Joey: Who will make up (GPC) Joey?

Step 3: Identify Joey's area of ministry: analysis of target area and people, geographical profile, population profile, economic profile, sociological profile, and religious profile, and

Step 4: Denominational partnership (Tira 2009; Wan and Tira 2009: 69-82).

As Tira suggested, "A healthy local congregation should always be pregnant but also be aware of favorable conditions and the best time to launch a joey. Many…local churches birth daughter churches without considering the health of the daughter church" (Wan and Tira 2009: 74).

THEMATIC RESEARCH ON FORMATION AND EXPANSION OF USA GPCs

Some of the sampled members expressed a variety of views on the histories about the formation and expansion of their various GPCs. They are obviously all first generation OBGs because most of the younger generations as immigrant children did not have any part in the formation of these congregations, societies, or assemblies.

Pastoral Insights on the Formation of USA GPCs

Four attaché mainline ministers in addition to one Pentecostal and two charismatic pastors were interviewed. The attaché ministers are posted by the PCG and the MCG from Ghana. Their visa requirements make them attached to these churches for a period of time only. When asked about the formation of the OMF, Gyang-Duah responded, "OMF has developed from the efforts of individual members who gather together. So far, I have supervised the inauguration of the Emmanuel PCG, Norton, VA in October 2006, New Jersey PCG in May 2007, Calvary PCG, Columbus, OH in August 2010, and Chicago Bethel PCG in April 2011" (Interview, May 25, 2010). Regarding his attachment to the Ebenezer PCG, Gyang-Duah said,

> I was the clerk of GA when the congregation informed the PCG of its formation. Ebenezer is a splinter congregation from Emmanuel, Ogden, NY that has affiliation with PCUSA. PCG realized that its prodigal minister was moving the congregation to affiliate with the PCUSA. Accordingly, when the group wanted to break and worship as Ghanaians they were encouraged. My first contact with Ebenezer was when I officiated, to the glory of God, its inauguration on October 23, 2003 with other officials. As the resident-minister, I have been involved with the Ebenezer PCG, Bronx congregation as visiting minister since 2006 and then regularly in 2008 (Interview, May 25, 2010).

When asked about how healthy it is for the PCG to leave individual immigrants to form congregations before coming in to supervise, Gyang-Dauh emphatically reaffirmed that the situation is very problematic. Yaw Asiedu described PCGNY's formation,

> I must confess that my involvement in congregational evangelization has not been much. However, having been a member of the PCGNY for the past 26 years, I have invited some members. Four Presbyterian congregations have been formed by members of PCGNY. They include Bethel Presbyterian Reformed Church, Brooklyn, Emmanuel Presbyterian Reformed Church, Ogden, Bronx, and Ebenezer PCG, Bronx, all in NY.

The Bible Study and Prayer Group (BSPG) also assisted to form the Presbyterian Church in Toronto, Canada. The most recent church PCGNY has helped to plant is Queens PCG, Queens, NY (Interview, June 2, 2010).

Joyce, 50, spoke about the Worcester congregation she ministers in,

> Worcester PCG congregation was formed out of crisis in 2004. When the former minister left with some members, the remaining ones urgently looked for another minister. I was contacted by Rev. Dr. Gyang-Duah and the elders of the congregation. I was asked to relocate from Lexington, KY to Worcester to pastor the congregation. One person who stood for the congregation at the time of the crisis was Abena Mansa
> (Interview, April 9, 2011).

Stephen Kwaku Owusu was not a founding member of the GEMC, Newark, NJ. However, his observations on the formation of the society were insightful. He said,

> Obviously, I was not involved in the formation of the GEMC. My observation is that the members in this society did not come from one society in Ghana. Rather, they have gathered from different societies of the Methodist Church in Ghana. Some are even from different Ghanaian denominations. The fact is some of them do not want to join the English churches of the USA. This is because Africans worship expressively. Methodists make the church an institution for vibrant singing of songs, expressive worship activities, and a place of socialization for the children where they are taught Scripture. In the diaspora, other activities by the immigrant Methodist churches include training of the younger generations for African values, introduction to other African networks, and provision of space for African Christian faith practice
> (Interview, November 19, 2011).

Ntiamoah Saka, 56, pastor of the Philadelphia CoP emphasized one reason why many of that church's assemblies have proliferated in the USA. He said,

> When our members come to the USA, they first start worshiping with white mainline churches. In these churches they speak English very fast, which becomes problematic for them; they do not sing, clap, and dance as we do in Ghana, and after the service the best one would get from any of them is "Hi!" Nobody would bother to know where one lived, how one came to church that day, or how one is going back. Sometimes one needed a ride home but it was nobody's business. However, the situation is different with us in this Philadelphia CoP assembly. One feels belonging and one's burden is another person's burden too
> (Interview, October 15, 2007).

Saka also gave an example of his explanation by quoting one of his members, "One of my members asked me, 'When I came to America, I worshipped in other places because I could not find any church of my people here. If today, by the grace of God, there is a Ghanaian Pentecostal church here why shouldn't I join?' This feeling is endemic among many of the members of this assembly" (Interview, October 15, 2005).

When David Ato Pratt travelled to the USA to further his education, he joined the Bronx, NY branch of his church. Later, the bishop and an assistant bishop came to America for a program and decided to ordain Pratt as a pastor. About the formation of the Irvington, NJ branch of VBC-I he said,

> I used to go with five other members to our Bronx branch from NJ to worship with them. One day the six of us met to discuss how to form a branch of the church in NJ that will eventually end our long driving to NY. We went on praying and made a firm decision to form a church under the direction of the Holy Spirit. We asked one of us to look for a place for us. He is now in charge of the Virginia branch of our church. Within two weeks we had a place in East Orange. We set a date to start worshiping and paid six months advanced rent (Interview, December 11, 2011).

Asked about what happened for the VBC-I to move to their current location, Pratt explained,

> As a result of the harassment of our Muslim neighbor, we worshipped in the basement of a member for a while. We then rented a hall from the Veteran Association in Bergenfield. Distance then became a challenge, which made us move to this place. One sister among us lived with a member of the NJ PCG. She connected them with us and we came to rent part of their upstairs worship premises. God blessed us because the NY branch under which we began to operate was already registered. In NJ, one can operate a church without registration. Though, we could have registered, we incorporated under the Bronx, NY branch. This initially helped us since we needed a tax exemption. All our tax exemption and documentation were done under the NY church
> (Interview, December 11, 2011).

Seth Anyomi, the founding bishop of the Portland International Church (PIC) narrated his version of the formation of the church. He said,

> My family and I arrived in Portland, OR, in the fall of 1991. I was invited to use Western Seminary as a base for the newly established World Link University (WLU) of the Third World Missions Association (TWMA). Upon arrival in Portland, I observed that many Africans in the metropolis did not attend church regularly. I took it upon myself to interview a few of my African friends and learned that some did not feel at home among Western congregations due to the style of worship and other reasons. I decided to respond to this great spiritual need. I discussed with a friend the plans to establish an international church in Portland. He gladly embraced the vision and introduced me to Kofi Nelson-Owusu who, at

that time, was a graduate student at the Portland State University (PSU). The three of us agreed to meet once a week for a year then launch the church. In the fall of 1993, PIC was born (E-mail, April 13, 2012).

Kofi Nelson-Owusu and Carroll of PIC, the two ministerial leaders, had different positions about its formation and their initial connections. While Nelson-Owusu was connected with the beginning of PIC, Carroll joined the church later. Nelson-Owusu had some basic reasons for his role in the formation of PIC. He said,

> My goal is to serve the Lord always. My initial connections with PIC had several reasons, three of which are first of all, circumstance. This is the circumstance of my coming to the USA instead of Canada where I intended to travel. I believe the sovereign Lord brought me here for a purpose. When I came to Portland, the person with whom I stayed was also schooling in PSU, Western Oregon. This helped me to have contacts with many of our colleague students. Second, close to our campus was a Baptist church with which I began to worship. After a year, the pastor asked me to speak to them in a retreat. Without my knowledge, God had revealed to them that somebody from Africa would come to minister to them. With this prophesy narrated to me I was convinced that God had brought me to them for a purpose. Third, I started to organize Bible studies and prayer in my room on campus. I also organized family Bible studies and all night prayer meetings (Interview, February 26, 2012).

Asked how these activities aided the formation of PIC, Nelson-Owusu continued,

> At this point I came in contact with one brother Francis. Later, I was also introduced to Seth Anyomi, the founder of PIC, who had a World Link assignment in the Western Seminary. We then linked together to fellowship. One day I was asked to preach in Salem where I met other African brothers, and after one year PIC was formed. My role as one of the three founding members of the church was for prayer because already my room was the meeting place for prayer on campus. We also had morning devotions. When the church started, I became the youth pastor. We started worshipping in the Western seminary cafeteria. Later we moved to the Bema hall before finally settling at our current place on 80th street (Interview, February 26, 2012).

Carroll, the Cameroonian, narrated how she started worshipping in Portland by saying,

> When I was coming to Portland, I knew only one Cameroonian family. While the husband is Cameroonian, the wife is a White-American. I stayed for one year with this family in Forest Grove. I had had no contact; nothing so far. Accordingly, my first church was the Four Square Church. Later in

the first year, I moved to the South West Bible Church in Beaverton, OR. I was introduced to PIC by a Cameroonian sister three years ago to attend an evening prayer meeting. On the second occasion, I was invited to speak during a PUSH (pray until something happens) night. I did not integrate into PIC until June 2011 when I became a member. Look pastor, when I came here, I joined the Four Square Church. My "mother" with whom I was staying introduced me to the pastor of the church. Could you believe that for a whole year, the pastor did not even remember me, my name, and let alone where I was living? Sometimes I had to remind him of my name. I had the feeling of being unwanted. Pastors are supposed to know members of their parishes, you know. The church is no more a preaching point. The church has to be a family. As a result people would like to go and worship with their own people where they feel understood, are loved, can get information about many things, and where they feel they are valued (Interview, March 11, 2012).

Asked whether such experiences compelled her to move to an African congregation she persisted,

Trust me; the integration process in the church is a challenging one. Integration itself is not an easy experience. I had similar experience in my second church, the South West Bible Church in Beaverton, where I was even allowed to lead women's Bible studies. My contention is that believers in the various churches should have a sense of belonging. Many people say there is diversity but in the grassroots this is not a reality. Before joining PIC, I had the opportunity to attend other African churches where sometimes the experiences were similar. I had the conviction to join this church. I don't have to sound spiritual but really I had the conviction that PIC is the place for me (Interview, March 11, 2012).

Untrained Leadership Insights on the Formation of USA GPCs

Some founding caretakers or untrained leaders were also interviewed about the history of the formation of their congregations, societies, and assemblies. Paul Asiama, 61, stated,

Someone invited me to attend a "PCG" congregation. I was not impressed by the leadership style. It was one-man authoritarian leadership. Three of us then decided to start a "real" PCG called Bethel. Later leadership conflicts between myself and James made me quit. I organized a small cell prayer group in my home in Chicago. Later when we were outgrowing my living room, we accepted a worship place in a PCUSA congregation at the

Rogers Park, N Greenwich Ave. We then worshiped in the afternoons (Interview, October 18, 2010).

Asiama explained why the Bethel PCG is no longer at the Rogers Park location and about the formation of the OMF. He said, "Distance to the North side became a challenge for many of the South side members. Therefore, in January 2010, the Baptist church offered us their old chapel and we moved to the Indiana Avenue as the Bethel PCG. Again, when there was a plot to destroy the USA PCG congregations, I teamed up with others who stood up to organize the OMF congregations" (Interview, October 18, 2010). Ansah Ntow, 53, was one of the staunch Ghanaian members of the Trinity PCUSA, Fairfield, OH. Later, the Ghanaians in the Trinity congregation decided to worship by using their mother tongue. About the beginning of the Cincinnati PCG, Ntow said,

> Gradually we were able to convince the leadership of Trinity to worship separately. We started meeting once a month. A single thing that helped to unite us was the organization of the welfare system. We realized that when a Ghanaian member had a problem in Trinity no help came from the majority of the church. Organizing welfare for us as Ghanaians really helped us to meet our challenges. One Sunday, we travelled to worship with the Calvary PCG of Columbus, OH. This Ghanaian worship experience encouraged us. One senior member of Calvary PCG became our advocate and encourager. He started to visit us every two weeks to worship with us. Another issue that brought us together was the organization of our welfare system. On September 21, 2009, a couple and his wife offered us their home to begin worshipping as PCG congregation. This was the beginning of Cincinnati PCG (Interview, April 11, 2011).

Other insights came from the lay ministerial leadership of the diaspora GPCs in the USA. All of them were also first generation OBGs. In the Newark GEMC, Opanyin Fosu, 70, stated, "Two families started the GEMC in 1998. When I joined them upon my arrival in 1999, I eventually became the caretaker. In the Methodist church we only have pastors and caretakers" (Interview, November, 19, 2011). Presiding elder Lawrence Owusu of the Philadelphia CoP also said, "It all started when in late 1995, five family members decided to meet and pray in my home. At this genesis prayer meeting of the assembly, the members present were resolved to meet weekly" (Target Group Interview, October 15, 2005).

Eldership Insights on the Formation of USA GPCs

Narratives from some OBG founding members and elders on the formation of GPCs' congregations, societies, and assemblies are reported. Afua Okobea of PCGNY recalled,

> My late husband and the first minister of the church were instrumental in bringing me to PCGNY. As one of the early members some 26 years ago, I had to work hard on the membership drive because we were not getting members. On the very first occasion that I was invited, I was given a pad and a pen and I instantly became the clerk of the congregation for 12 years. The late former Moderator who inaugurated the congregation told us that we could not have a minister without a session. Therefore, on the same day that our first PCGNY minister was ordained, we were also installed as session members. I was installed as the clerk of session. Eventually, I became also a founding member of the OMF (Interview, December 2, 2010).

Edward Ansong, a founding member of the OMF and the Ebenezer PCG, Bronx, gave extensive answers about the formation of diaspora congregations in the USA. He provided insightful answers on various issues. With regard to his involvement in OMF activities, he said,

> For me to live is Christ. I have a problem when it comes to having a condoning life other than the Bible, God, and God's work. I feel I have a mandate from God to work for Him. In the PCGNY, after a number of all-night prayers, we had church extension excursions to Virginia and Canada. These activities culminated in the Presbyterian churches in Toronto, Canada, and Woodbridge, VA. Now these congregations, unfortunately, are affiliated to the Presbyterian Church of Canada (PCC) and PCUSA, respectively (Interview, December 2, 2010).

Ansong also knew about the formation processes for immigrant churches in the state of New York. He had this to say on the matter,

> To form a congregation in NY, one needs three basic things: 1) registration; 2) place of worship, and 3) appropriate steps which include: a) federal identification number; b) registration with the State. Also (i) the church has to declare who will be responsible if it is dissolved, especially if there is a debt (ii) dissolution responsibility persons; c) offices of the church (Interview, December 2, 2010).

Encouraged to elaborate, Asong stated,

> The other important items include: 4) Federal Document. This is the famous Form 501C. It is the authority to collect money and not to pay taxes. Here, the church should declare: a) officials in the church, e.g. the

minister, the clerk, senior presbyter, the finance director, among others; b) declaration of those on the pay roll; c) how leaders will deal with influence: (i) nobody should influence decisions in the church; (ii) documentation of everything regarding the formation; and (iii) how the church will deal with conflict. Finally, iv) What arms length? This involves three things: a) Negotiation. It defines how the church's administration will do business. Here, all administration should be in the consultative body or council; b) 'American Way,' i.e. when the council of the church says 'this,' there should be somebody within the council who should say 'no;' c) working of committees. For Ebenezer, I wrote everything (Interview, December 2, 2010).

Joyce Baah, 47, is a founding senior Presbyter of the PCG nursery congregation in Atlantic City. She said,

My faith is very important to me. Human beings exist in this universe to obey, worship, and serve God in mission. Accordingly, I believe God sent me to this part of the world to help form His church. When we relocated to Atlantic City, somebody had started a Pentecostal church in his basement, which I attended. I was so much encouraged that as soon as my family bought a house, I started gathering some people in our living room to worship God, beginning in July 2009. My main concern is about my children. To protect them from the influences of the diverse neighborhood, I always send them to church to get some Christian values in them (Interview, December 2, 2010).

Michael Gyamfi, 60, is one of the two stewards of the Newark GEMC. When interviewed, he narrated how he became a member and his involvement of its formation by saying,

When I came to the USA, I joined an African-American church. Later, I joined a Ghanaian charismatic church because I did not get fulfillment. I was still not comfortable because their worship style was so much of the outward expressive form without any depth. Then I visited an African market owned by a Ghanaian. Here I saw a flyer that advertized the GEMC. When I joined them, I recognized that Opanyin Fosu, who knew my family background, was already a member. He introduced me to the church. Later I was appointed one of stewards. Through trials and tribulations we have been able to sustain this society in Newark (Interview, December 11, 2011).

Prompted to expound further on his involvement in the formation of the society, Gyamfi said,

When I joined the church it was in its formative years. This society actually started with many of the members who were not originally Methodists back home in Ghana. They joined because it is a Ghanaian community church. Therefore, we had to go back to the basics. We had to contact the mother church back home to inquire on what to do and how to go about its organization. Currently, the Methodist church in Ghana itself has gone through a lot of changes, which we have to be abreast with and go by. In a way, my little contribution in teaching these basics of the holiness movement in Methodism has helped all of us to reach where we are now in unity (Interview, December 11, 2011).

Kwadwo Osei Agyemang, 53, the other steward of the GEMC, had elaborate information about the formation of the society. He said,

I am a Methodist as I grew up in that church in Ghana. In fact when I came here to the USA, I went to worship in the United Methodist church briefly. I could not stay there because their form of worship does not conform to the way we worship in Ghana. Again, because of my Scripture Union (SU) background, their form of worship did not click with me. So I joined a Baptist church and worshipped from city to city, especially NY. One day, I met a school friend who had organized a prayer cell meeting who invited me to speak during one of their meetings and I eventually became a member. This friend of mine belonged to the Church of God; the group gradually resulted in a Ghanaian Community Church of God when it started to become larger and larger in Newark.
(Interview, December 11, 2011).

Asked to narrate how he eventually became a member of GEMC, Agyemang said,

One day, when we went to worship, we realized that another group was meeting in the same building. This group is now the GEMC. My wife on that first day just stood up and walked to join the Methodists. I could not join them immediately because of my leadership role in the Church of God. I was stuck with them until the year 2000. Unfortunately, my friend had documentation problems. He was arrested by the immigration officers and deported back to Ghana. The Ghanaian Church of God then folded. The situational crisis then made it easy for me to move to join my wife and my Methodists. When I joined them it was not long that I was asked to become the secretary of the church. Things began to happen in rapid succession and the church simply broke up. A faction, mainly made up of the younger generation, went away to form another Methodist church with the then minister. When that happened, those of us who remained had to organize ourselves to sustain the church. I then became the steward in 2006 (Interview, December, 2011).

Agyemang continued,

At the critical time that we needed pastoral care, a student-pastor studying in the Princeton Theological Seminary (PTS) came in to help us despite his being a Presbyterian minister. As a man of God, it did not matter for him to come from another denomination or to travel the long distance from PTS to Newark in order to help us stabilize the church. At times I even forgot that he is a Presbyterian minister because he functioned more than a Methodist minister. GEMC is a society that takes into account the complete individual person. We come to church, we sing our hymns and gospel songs, and we release much tension built up through the stressful socio-economic life of America. We also praise our Lord and Savior Jesus Christ, study the Bible in Christian education from our cultural perspective, and we create Christian fellowship among ourselves. The way the church treats members is about Christian love. That love remains among all members; it transcends to everyone. When individuals have activities, the whole church will mourn or rejoice with them. This is more precious. There is a lot of stress but when we meet together we endeavor to put stress outside to build and lift each other up (Interview, December 11, 2011).

About the formation of the Philadelphia CoP, Okyere Asiedu, 55, a member of the local presbytery stated,

The first crusade of the assembly was held in the Church of God on Chestnut Street in August 1995. The intent was to make people of the Philadelphia area aware of the existence of the church. Despite the wide publicity, most of the people who came for the crusade were members of the assemblies in New York, Newark, and Atlantic City. The then national Apostle, the main speaker and the international head of the church in New York, indicated that church planting was a spiritual activity and that the spiritual impact of the crusade could not be seen with the physical eye. He was optimistic that through the crusade, a devastating blow had been dealt to the kingdom of Satan. He emphasized that very soon the results of the crusade would be seen (Target Group Interview, October 15, 2005).

Brando Akoto, one of the members of the PIC board of elders narrated his own story of how he became a member and the formation of the church. He said,

I got married in Ghana and my African-American wife came back to the USA to do her masters. She lived in Massachusetts but had come to Ghana for a Peace Corps program. When she got back to the USA, she found out that she was pregnant. The issue now was whether I was going to come to live here with her because she was determined to complete her masters. She convinced me to move to America after our son was born. Before then, I had told her to find a church and she found PIC, which was being set up in 1993 (Interview, February 12, 2012).

Asked to come out with how his wife got to know of PIC and how he came to be a member, Akoto said,

Pastor Nelson-Owusu, one of the founding leaders of PIC was working in the same building with my wife. She was invited by the pastor and ended up attending PIC. On my part, I already knew Bishop Anyomi when I was a member of the Action Faith Church in Ghana. Bishop Anyomi had had repeated vision of church planting worldwide. Meanwhile, the members were meeting to pray, which they had done for a year. Bishop Anyomi had deep contact with the African community in Portland. He also knew many of the students who were schooling in the PSU and Western Seminary. It was these contacts, among others, who came together to pray and eventually form the church, including my wife. Therefore, when I came to the USA, I had no option but to join her in this church, which was in its formative stage (Interview, February 12, 2012).

Following the formation of GPCs the necessary follow-up is the development of the gathered members.

THEOLOGICAL DEVELOPMENT: "MINISTERING TO" USA GPCs

The gospel is embodied in five important developmental practices, namely, discipleship (*didache*), worship (*leiturgia*), witness (*marturia*), belonging (*koinonia*), and service (*diakonia*). For their internal development, the GPCs have engaged in three of these: worship, discipleship, and fellowship in "ministering to the diaspora." Development, the teaching ministry of the church, is further associated with the internal maturity of the general membership with regard to its cognitive and spiritual growth.

In development, "ministering to the diaspora" becomes intra-congregational functional pastoral and ministerial roles. Pastoral role suggests the winning of souls, the feeding and tending the flock of Christ through shepherding, and discipleship of the flock. Ministerial role indicates any other functional activities of the servant leadership of Christ. Two other major markers of the theological aspects of ministry are fellowship and the apostolate of the laity based on the tenet of the priesthood of all believers (1 Peter 2:9, 10).

Ministry as Fellowship
(Belonging and Team Building)—*Koinonia*

A major ministry practice is fellowship—belonging, otherwise known in Greek as *koinonia*. It includes the practice of hospitality, introduction of people, ushering, congregational care, and even dining together, among others. Small groups matter in every congregation where the individual is important. African communal "we feeling" philosophy is the cynosure of GPCs' theological development. Everything happening to the individual happens to the community and vice versa. "The individual can only say 'I am, because we are; and since we are, therefore I am.' This is a cardinal point in the understanding of the African view of man" (John Mbiti 1969: 106). Since the assimilated LBGs are prone to be individualistic through the influence of USA pop-culture, the diaspora GPCs offer the opportunity for enjoying some form of community life. This offers priceless context for their development.

Ministry as Lay Involvement

Another aspect of theological development is lay involvement. Movement away from ministry as the monopoly of the ordained (theology of the ordained) to ministry as the responsibility of the whole people of God (theology of lay ministry) is one of the most dramatic shifts taking place in this early 21st century era. David Bosch, in identifying the "apostolate of the laity" (2005: 472) and in addressing the tasks of the church and theology in our time, formulated six theses, one of which stated, "Christian theology… will no longer be simply a theology for priests and pastors, but also a theology for the laity in their callings…Lay persons…are not to accompany the office bearers. It is the office bearers who have to accompany…the latter's mission of the people of God" (Bosch 2005: 472). This shows that for any leader to consider ministry as a do it-alone-business is disastrous.

The theology of the laity does not mean that the laity should be trained to become miniature pastors. Their service for ministry is offered in the form of the ongoing life of the Christian community in stores, classrooms, offices, towns, villages, farms, and homes, among others. "Lay ministry is the phenomenon of 'base' or 'small' Christian communities…including house church groups in the West" (Bosch 2005: 472). In institutional development the laity is indispensable. In the majority or two-thirds world for instance, where the voices of the poor are silenced, the church should be the voice of the voiceless. Since God has deliberately chosen to be on the side of the poor, the needy, the stigmatized, and the marginalized, it is the ministry of the church to fight on the side of and for such people. This is a combined ministry of both the clergy and the laity to the extent that it becomes impossible to distinguish who is doing what. The GPCs should gather courage to perform this prophetic role by their USA congregations.

ORGANIZATIONAL DEVELOPMENT: "MINISTERING TO" USA GPCs

Organizational aspect of ministry consists of the various functional strategies of sustaining the development of congregational members. Two of

John Nevius and Henry Venn's "three-selfs" (self-propagation, self-governing, and self-finance) and Paul Hiebert's self-theologizing are relevant under the organizational dimension of ministry. Out of the "three-selfs," self-governing and self-supporting are important for our purpose.

Ministry as Self-Governance—Polity of USA GPCs

Most of the GPCs in the USA are self-governing. Their sessions, councils, boards, or ruling elders are made of members either appointed by the leadership or elected by the members. For instance, the agents (ministers, apostles, pastors, bishops, catechists, and caretakers) are appointed while the other members of the local elders are either appointed or elected. In the end, USA GPCs are self-governing without any external control except its own system. Gyang-Duah stressed,

> Some members think because they helped to start the congregations, they have the authority in arrogating to themselves very high and permanent positions. Others in the church want to monopolize the administration of the congregations. These are very challenging for the Ghanaian diaspora church. Taking power from such people by the rules and regulations of the various denominations should be a gradual process, though (Interview, May 25, 2010).

Finding it difficult to let go of their positions, even though they may have relocated from their neighborhoods, some leaders then drive long distances to attend church services and other activities of their congregations, societies, or assemblies.

Ministry as Self-Finance, Self-Reliance, or Self-Support

In the ministry of self-support, tithe payment is a ritual. It is believed that God bestows abundant life or withholds prosperity depending upon the attitude of the individual in order to uphold proper ritual behavior (Psalm 91, 126; Malachi 3:8-10; Luke 6:38; and 2 Corinthians 8, 9:6-15). "Humans participate in these blessings through proper ritual behaviour which includes the payment of tithes...and offerings...the *ritual* of tithing is believed to be the actual key that unlocks God's storehouse of prosperity and releases His protection against the onslaught of the forces of evil" (Kingsley Larbi 2002: 427). Philip Jenkins suggested the blessings received from Christian giving by stating, "Once Malachi is given this awesome status, the reader pays special attention to its rules for living, which strongly emphasizes giving God what is rightly His, especially in tithes and offerings. Christian churches...encourage believers to give according to their means, and ideally, to tithe" (2007: 92).

Diaspora GPCs in the USA are self-finance or self-reliant. They have used the biblical concept of tithing as a means of thanksgiving. As a ritualized performance, members are thus encouraged to practice tithing in order to receive divine blessings. Offertory and other fund raising activities are also organized. These include annual thanksgiving harvests. These finances are raised and controlled by members themselves without any external funding, whether foreign or local. The funds are used to run the congregations, societies, or assemblies and support their international head offices and their mother church back home in a transnational ministry.

THEMATIC RESEARCH ON THE DEVELOPMENT OF USA GPCs

There were mixed reactions with regard to the issue of development. Some of the OBGs, including some clergy, perceived development as physical infrastructure. Conversely, almost all the second-generation members decried the lack of development as spiritual growth in their congregations, societies, and assemblies.

Pastoral Insights on the Development of USA GPCs

Yaw Asiedu had a mixed reaction for development. He stated,

> I consider development as both satisfactory and unsatisfactory. PCGNY started with 11 adults and 1 child in 1985 and has easily grown to be the largest congregation of the PCG OMF. This is a positive development because it has grown to over 500 members. Since it has now acquired its own worship place at West 123 St, Harlem, development is satisfactory (Interview, June 2, 2010).

With regard to the PCGNY unsatisfactory development, he added,

> Development is unsatisfactory, however, due to some challenges. Members' participation in beyond-Sunday teaching activities, prayer meetings, revivals, deliverance services, and discipleship is most challenging. Lack of time for other ministry activities is the bane of many of PCGNY members. Even regular worship times should necessarily be adjusted to ensure maximum participation (Interview, June 2, 2010).

Joyce also had the following to say about development in her congregation,

> When I became a Christian, I developed an interest in praying, fasting, and Bible study without which I would not be able to become a minister. As a

minister, I give my members what I have. And what I have is Jesus Christ. At the moment, development is adequate. In Worcester PCG, teaching, guidance, prayer, and Bible studies are present and satisfactory (Interview, April 9, 2010).

For Stephen Kwaku Owusu the developmental process of the Methodists is based on the acronym IWA. He said,

> Methodists have an acronym upon which development is based. These are IWA—intellect, will, and affection. First, for intellect, there is the development of the mind. This is what we study and know about God. The Bible says that without knowledge, my people perish. Knowledge without wisdom is fruitless, though. Therefore, we seek God's wisdom in addition to knowledge as Methodists. Second, with regard to the will, there is the willing commitment of members. Again the Great commandment is to love our God with all our soul, heart, strength, and mind and love our neighbors as ourselves. In this society, members' commitment in terms of time factor and tithe payment is good. Third, affection is the whole gamut of the worship experience (Interview, November 19, 2011).

Asked to explain affection further, Owusu continued,

> African Methodists are noted for expressiveness in their feelings. We sing, shout, and dance, which exhibits our emotional feelings. In the Newark GEMC, for our development, we have Bible studies on Wednesdays (7-9 pm) and prayer meetings on Friday (7-9 pm). Various organizations such as the youth, women's and men's groups, and the choir, among others, also have their meetings in which they study the Bible, pray, and fellowship (Interview, November 19, 2011).

Owusu further expatiated, "Methodists have an important system—the class system—which, though somehow organized here, does not strictly work in the USA. Hindrances for the lack of the class system include work schedules, lack of time, lack of circumstances on the part of members to meet together, and the shifting system. For example, even for Sunday worship services members attend bi-weekly" (Interview, November, 2012). Asked for his opinion what should be done to improve individual development, Owusu said, "The grown—those who already know seek to mature. Others, however, are only in the church for the satisfaction of actual and felt-needs. Commitment and time factor make development good. Here, commitment would mean financial, time spent for God, and place and frequency of meeting. All these show individual commitment, growth, and maturity" (Interview, November, 2011). Saka Ntiamoah described how development has improved both spiritually and physically in the Philadelphia CoP. He said,

> When I was transferred to this assembly, we were worshipping in the old chapel of the Larchwood Street Christ of Calvary Baptist Church. I immediately instituted the Friday all-day prayer and Bible studies in which members came to participate according to their time schedules. I also encouraged them to attend the district Christmas, Easter, and Holy Ghost and Youth conventions. Participants of these conventions enjoy the fruitful teachings and worship experiences for their individual development. When the opportunity offered itself, we organized ourselves to purchase the sanctuary of the Catholic Church on the South 26th street with the attached conference hall from our own resources. Later we also purchased a house to serve as a manse for the pastoral leadership. What the members should realize is that all these are a reflection of God's glory and favors. They also show their maturity and growth with regard to their giving commitment to Christ (Interview, October 15, 2007).

Like Yaw Asiedu of PCGNY, Ato Pratt of the VBC-I also found development relatively unsatisfactory. He stated,

> Back home in Ghana, it is easier to organize Bible studies, prayer meetings, revivals, crusades, and the like. I think our development is not satisfactory. This is one of the major challenges as an immigrant church in the USA. Lack of time is a major cause for the unsatisfactory development. People claim they have come to America chasing the dollar. Thus, development is difficult. Moreover, many diaspora Ghanaians are looking for association. They join churches in order to associate with others in terms of celebrating the rites of passage such as births, marriages, and funerals. However, in the Christian faith, these are added benefits—bonuses. With the resurrection power, the propitiation of sin that Christ achieved for humanity is the basis for believers' faith. Accordingly, believers are to engage in developmental activities that will help them mature into Christ-like nature in discipleship (Interview, November 28, 2011).

Kofi Nelson-Owusu reflected on the development in PIC by saying,

> When PIC started, there was no church with African flavor in Portland. Thus, the church grew very fast. There was division, so I left, but the Lord asked me to come back in 1997. The church has a mission. Some people come to PIC and, after they are shaped, they go away. When I came back I became the associate pastor and now I am the pastor. Some of the people who leave PIC call me and thank me for their time here with us. Now our focus and passion of the church is the city of Portland. God says, 'I brought this church here for a purpose. I want you to stand in the gap for Portland." Accordingly, PIC is counted upon to intercede for the other churches to survive and grow. Thus, intercessory prayer is our means of development (Interview, February 26, 2011).

Carroll's views on development seemed slightly different from her senior pastor Nelson-Owusu. She stressed motivation several times by saying,

> If I have to be honest with you, pastor, I think the first thing for PIC is motivation to believe again. When people don't believe in anything done in the church they cannot do their best. They may hear the message but they will not be motivated to worship as genuine Christians. For example, to have a vibrant church is not a manifestation of technical skills. Rather members should be motivated. When people feel discouraged, bruised, or disillusioned, they may find it difficult to believe and difficult to do anything. Motivation must prevail; there should be revival. From motivation, ministries such as prayer, Bible studies, and youth ministry, among others, should be vibrant to satisfy actual and felt-needs. This will make the practice of Christianity meaningful to all the various sectors of the church. People should be motivated to do what they are supposed to do. That is when development will increase (Interview, March 11, 2011).

Untrained Leadership Insights on the Development of USA GPCs

The responses from four caretakers, a CoP presiding elder, and a board elder of PIC indicated that the presence of many untrained lay leaders in the USA GPCs reflects a lack of development. Paul Asiama admitted, "We have lacked much discipleship, leadership training, and other activities in the Chicago Bethel PCG. For me evangelism has an inverse relationship with the presence of manpower. Without manpower, there is no development and there is no resultant reaching out" (Interview, October 18, 2010). Dwomo Sarpong simply stated, "Lack of development for the lay leaders is where we have serious problems. I think activities that will help members develop spiritually should be intensified" (Interview, November 23, 2010). Ansah Ntow also confirmed, "Cincinnati needs more developmental materials and methods. For instance, most of the members are available for leading Bible studies. Therefore, I constantly call on the OMF leaders to come down to help us" (Interview, April 9, 2011). Opanyin Fosu stated,

> The society of GEMC has planned to organize revivals and all night services for its development. As the caretaker, I have helped the society to be organized into the Methodist class system, which we knew back home in Ghana. Trying to do our best here, it's organized into the day-born groups. Thus, we have seven classes in the system. Everyone in the society is given to a class leader to follow up. The system is reminiscent of the American senate. We believe that if well organized in terms of Bible studies, fellowship, and prayer, spiritual growth of members will improve tremendously (Interview, November 19, 2011).

studies, witness, and spiritual growth. If we do not have spiritual growth that is when the devil can strike and bring division. That's why Jesus said we should watch and pray. Watching and praying diligently will make the devil fail to destroy God's people. Thank God that we have gone back to the very foundations of our faith: prayer, God's Word, and witness. When these happen, they bring true fellowship and true fellowship brings growth. I thank God that we have slowly but surely started growing again (Interview, December, 11, 2011).

Second Generation OBG and LBG Insights on the Development of USA GPCs

Like Boye-Doe and others, the younger generations were not inspired about the OBG perception of development. Even worship, the most organized ministry, is found boring by some of them. For instance, Kwaku Boakye reflected,

> I was born into a Presbyterian home. In my family where every night we read the Bible and prayed together, the Christian faith played a large role as we grew up. I have two different kinds of friends. With my Caucasian friends who are outside the church, Christianity is a no-go area in our conversations. It is not the same with Ghanaian friends. Organizing separate youth services is very important for youth development. My advocacy for the youth service in PCGNY, separate from the sometimes-boring adult services, has yielded the current interesting results (Interview, November 12, 2010).

Tiwaa shared similar sentiments with Boakye about development. She said,

> My home and upbringing have informed my faith. In 1996, I became a member of the Junior Youth. I was confirmed in 1999. I did not receive fulfillment until an inter-Christian conference in College. Pastor George, the speaker, was influential in my becoming a Christian. At his altar call, I just moved forward to accept Christ. Thus, I accepted Christ in America. I then realized that Christian development entails having a personal relationship with Christ our Lord, praying unceasingly, and reading the Bible so much. These things I did not get in PCGNY (Interview, November 12, 2010).

Looking at development from the perspective of the youth, Tiwaa added,

> Youth services have influenced me and are very important in shaping the youth. The youth cannot relate to the adults more than they can relate to their peers. We see the adults as boring. I want to be frank with you,

pastor. No! I don't see any development in this congregation because in my view it is unspiritual. There is no Christ present. We just go through motions and our emotions. For the next five years, I want to see leaders who are listening to Christ and I want to see more Christian education for development (Interview, November 12, 2010).

Expressing similar sentiments from Tiwaa, for Moet, development is vital for the youth. She said,

The youth is a group of people I call "baby Christians." We have to do things to entice them. We have to make them youth for Jesus in the Christian faith. We have to engage them. Every Sunday, activities should be different for them. For instance, every Sunday, I feel lifted up in a different ways. Different pastors deliver different inspirational messages. I, therefore, grow in answered prayer through these pastors. This is what should be done for the youth. I am a member of the Contact Teens Ministry. We use English language, English music, and other activities to redirect their misplaced priorities to meaningful use. Development for the church's future will be guaranteed and assured through such activities for the youth (Interview, December 20, 2011).

Billy, 11, expressed one of the most emotional statements. "Pastor, this is not a church," he said. Asked about why he was making such a statement, Billy explained, "Because the adults don't care for us as their children when we go to church" (Interview, March 14, 2010). For Billy, development simply means caring for the innocent and vulnerable young ones in the children's services of the GPCs.

MOBILIZATION FOR "GLOCAL" MISSION ("THROUGH" AND "BY/BEYOND")

Transformational development necessarily culminates in the passion in mobilization, which constitutes motivation, engagement, and encouragement in the practice of mission. Whether for traditional or diaspora missiology, congregational maturity is a direct reflection of how members are motivated, mobilized, and engaged in carrying out missions. In other words, developmental maturity is a reflection of the positive relationship between the passion for witnessing and their fellowship, worship services, and other activities as Christ's disciples. Ralph Winter stated, "Essentially, mobilization refers to any process by which God's people are awakened and kept moving and growing until they find their place for strategic involvement in the task of completing world evangelization" (Mission Mobilizers 2007: c6).

"Mission/Ministering through the diaspora" expresses the fact of "glocal mission." The term "glocal" combines global and local to demonstrate that "missions through" diaspora can be both (Bob Roberts <http://www.amazon.com; http://www.christianitytoday.com; http://mattstone.blogs.com/Christian/glocal; http://www.christianitytoday.com; http://www.elca.org> October 1, 2011). On one hand, in its global perspective, it is the practice of mission to an ethnic group's own members elsewhere—that is, wherever they are found globally. On the other hand, it is the diaspora reaching out to their own groups back in their motherland. The Christian story essentially summarizes who Jesus Christ is and why He is special in the proclamation of the reign of God. As a result, mission should strive for the inseparable quantitative and qualitative development in the GPCs because unmobilized membership is a reflection of the lack of transformational discipleship.

"Missions Through the Diaspora:" Foreign Land Ethnic Consciousness

"Missions through the diaspora" is the nurturing of GPCs' members for external missions toward other members of the generic Ghanaian diaspora in the USA. It is "reference to the missions whereby the diasporas are evangelizing their kinsmen in their homeland or elsewhere" (LDLT 2010). The Ghanaian diaspora has had a "strong ethnic group consciousness sustained over a long time and based on a sense of distinctiveness, a common history, and the belief in a common fate" (Robin Cohen 1997: 177-196). Ethnic Associations (EAs) are one of the social institutions set up in the Ghanaian diaspora to solve physiological, psychological, spiritual, and socio-economic needs.

Three of the reasons for setting up EAs are identified. These reasons are similar to those for the formation of GPCs. First, like all African societies, the foremost underlying principle for EAs is that the individual is not an island. Consequently, family relational core values such as community, communality, and commonality are the overall objective of the EAs. Second, *Nnoboa* is an *Akan* term that literally means self-help. It comes from the subsistence farming system of the *Akan* in which farmers help each other to prepare their lands. *Nnoboa* and fraternizing serve the function of providing the needs of EA members. The concept provides communal support to diaspora Ghanaians in the USA. This concept was found in the constitutions of all the EAs. For instance, one of the objectives of an association stated, "Consolidating individual efforts in their sojourn in the USA to help one another" (*Kwahu* Association Constitution: 2). Other EAs had similar objectives. Third, networking is the major objective of the National Council of Ghanaian Associations (NCOGA) Inc. The objective affirmed in its constitution stated, "The Council shall be an umbrella association of all the Ghanaian associations in the tri-state area and shall be oriented towards: Fostering unity, harmony, understanding, and cooperation" (NCOGA, Inc.: 2)

March 6 is the anniversary of Ghana's political independence. Ghanaians all over the world celebrate this national Independence Day. On March 6, 2010, one such celebration was organized in Portland, OR, where all Ghanaian ethnic groups gathered to celebrate Ghana's independence. Another celebration on October 17, 2010, was the GHANAFEST (Ghana Festival), a joyous celebration and festival of Ghanaian culture by the various ethnic groups in Chicago, IL. The celebrations included cultural displays, recitals, singing, drumming and dancing, and Ghanaian foods. Following the EAs, Ghanaians have changed some homes, garages, warehouses, and dilapidated buildings into impressive chapels. Indeed, if GPCs want to practice "missions through diaspora," the obvious breeding grounds for membership drive are the EAs because it will be easier to strategically mobilize members for the practice of diaspora missions there.

"Missions By and Beyond the Diaspora:" Ministry as Witness—*Marturia*

Witness, evangelization, or *marturia* involves bringing individuals, households, and communities to repentant faith in the Lord Jesus Christ. This leads to salvation through conviction of sin by the Holy Spirit. As Paul suggests, believers are made holy in order to make Christ visible in their bodies (2 Corinthians 3:2). The goal of witness is to make Christ visible to others. Since God comes to people through other people, members of the diaspora GPCs must not imprison themselves in the four walls of chapels and refer to themselves as Christian. They should "go and make disciples" (Matthew 28:18, 19).

Coupled with "missions through the diaspora," witnessing will help "missions by and beyond the diaspora" reach out to indigenous peoples and other ethnic groups in the USA multi-ethnic context. Here, diaspora GPC members are obligated to be obedient to make disciples out of unreached Americans and members of the other ethnic groups. The mandate is to teach them to obey what the Lord Jesus Christ has commanded all believers in the Great Commission. "When members…have adjusted to the culture of the host country, they are the natural bridges for 'ministering beyond them' to reach residents of the host country" (Enoch Wan 2010; Cho and Houston, eds. 2010: 95). While "missions by the diaspora" is the means (what), "missions beyond the diaspora" is the method (how).

THEMATIC RESEARCH ON MOBILIZATION FOR MISSION OF USA GPCs

Mobilization for "mission through diaspora" and "mission by and beyond diaspora" seem challenging for the USA GPCs. While the former is relatively encouraged, the latter is the most challenging because of legalities, secularization, and extreme religious rights, and non-acceptance, among others. Some of the GPCs have decided to practice the "mission by and beyond the diaspora" from their inception. The PIC in Portland, OR, is one such congregation that was chosen as the fifth case study in Chapter 7.

Pastoral Insights on Mobilization for Mission

The ministerial leadership conceded the slow pace of mobilization for mission. Gyang-Duah deemed this slow pace frustrating by saying,

> Reaching out? Hm! This is a problem. It is so frustrating for us as leaders. The best way is to recognize that Christians have a mandate for outreach. At the moment, reaching out to the unreached Ghanaians is first step. Reaching other ethnicities is, then, the ultimate goal. The question, however, is do Americans accept immigrant churches as such? Do they recognize us as fellow Christians serving the same God they serve? I doubt if Americans have accepted immigrant churches as part of the Body of Christ in their midst (Interview, May 30, 2010).

Yaw Asiedu also expressed similar frustrations,

> Mobilization for mission has been unsatisfactory. Because of the laws of America, missions and evangelization are difficult. Attitudes of "being politically correct" or "who are you to tell me how I should practice my faith?" are detrimental to mission in the USA. Financing mobilization for mission is another tough issue. For instance, PCGNY, has been extremely nonresponsive—to contribute $500.00 a month for evangelism. New strategies have to be aggressively used rather than the traditional mission and evangelization means. The session should liaise with the professionals in the congregation for mobilization and outreach activities (Interview, June 2, 2010).

The sentiments expressed by Joyce are no different,

> I concede that in this area the congregation is not doing well. I continue to tell the members that, as Christians, all believers must be prayerful and go out there to proclaim and witness for Christ. I, therefore, see motivation and encouragement as individual effort. It is a fact that the general institutional training, mobilization, motivation, and engagement for

mission and church planting are lacking. I have tried to mobilize members to plant a congregation in Leominster, a suburb of Worcester. The challenge is finding a worship place (Interview, April 9, 2010).

Stephen Kwaku Owusu enumerated about five means of mobilization for mission. He, however, concluded that mission by/beyond is problematic. He said,

> In the GEMC there are several methods of mobilization and engagement of the members for mission. First, during social gatherings, members use the opportunity to spread the gospel. They then invite their relatives, friends, and contacts. Second, self-help is another means through which the church is attractive. Members help themselves during times of birth, marriage, and funerals. Third, the phone is used for the contacts and invitation of distant, new, and other members. Fourth newsletters, flyers, and leaflets are used to advertize the church. Newspapers such as the quarterly Methodist Herald for Builders (MHB) are written to advertize the church to attract members in the Ghanaian community. Fifth, picnics are organized periodically. In these picnics non-members are invited and when they come to enjoy, they decide to remain and join the society. These make the church attractive to the Ghanaian community. The part that is challenging is the ministering by/beyond the Ghanaian community. We engage in help for home people. Through this we believe some may be won for Christ (Interview, November 19, 2011).

Ntiamoah Saka suggested two reasons for the CoP mobilization, encouragement, and engagement for mission in the USA that have resulted in its growth. He said,

> For me, the first and foremost reason for the spread of the church planting movement by the CoP is deeply rooted in the well-planned global training of evangelists. These are usually commissioned to plant assemblies of the church wherever they are. I am an example of such a strategic program. The second reason is the community-based church panting strategy. The main strategy here is the idea of conventions organized with the ultimate goal of planting a church. This has been an age-long strategy and the CoP-I considers it as the gathering or assembling of the people of God to worship and praise Him. These conventions are organized annually in areas targeted for evangelistic work. They include Christmas, Easter, Holy Ghost, and Youth conventions. During these conventions, training of leaders, teachers, and evangelists are done in Bible studies, church administration, and general ministry. At the end of each convention, an assembly could be established and leaders appointed and commissioned to take charge.

Ntiamoah Saka continued,

Witness and aggressive evangelization for growth are synonymous to Pentecostalism. Mission and evangelization starts with the experiential encounter with the Lord Jesus Christ. The experience is referred to as "conversion growth." For Pentecostals, there is the need for the second experience for the baptism in the Holy Spirit regarded as empowerment for mission. When I was transferred to Philadelphia, our church had only one assembly, which was part of the Newark district. By the grace of God the Philadelphia district was inaugurated in 2005 when we planted assemblies in Delaware and other suburbs of Philadelphia.

David Ato Pratt said,

Mobilization for mission is challenging but we in VBC-I are trying. In mobilization and engagement, we select people with similar understanding or people who are matured and get along to use them as core group for witnessing to propagate the gospel. These core people are then trained and they are used to reach out. At the moment we are into "ministering to the diaspora" and "ministering through the diaspora" to a limited extent. Recently at our leaders' meeting, there was the proposal for reaching out to the prisons, old-aged homes, social centers, and the homeless in the subways, under bridges, and bus and train stations with the social gospel. So far these have not started because they are still on the drawing board. We are learning from our London branch, which has prisons and nursing homes ministries (Interview, November 20, 2011).

Kofi Nelson-Owusu indicated that mobilization for mission is a major objective of PIC. He said,

Reaching out to the lost of our society is the objective of PIC. We encourage members to reach out to people with friendship. We encourage our members also the share the life of our Lord to others. In addition, we engage and support short and long term external missionaries passing through PIC. Honestly we have not reached to the high level of sending missionaries yet. However, we support and pray for missionaries who are on these long and short-term missions. One time we joined a Presbyterian church to hold a missionary conference. The purpose was the mobilization for mission (Interview, February 26, 2012).

Unlike his fellow pastor in PIC who sees mobilization as internal and individual process, Carroll sees it as external and networking. She said,

The first thing is about understanding; I mean both internal and external understanding of each other in the African diaspora. Here, I propose networking for the African church leadership. I have also noticed that I could assume, conclude, and/or judge who you are until I get near you. This will break the barrier of differences. Again what PIC is struggling with are the same things other Africans churches are going through in the USA. This means that we all have a common enemy. In terms of motivation and engagement for mission, I will again stress that leading from behind or beneath is meaningful. To motivate others, relationship building is the key and it also includes building bridges. For instance, in the PIC, I visit the elders and engage them in conversation. This is helping me to know them and helps to resolve some of the issues and challenges raised. In trying to mobilize, organize, and network, the people of God could use their time, love, and prayer for each other and reach to others in the world (Interview, March 11, 2012).

Untrained Leadership Insights on Mobilization for Mission

The untrained leadership contended that the lack of training is the cause for the lack of mobilization for mission. Dwomo Sarpong observed, "General mobilization is difficult. Members have no or little time for God and God's work. Consequently mobilization for mission is unsatisfactory. The congregation can mobilize members through prayer. However, we are trying to do our best" (Interview, November 23, 2010).

Paul Asiama said, "Mobilization for mission is not part of my congregational goals. I do not engage in evangelism because I hardly involve myself in the parties and other activities of Ghanaians in Chicago. What happens in such activities is immorality" (Interview, October, 18, 2010). When asked whether his assertions are not judgmental, Asiama continued, "I do not have the moral courage to mobilize members for mission in the midst of drinking, eating, and compromised dancing. To improve the mission and evangelism of the OMF congregations, there is the need for manpower development. Internal training has also been difficult. For fear of losing one's job, many potential ministers do not like to leave their own jobs to train" (Interview, October 18, 2010).

Ansah Ntow also stated, "Our congregation has been only one-and-a-half years old. Thus, corporate mobilization for mission in Cincinnati PCG has not been so much so far. Mission and evangelism are not so much. Recently, one of the session members suggested engaging in mission by collecting food items and clothing for the poor. For us this is laudable suggestion for mission practice" (Interview, April 10, 2010).

Opanyin Fosu collaborated some of his minister's activities of the church's mobilization for mission among the Ghanaian community by saying, "Honestly, no house-to-house evangelism has been engaged in. GEMC's major outreach is done during various Ghanaian gatherings such as funerals, birthday parties, and outdooring. To begin with, we make flyers to inform people about such activities in the church. Then, during such occasions I am normally given ten to fifteen minutes to speak about the activities of the church and membership drive (Interview, November 19, 2011).

Laity Insights on Mobilization for Mission

A mixture of positive and negative expressions was received from the laity as they shared similar opinions from the clergy, the untrained caretakers and leaders. Witnessing has also been a marked developmental issue. Michael Gyamfi affirmed the activities that the pastor and caretaker of GEMC are using for mission by saying,

> With regard to mobilization for mission, apart from the spiritual life, we also engage in outdooring, funerals, picnics among others. Through such activities those who attend from outside are attracted to join the society. We have also participated in visitation and in religious activities such as the dramatization of some of the biblical stories in Lancaster, PA. This also attracts those who join us for such trips. Another form of mobilization depends on the activities of the various groups in this society. Men's fellowship, women's fellowship, the youth, and the like, who organize their own activities help in mobilizing members for mission because they invite their friends for such meetings. The choir, for instance, keep singing at various functions which witnesses to people outside the church. Put differently, witnessing has been one of the values of this church (Interview, December 11, 2011).

Collins Kwasi Asamoah Afriyie said, "Having been part of this church for a while, I have realized that members feel loved when they are mobilized and engaged. For instance when one is sick or perhaps something happens and many of the members visit, one feels loved and belonging. That helps them to reach out to others who are outside the church and this helps to attract other Ghanaians to join us" (Interview, December 11, 2011). Kwadwo Osei Agyemang conceded as a failure the inability of GEMC to practice mission by/beyond and suggested that members have to change their inward looking mentality and attitude in order to transform the society. He said,

> We have to change our mentality about a native church that remains a native church. I think this is one of our failures because we are not doing much to affect and transform the society we find ourselves in. We come to church, we worship, we sing our hymns, and we fellowship together among ourselves and we are done. Given the culture of America, we may find it difficult to engage in witnessing. However, we have to strategize well to do it. We have no other option because it is a commandment from the Lord and our mandate. For instance, if we were to be in Ghana, it would have been easier to organize crusades to affect our neighborhoods but this is not so in the USA. Here, maybe we need to do community work. In doing so, we need to involve other people in those communities. This will build bridges among the races. In addition, we can form teams to visit members of the community one-on-one. Indeed, we should change our

attitude and try to do our best. The ministry is not about us but so much to show that we care about others too (Interview, December 11, 2011).

Brando Akoto suggested that the lack of mobilization in any congregations lies with leadership by saying,

> Leadership makes a big difference with regard to mobilization for mission. I know that the founder of PIC is mission oriented when he was here. Members know this. The current pastor loves missions but he is different; members know this too. Members know that the church is mission oriented and every member has to be a missionary. For some time the pastor was interested but his disposition is supportive rather than participative. The point is that it is easier to lose focus of mission if the leader loses such a focus. Gradually, the pastor seems to change in attitude and this is positive (Interview, February 12, 2012).

For D. J., 28, the issue is with the attitude of some Christians. He said,

> Most young Ghanaians in the USA are perceived by the church as drunkards, fornicators, drug addicts, and good-for-nothings. Some of the churches such as the Church of Pentecost brand us as sinners and reject us with the 'holier than thou' attitude. Thus, I had come to my tribal association and found love, unity, and enjoyment of the family spirit. I find a 'we-feeling' in this Asante association. If any Ghanaian church wants to have converts from most of the members of the ethnic associations, it should come down to our level and listen to us (Target Group Interview, December 4, 2009).

Youthful Tiwaa also expressed the obvious by stating, "There is no mobilization for mission activities in this church. I want to be honest with you. When I meet people, I witness to them, but I will not recommend my congregation for them. It will just put me to shame. I blame the leaders. They have succeeded in making this church a social group" (Interview, November 12, 2010). Another youth from the same denomination as Tiwaa, Sandra Ampadu Asiama, had a different attitude towards mobilization for mission. Even though her congregation has not strictly gone into mobilization for mission, she has gone out personally to engage in social gospel. She said, "Right now, I would rather invite people to worship with us. So far I have invited five young people who visit us to enjoy our worship services, revivals, and other youth activities such playing soccer, picnics, and screening of discipleship DVDs. Since the mission of the church is not so much developed for reaching out, I am collecting clothing and other materials for the poor" (Interview, April 26, 2011)

SUMMARY

In Chapter 3, the first discussion was "missions/ministering to the diaspora" in light of the formation of USA PCG congregations through CPMs and planting of viable churches. The second discussion consisted of another "missions/ministering to the diaspora" Ghanaians with regard to development. The final discussion took together "missions and ministering through diaspora" and "missions by/beyond the diaspora" which discussed the mobilization for mission of the USA GPCs. Moving on, Chapter 4 explores the diversity, identity, and receptivity of the gospel of the Ghanaian diaspora.

QUESTIONS FOR DISCUSSION

1. What can we learn from the historical account of the formation and development of USA GPCs?
2. Are those insights relevant to other diaspora communities in the USA?
3. From the extensive quotations of data collected through personal interviews, what specific insights can be screened from the perspectives of pastoral staff, untrained leadership and 2nd generation of OBG and LBG?
4. What is "glocal" mission among Ghanaian diaspora in the USA?

Chapter 4
DIVERSITY, IDENTITY AND RECEPTIVITY OF GHANAIAN DIASPORA IN THE USA

INTRODUCTION

Discussion of the ethnographic distinctive markers such as diversity, identity, and receptivity of the gospel is critically important for this volume. The Ghanaian diaspora finds its unavoidable presence in the USA multi-cultural context. In view of this, OBGs and LBGs relatively cherish their identity formulation in their attempts to assimilate or not. At the same time, having immigrated to the USA with their religiosity from a high-context culture, the receptivity of the gospel sometimes become challenging in the USA low-context cultural milieu. The composition of Chapter 4 is an ethnographic understanding of the above distinctive markers by the Ghanaian diaspora in the multi-cultural USA. Utilizing three case stories, the chapter covers a description of diversity and its markers, addresses identity and its formulation in the USA, and concludes with the receptivity of the gospel by the USA Ghanaian diaspora.

DIVERSITY OF THE GHANAIAN DIASPORA IN MULTI-CULTURAL USA

Diversity expresses itself in ethnic, cultural, religious, and linguistic dimensions (Wan and Edu-Bekoe 2010, 2011; Moreau and Snodderly 2011: 35-

62). It also includes generational variation. Case story 4.1 is an example of the generational variation of the Ghanaian diaspora in the USA.

> **Case Story 4.1: Teenage Disconnection with Adult Generation**
>
> In November 2009, a Ghanaian boy, 13, jumped from the balcony of the 22nd floor of the Tracy Towers in the Bronx, NY. The mother had prevented him from going out to play basketball after school. She had told him to finish eating his lunch, which she was preparing in the kitchen. He was also to finish his homework before she would allow him to go. On the spur of a moment the mother went from the kitchen to the balcony only to witness her son falling downward to his death on the pavement.

One cultural and moral value in this case story is obedience. Ghanaian traditional orientation of the mother would have been to obey the parent. However, this boy was born in a different cultural context altogether. Diaspora LBGs in the USA are born in a diverse society with different ethnic groups. Therefore, their identity formulation is different from their OBG parents. In the USA, apart from the home the school, peer pressure, and the neighborhoods are all nurturing grounds.

Categorization of Diversity

Some scholars differentiate diversity into two-dimensional contrasting categories. Lingenfelter and Mayers regarded the two dimensions of diversity as cognitive and categorized them into dichotomistic and holistic thinking. In Figure 4.1 is a representation of the two types of thinking (2003: 54).

"Dichotomistic thinkers tend to categorize people into specific roles…In contrast, Holistic thinkers…are somewhat suspicious of people who appear faultless and are more tentative about condemning the faulty" (Lingenfelter and Mayers 2003: 54, 55). James Plueddemann also categorized high and low contexts that fit the above cognitive thinking. "A high-context culture is made up of people who pay special attention to the concrete world around them. Everything in the physical setting communicates something significant: the atmosphere of the room…and the body language" (2009: 78). Culturally, southern continents have high-context people, exhibiting holistic thinking. In low-context cultures, "people pay attention to explicit communication and to ideas. The context of these ideas is not as important as what is specifically said. Precise words are more important than the tone of voice…High context peoples are deeply embedded in the immediate surroundings around them…low-context people are immersed in the world of concepts, principles, and ideas" (Plueddemann 2009: 78). Caucasians in Western nations and people of some other technologically advanced "nations" have low-context cultures and belong to the holistic thinking.

Figure 4.1: Contrasting Dichotomistic with Holistic Thinking

Dichotomistic Thinking	Holistic Thinking
Judgments are black/white, right/wrong—specific criteria are uniformly applied in evaluating others	Judgments are open-ended—the whole person and all circumstances are taken into consideration
Security comes from the feeling that one is right and fits into a particular role or category in society	Security comes from multiple interactions within the whole society—one is insecure if confined to particular roles or categories
Information and experiences are systematically organized; details are sorted and ordered to form a clear pattern	Information and experiences are seemingly disorganized; details (narrative, events, portraits) stand as independent complete in themselves

Figure 4.2: Comparison of Ghanaian Traditional and Western Mindsets

Ghanaian (*Akan*) (High-Context; Holistic Thinking)	USA (Western) (Low-Context; Dichotomistic Thinking)
Cognition and Emotion	
Conservative - always repeating Emotional - individual lives on emotions; gives expression to feelings Mystical, fantasy and meditative Intuitive and imaginative – emotional, mental acceptance, and responsive	Dynamic - always creating Volitional - individual expresses own will; lives under control of will Empirical - preoccupied with details Independent - self-sufficiency, self-reliance, and self-determination
Individual in Social Organization	
Causative being dualistic; both physical and spiritual causes of phenomenon Communal – community-oriented, family emphasis, nobody an island Content with and passive to reality Tribal and traditional. People-oriented; relationally based	Causative; rational - Always asking 'why?' Exploitative, discovery, scientific Individualistic; venturesome Universalistic – transnational; global perspective Individualistic – competitive; achievement-oriented
Socio-Economic Orientation	
Existence; subsistence-oriented Socialism; personality consciousness	Goal; success-oriented, business-oriented. Capitalism; time consciousness
Religio-Cultural Orientation	
Religion: holistic worldview; related to whole Ontologically, person is small part of cosmos; subject to cosmic laws	Dualistic worldview: sacred vs. secular Utilitarian; world—person-controlled object

Since globally, people belong to either dichotomistic or holistic thinking, diaspora people in the multi-cultural America may belong to either of them. Their cognitive orientations are a reflection of the contexts from which they came to the USA. The Ghanaian diaspora, though ethnically and culturally unique, has obvious inter-connectedness with other ethnic groups in the USA. Thus, diversity is strongly exhibited by the presence of the various ethnic groupings. Figure 4.2 compares the Western low-context culture mindset with the Ghanaian traditional mindset from high-context culture. The table is an adaptation from Wan's comparative study of Chinese and American Western mindsets with modifications to suit the Ghanaian diaspora issues (Wan and Edu-Bekoe 2011; Moreau and Snodderly 2011: 35-62).

Ethnic, Cultural, and Linguistic Diversities

Ethnicity consists of "shared racial, linguistic, or national identity of a social group" (Atur Aghamkar 2009 DIS 751I Hindus in the Diaspora Course). Existence of ethnicities in a particular geo-political context signifies cultural diversity. Even within a particular ethnic group there are diverse sub-cultures. In the pluralistic American society, various ethnic groups are at different stages of integration. Ethnic communities in the diaspora form when members of an outside group, accustomed to a different way of life, find themselves as guests of a complex community. Ethnic communities are also formed only if the receiving host society is open to outsiders, and if there are reasons why the guests find it possible, necessary, and advantageous to band together into a sub-community of their own (Aghamkar 2009 DIS 751I Hindus in the Diaspora Course). Every ethnic group in the host nation becomes a part, partially or completely, of the host culture through various mechanisms such as adaptation, absorption, and assimilation. Naturally, there is an ongoing dynamic interplay between traditional Ghanaian culture and the influences of dominant USA pop-culture including thought patterns and lifestyles.

Two hypotheses observed among the ethnic groups are structural and cultural assimilation or acculturation with regard to cultural diversity. Structural assimilation involves the process where the immigrant ethnic group tries to learn the manners and style of the new society (Aghamkar 2009 DIS 751I Hindus in the Diaspora Course). Cultural assimilation arises in a situation "in which members of the immigrant group relate to members of other groups, particularly on the intimate levels of friendship and family formation, without regard to ethnic differences" (Aghamkar 2009 DIS 751I Hindus in the Diaspora Course). At this deeper level, the change involves worldview, values, and faith, among others. One option is the host culture-conformity where various immigrant groups conform to the mores and value-systems of the dominant host group. Cultural pluralism illustrates how different immigrant groups maintain their particularistic identity even when they have integrated into the host society. For instance, the traditional Ghanaian mindset is diverse. The process of adjustment of USA OBGs for integration is also diverse.

A major indigenous knowledge is language. English is the official language of Ghana—a British colonial-heritage. However, there is a heterogeneous linguistic diversity. Moreover, different dialects are spoken in the same linguistic-stock. Ruth Benedict expressed linguistic differences as important in understanding cultural diversity, "The numbers of sounds that can be produced by our vocal cords...are practically unlimited...a great deal of our misunderstanding of languages unrelated to our own has arisen from our attempts to refer alien phonetic systems back to ours as a point of reference" (1989: 23). The major challenge of the OBGs is forthrightness to teach their mother tongue to their children in the multi-ethnic USA. Some other ethnic groups in the USA such as the Hispanics, Chinese, Koreans, Japanese, and the like, are doing this. As Chin Wang stated, "The Chinese and Hispanic churches also provide classes to learn their home language—Chinese and Spanish. However, their targets and purposes differ" (2011; Moreau and Snodderly 2011: 21-33). The existing generational variation between the OBGs and LBGs create challenges. Another reason may be that while English is the official language in both Ghana and America, it is not so in Hispanic or Asian nations.

Worldview and Religious Multiplicity

In multi-cultural USA, differences in worldviews create wide cultural gaps. "Comparing the Ghanaian worldview-controlled mindset with that of Westerners, the former is more people-oriented, conservative, and holistic whereas the latter is individualistic and time-oriented...For both cultures, the worldview impinges on values which in turn influence beliefs that control behavior" (Wan and Edu-Bekoe 2011; Moreau and Snodderly 2011: 35-62). The challenge is how the OBGs fit into the industrialized socio-cultural worldview of the USA. The separation of state and religion experienced in the USA is relatively non-existent in the Ghanaian context. Generally, therefore, the Ghanaian perception and involvement with religion is different from the style in USA popular culture.

THEMATIC RESEARCH ON DIVERSITY OF USA GHANAIAN DIASPORA

A fascinating variety of views on diversity was expressed in the ethnographic interviews for this book. The views included those of OBGs, 1.5 OBGs, and LBGs. For this volume, I interviewed persons of various ages in multi-cited GPCs in the USA.

First Generation OBG: Insights on Diversity

Stephen Kwaku Owusu, 54, said,

> I think diversity is good because of the freedom of expression in America, and it allows people to live the way they want. However, it is problematic for the immigrant younger generations. They become assimilated and lose their ethnic identity to the diverse American popular culture. With some of us as adults, we have the mind to go back home. Therefore, we do not care about our accent. This is not so with the younger generations for whom diversity becomes problematic (Interview, November 19, 2011).

Adomako Kwame Afram, 71, saw diversity as problematic for diaspora Ghanaians. Afram contended, "Diversity is not helping Ghanaians in the USA. It is important to bring the good news to people in their own language and culture. There is a conflict of cultures in diversity" (Interview, November 21, 2010). Conversely, Emmanuel Kwame Gyan, 50, considered diversity as positive. Gyan argued, "The USA is a melting pot. Some people do get along despite their differences. For me, diversity is positive because most people get along if they are Christians. Such Christians go along with people of different cultural and religious affiliations" (Interview, November 28, 2010).

Collins Akwasi Asamoah Afriyie, 49, finds the USA an interesting country to live in because of diversity. He insisted, "I see America as an interesting place to live in. As a result of diversity, America gives opportunity for everybody to fit in. One is not a loner because one would by all means fit into the American context and interact with different people. You can find every culture in America and that helps many people to blend in" (Interview, December 11, 2011).

Abenaa, 49, strongly maintained,

> Me? At 36, I was already grown before coming here. Comparatively, our children back home have more cultural and moral values imbibed that make them grow as responsible adults to fit into society. But in America, firstly, because of the schools, the television, and peer pressure, it is not like home. Secondly, there are differences of the teaching patterns here. Teachers, peers, the church, and the home are all teaching different things to children. Younger ones definitely get confused. Diversity is the cause of the lack of Ghanaian cultural and moral values of our children in America (Interview, November 27, 2010).

Michael Gyamfi, 60, sees a positive reflection of diversity on American life whereby though the country is made up of diverse people groups, all see themselves as Americans. He stated,

> Life in America is so diverse that it is described as a melting pot—a context with variety of various cultures that have come together as a whole. There

are the Spanish, Puerto Rican, and Irish days, among others, that are celebrated in America. One important thing is that all these different peoples see themselves as Americans. Even those who are historically not from America identify themselves with hyphenated identities such as African-Americans, Japanese-Americans, Chinese-Americans, Cuban-Americans, and the like. The beauty of this is that everyone tries to accommodate one another (Interview, December 11, 2011).

Edward Ansong, 61, had mixed views about diversity. He said,

> Personally, I have lost something Ghanaian because I used to speak English all the time. When I met Ghanaians I could not speak Twi, my language, well. Worse still, since my wife is non-Ghanaian I felt estranged from Ghanaian life and culture. Hence, a greater part of my "Ghanaianess" was wasted away. That is what diversity has done to me. Moreover, by learning the laws, the culture, and ways of Americans, education alienated me. At a certain point I decided to turn my mind back to Ghana and Ghanaians. That was when I joined PCGNY in 1996 (Interview, December 3, 2010).

In serious disagreement, when Emmanuel Presbyterian Church of the Ogden, Bronx decided to affiliate with the PCUSA, Ansong and three others broke away to form the Ebenezer PCG in Bronx, NY. Deeply rooted in Ghanaian culture and worldview, Opanyin Fosu, 70, considered diversity as generally good for America by saying,

> Diversity means different people groups from Africa, Asia, and South America, among others, who are living together in the American context. Even Africans are different peoples from various nations. Such diversity is very good for America. The USA is the end of the world because people from all over the world want to be here. When such diverse people meet together, it exhibits the creativity of God. In the American diversity, therefore, there are different groups of people with different languages. For me, God wants such a context for America (Interview, November 19, 2011).

Kwadwo Osei Agyemang, 53, looked at diversity from two contrasting angles by stating,

> American society is one that—when you live outside—you tend to perceive and visualize it through television, movies, and books. However, when you get in here, you will see different situation altogether. In America, there are different cultures. Sometimes one marveled so much that one does not believe that human beings have the same God for all. This is in reference to the perception about immigrants by some Americans. At the same time some other Americans have displayed real community care that makes it bearable for one to pursue one's education

and work among diverse groups of people. The point is, you live among some people who will look down on you because you are an African but at the same time you get other people who would consider you as God's child. That is the essence of American diversity (Interview, December 11, 2011).

Sandra Ampadu Asiama, 26, stressed that because she had lived among the Ghanaian diaspora, she does not see any differences brought about by diversity in her community life. However, in her educational life she recognizes diversity in America. She said,

On one hand, when I came to Cincinnati I found myself in the Ghanaian community. Therefore, socially, I don't see much difference in the community around me. For instance, in the Cincinnati PCG, the mother tongue and worship style are not problems for me. On the other hand, however, I was usually the only black girl in class in the Miami University in Cincinnati, OH. I could not feel like joining conversations of the members of my class who were so different. I was just lucky to find another black, a Nigerian. Group study, which is so helpful, is not popular here unlike Ghana. So I studied with my Nigerian colleague (Interview, April 21, 2011).

Kofi Nelson-Owusu, 48, considered diversity from the church and secular contexts differently. He said,

I am a tent-maker pastor. The Christian family is so broad. When I call people my brothers and sisters, I mean it. Within the church, color is not an issue for me. Someone once told me, "I feel what I feel inside you." In the church, the context is to collectively have Christ. That is most important rather than focusing on our differences in ethnicity. However, outside the church, the situation is different. All people compete on merit. This is where diversity in light of differences among various people groups becomes an issue (Interview, February 12, 2012).

As an ordained pastor of VBC-I by its bishop, David Ato Pratt, 45, contended that in the Kingdom of God believers are one which reflects on the beauty of diversity by saying,

Judging from our background, we have included in our name the word "international" because of our vision of including people of cultural differences among our membership. Currently, our membership is made up of people of our kind. Some other Africans have easily identified with us. To a limited extent, some people from other areas who have similarities with us have also been attracted. We get persons with similar backgrounds like us such as Caribbean, Jamaicans, and West Indians, among others. For example, mixed marriages make it relatively easier to accommodate spouses of both similar and different backgrounds. In the Body of Christ, we are all one. That is the beauty of diversity in God's creation. So far we have not been able to achieve a harmonization of other ethnicities in our congregation. Evangelization has been a little bit challenging because of religious and other rights; Africans find it difficult to witness freely. However, we must strive to attract others. For me, I don't see it in our days (Interview, November 28, 2011).

Brando Akoto, 48, does not find diversity in America anything new because he had organized so many cultural exchanges among Europeans, Canadians, and Americans before he travelled to the USA. He said,

Since I consider everything from the value-added perspective, diversity is valuable in the USA. Living with different kinds of people has lots of advantages. Most American life regarding diversity has not been new to me because I had the opportunity to live with different kinds of people in Ghana before travelling to the USA. I was in contact with and lived with Germans, French, and the Dutch, among others in Ghana. Others included the people of the Scandinavian countries such as the people of Denmark, Sweden, Finland, and Norway. Of course North Americans were included as I also lived with people from the USA and Canada. I also organized some cultural exchange programs among these people so much so that what is happening with regard to diversity is not new to me. For me, diversity is valuable and beautiful.

For Carroll, diversity has helped America. She does not see why the church in America has been segregated between White, Black, Hispanic, or African, among others. She contended,

God is diverse. God reveals Himself in diverse ways to human beings. Diversity has helped America. It has helped to get the best from other ethnicities from all over the globe. Diversity is strength when we know our limits. If we can discover our differences and we know our limits we can use diversity to our advantage. I have a question. In the church, how do we conquer the negatives of diversity? Unity is the word for our actions, being, and operation. In Christ, there is no Jew or Gentile. That is the beauty of diversity in the Reign of God. I don't even understand this situation. If we are to present a communion of believers, I don't understand why there should be White, Black, Hispanic, Asian, and the like churches in a Christian nation such as the USA. Maybe there is a root cause for this. Maybe America's experience of slavery when there were clear distinctions of segregation caused this situation. America is a multi-cultural society where various people groups are clearly distinguished and the church is unfortunately an exhibition of this (Interview, March 11, 2012).

Second Generation OBG: Insights on Diversity

With insightful opinions, both Mr. and Mrs. Addo-Prempeh expressed interesting views about diversity in the USA. Victoria, 31, acknowledged, "American community is very diverse. There are different people everywhere. I doubt if there is a people group in the world that does not have a representative in America. New York, for example, is made up of people who come from various nations. It seems everybody in New York is from somewhere else" (Interview, November 23, 2010). Victoria Addo-Prempeh joined her parents in the USA after high school in Ghana in 2004. Victoria works full time as the secretary of PCGNY and studies part time for her Masters in Social Studies. Like many diaspora Ghanaians, she thinks that study is the only way to move up the social ladder in the USA. Kwadwo Addo-Prempeh, 42, Victoria's husband supported and affirmed,

> I agree with Vic. that there is more diversity in the USA. The American society is changing forever. What is peculiar, in my opinion, is that more people are coming to the States every day. One may meet a different person in the train or in the bus each day. One would want to meet this new person, know him/her, or even learn his/her language. However, the next day one meets a completely different person altogether. The cosmopolitan nature of the USA makes it imperative for the individual to make adjustments in order to accommodate others. That is not going to stop today. This makes diversity in the America unique (Interview, November 23, 2010).

Addo-Prempeh and his wife were interviewed together in Victoria's office. He is an attorney who met and married Victoria in the PCGNY in 2007. Eric Kyeremeh, 29, initially encountered challenges with diversity in the USA. He affirmed,

> Diversity was initially challenging for me in the USA. In my school in Ghana, I experienced deep diversity to a limited extent because Ahmadiyya Islamic High School was diverse. Therefore, I had overcome diversity before coming to America. However, I was exposed when my accent betrayed me. When people kept referring to my accent, I felt deepseated incompetence and withdrew into myself. I felt very uncomfortable. It was so unfortunate and overwhelming. Nevertheless, I never allowed my accent to overcome me. I rather pushed forward to overcome it (Interview, November 28, 2010).

Abigail, 17, said about her experience of diversity,

> I came to America with my parents and two siblings when I was eight years old. In fact, I did not know what was happening since I was so young. I remember I was crying and wanted to be home in Ghana. All I

realized was that we were in an aircraft that landed at an airport in America. At school, I was admitted to grade 3 where I met different ethnicities. Some of the things my peers do are quite different. I don't have a boyfriend. I don't do drugs. I don't smoke, I don't drink, I don't attend wild parties, I don't attend pubs, and the like. These are some values from my Ghanaian home. Some of my teenage peers in school do not share these things with me (Interview, November 28, 2010).

Second Generation LBG: Insights on Diversity

The views of LBGs about diversity were stated from different angles. Adjoa Debrah-Dwamena, 32, took it from a linguistic perspective. She said,

> English is my first language. My parents speak Twi, Guan, and Ga. But they spoke English with me in the home when I was a child. My dad told me the reason for not stressing on the mother tongue. I grew up in NY but in a diverse neighborhood with different languages such as Haitian Creole, Spanish, and English. Therefore, my dad did not want me to be confused with the many diverse languages in the neighborhood. Since English was common to all, my parents chose to communicate in it with us in the home (Interview, November 12, 2010).

Debrah-Dwamena is an attorney. She was born in and grew up in NY. Whenever anybody chats with her in *Twi*, she would always respond in English. She understands it a bit. There are several diaspora Ghanaians who have had this issue of their children unable to speak their mother tongues. Many of them regret it later. But others just do not care. In Portland, OR, Effe, 20, looked at diversity from building relationships,

> Diversity can be viewed from the relationship one builds with different people. I was born in Guelph, a small university town in Ontario, Canada. I have been nurtured in different countries with many different kinds of people. My parents wanted us to know different people. My best friend is Alexander with whom I went to school since the 7th grade. He is African-American guy. He is not a Christian, though. This is unfortunate. I have tried but he seems not to change. I respect him for that. When anything happens to me I call him. Like when I am mad at my parents or some boys I call him. Though we are different, we both understand each other. And we know what is good for us. It sounds good. Alexander is not Ghanaian but I connect well with him. For me this is diversity in the USA (Interview, February 2, 2011).

Effe is a pre-med nursing student at the Portland Community College. Her parents relocated to the USA from Guelph, Ontario, Canada when she was 9 years old. She is fluent and comfortable with communicating in English. Her

The two major dimensions in the process of cultural integration are: objective predisposition ("the degree of resemblance of an 'OBG/LBG's' own culture to the host culture"), and the subjective preference ("an 'OBG/LBG's' personal choice in terms of motivation, emotion and volition towards cultural integration). These two can also be the deterrent factors against cultural integration with resultant cultural variation—the A-B scale in figure 4.3 (Wan ed., 1995: 162; Wan and Edu-Bekoe 2011; Moreau and Snodderly 2011: 35-62).

Ian Yeboah and other scholars suggest several major themes in "respect of identity creation of second generation immigrants" (2009: 158-166). Figure 4.4 summarizes the diaspora Ghanaian generations.

Figure 4.4: Generational Composition of the Ghanaian Diaspora

Generation	Location of Birth	Cultural Orientation	Designation
First (1st) Generation	Ghana	80-100% Ghanaian Culture	Overseas Born Ghanaians (OBGs)
Second (2nd) Generation 1	Ghana	50% Ghanaian-50% American Culture	1.5 Second Generation OBG
Second (2nd) Generation 2	United States	80-100% American Culture	Local Born Ghanaians (LBGs)
Third (3rd) Generation	United States	95-100% American Culture	Local Born Ghanaians (LBGs)

The hybrids are not separated but are all included in the second and third generation LBGs. The various Ghanaian generations of immigrants vary in the preservation of traditional Ghanaian culture and adaptation to the USA pop-culture. The retention of cultural values of the OBGs is illustrated in connection with Figure 4.4 above. The first generation OBGs retain their cultural values as central, making USA culture peripheral. Individualism and assimilation are eschewed. The second generation (1.5) immigrant OBGs become culturally absorbed by the conditions of the host context through adaptation and assimilation. Their absorption happens through gradual adaptation. However, they may not become totally absorbed. There always remain some cultural values they would cherish and keep. Therefore, they are sometimes divided equally between cultural integration and cultural variation, as indicated in Figure 4.4. This is with regard to the original identity, cultural values, and the host culture. Many LBGs acquire some external expressions of the USA pop-culture. Ghanaian culture may remain faint at the core of their thinking while USA culture is dominant through integration or cultural assimilation (acculturation). They are so much impacted that at certain stages the cultural identity of the motherland becomes nil as shown in Figure 4.4.

There is the generic perception of the likelihood of LBGs losing their ethnic identity. Sometimes, some of the LBGs lose their identity through actions of their OBG parents. Case study 4.2 is an example. In addition to the disappointment of their children losing their cultural and moral values, OBGs in the USA sometimes express their frustrations in their children's loss of cultural identity. Nonetheless, unlike the era of their parents who needed to assimilate to be accepted for job openings, the contemporary younger generational situation is not as urgent because of globalization. "Recently American firms have subcontracted most of their jobs abroad as part of globalization…Immigrants are faced with a modicum of marginalization, discrimination, and tyranny as expressed by Haitians, Cubans, Mexicans, and Vietnamese in the United States" (R. Waldinger 2007: 3-39). Though the situation has put restrictions on LBGs in terms of absolute assimilation, social mobility through education has made the situation less urgent in the USA.

THEMATIC RESEARCH ON IDENTITY OF USA GHANAIAN DIASPORA

Definitely, some LBGs lose their identities in the USA. Some OBGs and LBGs who expressed mixed perceptions of their identity and identity formulation were sampled. These views, even though mixed, had one central focus of basic Ghanaian identity.

First Generation OBG Insights: Individual Identity

Opanyin Fosu, 70, stated his happiness to be Ghanaian by saying, "I am Ghanaian and I am very happy that I am. In the type of Christianity that I was trained, the fear of God was embedded into us. We as Ghanaian Christians have moral values such as honor, respect for the elderly, and shame for sin, among others. I am, therefore, proud to be Ghanaian. My identity makes me have the true teachings from the Lord for my salvation" (Interview, November 19, 2011). Afua Okobea, 65, simply identified, "I see myself as Ghanaian; circumstance may make one change one's identity to suit a situation, though. Otherwise one will not survive" (Interview, December 3, 2010). Edward Ansong, 62, saw identity cognitively. He explicitly explained,

> People don't understand why I do not connect so much with Ghanaians. My family is American. My children are not Ghanaians. They are Jamaican-Americans. These are realities in my life. For me, I am really diversified psychologically. I am what I call "a breed apart." That is somebody removed from his context or environment and nurtured in a different way for a special work. I do not put on Ghanaian clothing but American clothing. However, I am still a Ghanaian but my thinking is different from Ghanaians (Interview, December 2, 2010).

Unlike Ansong, Kwame Gyan emphatically said,

> I am definitely Ghanaian. My family is foremost Ghanaian because of our moral values and culture. However, I also learn American values and culture. In every culture there are both positive and negative aspects. I try to balance the two cultures. For example, two important American cultural values are respect for the law and to be responsible. These are positive (Interview, November 28, 2010).

Stephen Kwaku Owusu insisted, "I want to identify myself and my family as Ghanaian; my wife and children are Ghanaians. We enjoy Ghanaian music and foods such as fufu, kenkey, gari and mashed yam, among others" (Interview, November 19, 2011). Collins Akwasi Asamoah Afriyie, 49, related his identity with both his faith and culture by stating, "I try to be someone who believe in God, understands the value of life, and try to understand the value of culture. Though, I have been in America for almost half my life, I know that I have great respect for my culture. I do not want to lose my cultural values. I am truly and fully Ghanaian" (Interview, December 11, 2011). In the midst of different people groups, David Ato Pratt, 45, identified himself as full-blooded Ghanaian by saying,

> I see myself as Ghanaian among other ethnicities such as African-Americans, Haitians, Jamaicans, Caribbean's, and the like. In certain situations, we can compromise to forgo some things. For instance, because of documentation, one can become Ghanaian-American. As a pastor, it is difficult to open up to only people of your kind. VBC-I has an internal policy of all inclusiveness. We try to eschew ethnocentrism, discrimination, and marginalization. Thus, we do not sing any of our local lyrics when we come to worship publicly. We are supposed to be strictly international. Nevertheless, we do have our accent. So no matter what we do, we will never be Americans (Interview, November 20, 2011).

Kofi Nelson-Owusu, 48, said, "My Father is an *Ashanti* and my mother is *Kwahu*, both of the *Akan* extraction. Most of my friends are *Ewe* because they show love to me. I don't speak American slang; I don't enjoy their sports. My identity is in connection with everyone who is for the Lord Jesus Christ" (Interview, February 26, 2012). Carroll, 36, insisted, "I was born in Cameroon. I am, thus, a Cameroonian in the midst of many other ethnic groups but I am a citizen of heaven first. Though French is my first language, in the USA context, English is the common language. Since Cameroon is bilingual, I do not have any challenges with the English Language" (Interview, March 11, 2012). Brando Akoto, 48, also maintained his Ghanaian and African identity by stating,

> I was born in Ghana and I am a black man—an African. Yes, that is who I am. My family make-up, the way I was brought up, and the name I carry around are what make who I am. Am I in America? Yes, that is factual.

> Am I Ghanaian? Yes, I am. Am I African? No doubt, I am. However, I try to adapt and acknowledge the cultural context and the existence of other ethnicities with different cultures. My identity is informed by my uniqueness within these different cultures (Interview, February 12, 2012).

Sandra Ampadu Asiama, 26, said, "I am Ghanaian. I am even unique among other African groups of people because most of them communicate in their mother tongue. When I meet other different people from my own, I work hard to be affable to them. I am a lovely person; I do smile so much. Indeed I find myself privileged to be in American multi-cultural context but I am unique—a distinctive identity from others" (Interview, April 21, 2011). Unlike some Ghanaians such as, Afriyie, Akoto, and Sandra Asiama, whose stay in America has not changed them a bit, Kwadwo Osei Agyemang, 53, thinks otherwise. He insisted that he is African-American to answer the question about his identity. He stated,

> This is one question that baffles me because I consider myself as African-American. Normally, when one is considered "African-American," one is considered native black. I consider myself African. That is no problem. Truly, I am. However, the American culture has seeped so much deeply in me that I am not the same when I left Ghana. I prefer putting on the formal professional suit as a pharmacist. When I go back to Ghana, the first question people who see me do ask is "You are not living here, are you?" Yet, Americans will not accept you as one of them. In brief, therefore, I am not fully American but somehow, I am not fully African" (Interview, December 11, 2011).

Second Generation OBG: Insights on Individual Identity

Tiwaa, 29, expressed her identity as hyphenated Ghanaian, but not hybrid. She considers her Ghanaian-American identity derived only from her documentation. She stressed, "With regard to my identity, I am a Ghanaian-American. This is because with an American passport I am also an American citizen. With identity formulation of diaspora Ghanaian children, OBGs are not open-minded. Comparing their children with themselves is problematic" (Interview, November 28, 2010). Unlike Tiwaa, Mary, 16, was not enthused by the differences between her identity as a Ghanaian or a Ghanaian-American. When asked whether she would prefer a Ghanaian or American for a spouse, she replied, "It depends. I do not care actually. If I choose a Ghanaian, that will be all right because we will share many things in common. If I get an American, that's not bad too. I am too young to make a choice, however" (Interview, November 28, 2010). Mary's position exhibited the attitude of some 1.5 OBGs about their self-identity negotiations, especially the younger ones. Nonetheless, Abigail, 17, said,

> I am a Ghanaian. Ghana is where I was born. In the USA my family has a Ghanaian home. I see my home as different from my school. In the home, things that I am supposed to do as a teenage girl seem different from some of my colleagues in the school. I always make sure I do my homework. I am supposed to do some house chores too to help my mom: wash dishes, hang washed clothing, and help to cook. In addition, I am supposed to go straight home from school. These are facts (Interview, November 28, 2010).

When Abigail was coming for the interview she had an iPod with which she listened to popular music as many younger generations are prone to do. Jonas Sulemana, 33, now pursuing his doctorate at Sage Graduate School, NY said, "I was born at Yendi in the Northern region of Ghana. Therefore, I am a Ghanaian. This is not withstanding the fact that I am an American citizen holding an American passport. However, no matter whom you are or what you do, Americans will never accept you as one of them" (Interview, November 28, 2010). While Jonah's mother is from Jamasi in the Ashanti region of Ghana and is a Christian, his father is a Muslim from Salaga in northern Ghana. He grew up in his mother's family and it was through his maternal uncle that he immigrated to the USA.

Second Generation LBG: Insights on Individual Identity

Interestingly, not withstanding their structural assimilation, all the LBGs insisted they were fully Ghanaian contrary to the general expectations. Rex Agyemang, 31, was born and grew up in NY. He emphatically stated, "I am proud to be a Ghanaian. Other people may feel ashamed of their roots. I just love Ghanaian culture. For me, I don't feel American. When I visited Ghana and saw its culture, I immediately connected with it" (Interview, November 28, 2010). Moet, 29, an LBG simply stated, "I see myself as African-American but my roots are in being Ghanaian. Though, I was born in Atlanta, GA, my training in the home to speak the mother tongue made me connect with my culture easily when I visited Ghana. I cherish my Ghanaian roots" (Interview, December 11, 2011). Felicia Agyare, 34, also insisted that she is Ghanaian though she was born over three decades ago in Chicago. Agyare maintained,

> I am Ghanaian because I have Ghanaian parents. Although I am an American citizen by birth, I am still Ghanaian deep in my heart. I am so passionate about this. After I was sent back home to Ghana, a couple of years ago by my mother, I came back with a different perception about my nation. I just felt connected with my people and everything: the culture, food, and morals. Though, I was born here in Chicago, my parents just happened to be here to give birth to me. I am only American by chance (Interview, November 15, 2010).

The interview above was conducted at the family home in Bolingbrook, Chicago, IL. Felicia is the wife of Agyare from the Kwahu ethnic group. Agyare was not a believer when as the researcher I stayed in their home in Bolingbrook where I interviewed Felicia. It was here that I also met Kwarteng whose narrative is recorded in the case story 4.3. Effe of the PIC also confidently said, "I am definitely not an American because my name is Effe and my skin is dark. I am not Ghanaian. Neither am I American. No matter what you do Americans will never accept you as one of them" (Interview, February 8, 2011). This agreed with Sulemana but when pressed to explain why she sounded so vague, Effe explained,

> Look, uncle, I am more comfortable with English but I wish I could speak more Twi than I do now. I blame my dad and mom for that. I understand everything when my family or anyone else speaks to me in the mother tongue. But I feel reluctant to use Twi because I have my American accent. When I want to speak Twi, I feel like I would say something wrong and people will laugh. When communicating I just avoid the Twi because of saying something wrong (Interview, February 8, 2011).

George, 17, Effe's younger brother, shared a different perception about his identity. He conceded that he is Ghanaian by parentage but not a full Ghanaian. He stated, "I represent a group of Ghanaians who were born in the diaspora. I was born in Guelph, Ontario, Canada. I bring ideas of Ghanaian culture and American culture together. I am thus a hybrid. American culture is alright" (Interview, February 13, 2010). George's position here represents a small segment of the LBGs interviewed by the researcher. Again, interestingly, few considered themselves as hybrid. Some OBGs bemoan the assimilation of their young generation in the USA pop culture. This research, unpredictably however, indicated that with regard to identity formulation most LBGs consider themselves Ghanaians. They might have structural assimilation in the externals. Nevertheless, depending on their home training, deep down in their hearts, they consider themselves as Ghanaians. These interviews also revealed that diaspora Ghanaian identity formulation is strictly tied to the sort of home in which OBGs nurture their children.

GOSPEL RECEPTIVITY BY THE GHANAIAN DIASPORA IN THE USA

Among the Ghanaian diaspora are adherents of all the three major religions of Ghana. Christianity comprises the majority, though. In general, the concept of receptivity with regard to diaspora Ghanaians in the USA consists of two aspects: the socio-cultural and the gospel receptivity.

Challenging Context of Socio-Cultural Receptivity

One major but neglected aspect of identity receptivity is the socio-cultural. This dimension is in relationship with ethnicity. With regard to their strong accents, and that of their parents, receptivity of some LBGs by Americans is questionable despite some of them acquiring citizenship by birth or documentation. It is a fact that the LBGs have cultural integration in their way of life. They are predisposed to African-American lifestyles. However, their socio-cultural receptivity as American citizens is negligible.

Cultural Integration and the Receptivity of the Gospel

Most Ghanaians are generally receptive to the gospel. However, the mindsets and strategies used by some GPCs should perhaps be revised by using attractive approaches such as understanding, listening, and conversation. This crucial subject is important because as Ghanaians, the issue of receptivity of the gospel is strongly related to identity formulation. Case story 4.3 illustrates the challenging situation of gospel receptivity by Ghanaians in the USA.

Case Story 4.3: Difficulties in Proclaiming the Gospel for Receptivity (USA)

When approached with the gospel in the USA, some unbelieving Ghanaians claim they came to America to find money (the dollar power) but not to worship God. I had a conversation on November 13, 2010, with one Kwarteng, 53, in the home of the Agyares, in Bolingbrook, Chicago. Kwarteng had immigrated to the USA in the 1970s. According to him, he was 10 years when his father, a senior Presbyter, married a second wife and was suspended by the PCG in Kumasi. His late father became backslidden. Kwarteng also never stepped into a chapel since the age of ten. Kwarteng's perception of charismatic and prophetic ministry was very negative. Without any significant proof, he insisted that Ghanaian pastors parading as prophets in the diaspora are "fraudsters." According to him, he was a witness when the late prophet of the Bethel Prayer Camp arrived in Chicago from London. Kwarteng claimed when the prophet was returning to Ghana he had enriched himself by "defrauding" some vulnerable Ghanaian immigrants in Chicago under the pretext of solving their needs. Kwarteng does not believe those needs were solved, anyway. For a second time Kwarteng had been put off from receiving the gospel. How can this man and his friends be outreached with a new approach of receptivity of the gospel in the USA?

This case study illustrates the challenge of approaching some diaspora Ghanaians with the Christian faith message in the USA. Enoch Wan has suggested a positive relationship between a Christian home and receptivity of the gospel for diaspora people groups. Figure 4.5 (see next page) indicates the relationship between cultural integration and gospel receptivity (Edu-Bekoe and Wan 2011; Wan ed. 2011:220).

> If an 'OBG/LBG's' cultural background is more integrated with or similar to the "host culture," then generally there is more flexibility for that person to enjoy the freedom of accepting Christ...Christian's conversion and majority and the evangelization of non-Christians. (C...D of Figure # 4.5 is an evangelism-discipleship scale) (Wan 1995: 165; Edu-Bekoe and Wan 2011; Wan ed. 2011: 220).

Wan's statement above denoted the fact of differences of integration by the different generations of the diaspora Ghanaians with regard to the level of their disposition to the Christian faith. Case story 4.3 illustrates the reason for a change of strategy to attract diaspora Ghanaians. In the meantime, the generic receptivity of the gospel in the USA context is very challenging making receptivity of the gospel by Ghanaians complex. However, the level of integration or assimilation has little influence on receptivity of the gospel. Regardless of cultural integration, receptivity has a dimension related to accessibility of the gospel—the proclamation of the salvation of God in Jesus Christ, or the good news (within the popular USA culture).

THEMATIC RESEARCH OF USA GPCs ON THE GOSPEL RECEPTIVITY

The sampled individuals again shared their views on receptivity of the gospel among the Ghanaian diaspora in the USA. A mixture of OBG or LBG responses indicates a positive relationship between receptivity of the gospel and being born in a Christian home, and vice versa. Coming from a Christian home or being born to Christian parents does not necessarily make one a Christian, though.

First Generation OBG: Insights on the Gospel Receptivity

Charles Gyang-Duah, 65, looked at receptivity from both personal and congregational levels from the American context. Commenting on the challenging situation of the receptivity of the gospel in the USA, he said, "Making other people receive Christ in the USA context is a challenge. With the extreme individual rights, many immigrant Christians find it difficult to

Figure 4.5: Cultural Integration and Spiritual Formation Scale

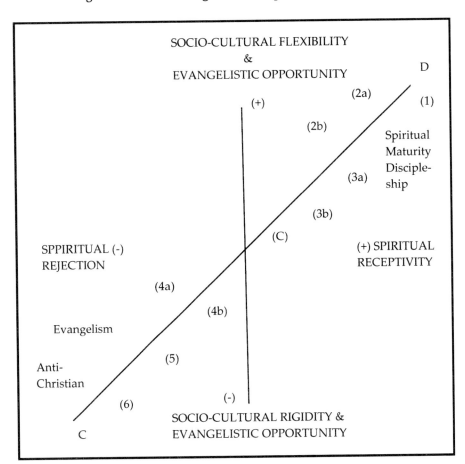

NOTES:
1. Mature Christian (from spiritual home, with teachable spirit)
2a. Born Again—Christian (from Christian home)
2b. Born Again—Christian (from other religious (ATR) home)
3a. Born Again—Christian (from Ghanaian home with teachable spirit)
3b. Born Again—Christian (from Ghanaian home without teachable spirit)
4a. Unsaved, unchurched (of another religion parents)
4b. Unsaved, unchurched (of Catholic parents)
5. Unsaved… (church going, mildly resistant to the gospel)
6. Unsaved… (unchurched, strongly resistant to the gospel)
(C). Point of conversion—point of intersection.

The following excerpt from Wan is informative on this point:

approach others with the gospel in America. to recognize other Christians next door" (Interview, May 25, 2010). Stephen Kwaku Owusu, 54, a converted Buddhist, described his reception of the Christian faith by saying,

> In 1980 I converted from Buddhism to the Christian faith. My uncle with whom I stayed to go to school introduced me to his religion. America is a country where any religion goes so my Christian faith determines everything I do. It determines what I wear; it determines my calling, character, charisma and the general relationship with other people. It is in the link with other people that I strive to make others receive the gospel in the USA" (Interview, November 19, 2011).

David Ato Pratt, 45, expressed his views about the receptivity of the gospel in the USA by saying,

> Receptivity of the gospel has not been easy with the Ghanaian community in America. It is worse with other people groups. Many people do not even know what Christianity is. Again, with our accent, many Americans do not want to hear the gospel from us. This is one of the major reasons why immigrant community churches are having so little impact on the American society. Basically, schools, the media, and other social institutions do not want to know about Christianity. It is increasingly difficult for immigrant churches to be transformational in the USA. Back home in Ghana (Africa), one can go and knock on the door of a neighbor to share the life of Christ. Relatively speaking, in America, this might be illegal now (Interview, November 27, 2011).

For Kofi Nelson-Owusu, one has to prove oneself before the gospel can be received. He said,

> The culture here is one in which you have to prove yourself before you are accepted. For example, in the secular context, to prove myself, I have to work double schedules. Similarly, in the church context, you need to prove yourself before the gospel is received from you. Friends who would not come to church need to be convinced. We in the church have to prove to those outside something positive and beneficial to them before they may accept to join us. For instance, if we in PIC have to get whites to join us, we need God's intervention for them to see that we have something that they do not have. This is tough. In fact, we have the focus to reach out to white Americans, African-Americans, and other ethnic groups. We have what they do not have and vise versa. At times, however, they do not give you the opportunity to prove yourself. That is the tough part of receptivity of the gospel in America (Interview, February 26, 2012).

Carroll, 36, had an insightful perception about receptivity of the gospel. She said,

> The USA is a beleaguered nation that does not want to hear the name of Christ. Success of the USA has eliminated the name of God to the background. In other words, achievement in development has resulted in secularity, scientific advancement, and enlightenment. Even worship is now a ritual that is not relevant to the present day technological advancement. In the end, the nation has lost its flavor, favor, impact, and influence in global Christianity (Interview, March 11, 2012).

Opanyin Fosu, 70, compared receptivity of the gospel in America with that in Ghana by stating,

> It is not easy to evangelize for the receptivity of Christ in the USA. Some people work almost 24/7 here to survive. Thus, it is not easy to proclaim and receive Christ. In Ghana if one stays in someone's home for a long time, it is not strange for that person to adopt the religion of the head of the household. Whatever is done in terms of faith and worship in such a home becomes the guest's life style. This is not so in America where work schedules have made it impossible to have weekends and religious vacations to worship. It is not easy to engage in reaching out activities because of busyness. More complicated is when family members of diaspora Ghanaians at home expect remittances. Lack of time for God's work is the issue here (Interview, November 19, 2011).

Kwame Adomako Afram, 71, perceived receptivity institutionally in the USA context when he said,

> Sincerely speaking, if receptivity is about spirituality my answer is no. Receptivity of the gospel is not a reality among most Ghanaians in America. There has been much change in Ghanaians who have immigrated to America. Some Ghanaians even perceive themselves as Americans. However, they are not. Most Ghanaians are just mere church-goers; they are not Christians. Such Ghanaians have not received Christ as their personal Savior (Interview, November 21, 2010).

Gladys Naykene, 49, said, "My life is Christ-dependent for He always delivers me. Sharing the abundant life in Christ in the USA, however, is difficult because of religious rights" (Interview, October 24, 2010). Kwame Gyan expressed, "I accepted Christ in America when I was invited to study the Bible by a friend in the Church of Christ. But it is not easy to share Christ in America" (Interview November 28, 2010). Michael Gyamfi who considers the Christian faith a way of life but sees its application as superficial stated,

> From my perspective, I see Christianity in America as superficial. People would like to show up as Christians but really I do not see Christianity applicable. Even in my work place people claim to be Christians but when it comes to living the faith out it becomes problematic. For me Christianity is a life to live out our salvation, which comes from the Lord. Personally, I

try to follow the ways of the Lord. The Christian life for me is to live out the faith realizing that it is not one's self-dependence but about being controlled by the Holy Spirit. I try so much to live as a Christian. This is what is lacking and conforming to discipleship makes receptivity of the gospel relatively difficult (Interview, December 11, 2011).

Sandra Ampadu Asiama said, "Without faith it is impossible to please God. The Bible says so. The Word of God is sharper than a double-edged sword. When I have a problem it is Christ who solves it for me. Sometimes, you'll have to have faith; in other times, you'll have to have doubt. With faith, I believe things will be OK for me. This is what I have to share. Its reception in the USA is challenging, however" (Interview, April 21, 2011).

Collins Asamoah Afriyie confirmed that it is difficult for Ghanaians to proclaim and receive Christ in the USA by saying, "Receptivity of the gospel and serving Christ in America are difficult because of time constraints. I love serving God but we all came to America to better our lives. The challenge here is how to combine the practice of one's faith with commitment to Christ. Thus, many people avoid commitment to the church" (Interview, December 11, 2011).

Brando Akoto also indicated how his faith is important to him by saying, "Faith is very important to me because I see it as the source of my life. I am committed to the cause of Christ on a daily basis and that is why I yearn for Christ. For me, commitment to the cause of Christ is forever" (Interview, February, 12, 2012).

Kwadwo Osei Agyemang declared, "My whole life is based on my faith in the Lord Jesus Christ. I do try to reflect and think about every action I take to see if Jesus would do it that way. I may not be perfect but my ultimate is to be a disciple who tries to follow Christ his Lord. That influences most of my decisions. Every decision, therefore, is made through that prism" (Interview, December 11, 2011).

Second Generation OBG: Insights on the Gospel Receptivity

From the second generation (1.5) OBG, Kwaku Boakye, 32, answered, "My Christian faith is very important to me because of the way I was brought up. My faith is part of my life. Unfortunately, to share this faith is difficult in America" (Target Group Telephone Conference Interview, October 3, 2010). Kwame Adu Gyamfi, 35, said, "As a believer, I should be much grounded in my Christian faith. Otherwise, I cannot progress upwards to what level I would like to be. I see most of my colleagues stressed out. I am not. My energy comes from my Christian faith. The problem is how to share this faith with others in America" (Target Group Telephone Conference Interview, October 3, 2010).

A serious Abigail concurred,

> I am a Christian. My mom has been so important to me in my Christian life. As a child I followed her everywhere she went. I followed her to the Women's Fellowship meetings. Becoming a Christian is not so important in the USA. But I became a Christian not so long in America. Here, I learn new things. This learning situation has impacted me to receive Christ. My older siblings are also inspiration to me (Interview, November 28, 2010).

Second Generation LBGs: Insights on the Gospel Receptivity

With regard to her receptivity of the gospel and the importance of her faith, Adjoa Debrah-Dwamena, 32, responded, "My relationship with God is very important to me. My Christian faith is an important part of my life. Three persons were important to me when I became a Christian. My father was. The other two were Rev. Dr. Kumi-Dwamena when I was a child and Rev. Comitheir when I was in law school" (Target Group Telephone Conference Interview, October 3, 2010). In a separate interview Debrah-Dwamena affirmed, "Jesus Christ is my Lord and Savior. I believe I cannot do anything without Christ. Two of us, one of my friends and I, whenever we chat, our conversations always turn to Christ. Whenever anyone of us has a problem, the other would say, 'Look at this passage. Christ will give an answer'" (Interview, November 12, 2010).

Most in response to the receptivity of the gospel considers it in relationship with a person's regional location in the USA. She said,

> In America where one is born determines one's religious commitment. I was born in the south of the USA where the nation is more cultural. The southern belt of America is relatively religious where receptivity of the gospel is more open. My Christian commitment is shaped because I was born and grew up in Atlanta, GA. However, the east coast such as NJ is more work oriented. Thus, if care is not taken one might lose one's religious commitment here (Interview, December 11, 2011).

Rex Agyemang also responded, "Christianity was all around me when I was growing in NY. As a child, I used to pray; I also used to view and listen to messages of televangelists. Who was important to me? It was an African-American guy. At the end of each message he used to say 'You need to accept Christ.' This was when I was about 13 or 14 years" (Interview, December 2, 2010). Effe reaffirmed her faith and described how she received Christ. She insisted,

> "I am a Christian. I became one since my adolescent age. In 2003, I went to a youth camp of an all white church. The camp was all wood and all white.

I really felt awkward. I felt very uncomfortable. I was like, 'You don't fit here. What are you doing here?' See, uncle, I was really struggling to fit in because of my dark skin. It was in the midst of meditating that I heard God saying to me, 'You belong to me. You belong to Jesus.' That was the first time I was so happy. I was about 16 years. I had friends from my high school peers: one committed suicide, another tried to kill himself, and three friends got pregnant. For my personal relationship with Christ, I just said, 'God, I give my life back to you'" (Interview, February 8, 2011).

George simply said, "I was born into the Christian faith. I have just realized my faith and just knew that God is good" (Interview, February 13, 2011).

SUMMARY

Chapter 4 has been an ethnographic description of diversity, identity, and receptivity of the gospel in the USA. Accordingly, having utilized three case stories, the chapter covered a description of diversity and its markers, addressed identity and its formulation in the USA, and concluded with the receptivity of the gospel by the USA Ghanaian diaspora. The relevance of leadership and discipleship in the USA GPCs is discussed in Chapter 6.

QUESTIONS FOR DISCUSSION

1. How Ghanaian traditional mindset is different from Western mindset?
2. How do 1st generation OBG, 2nd generation OBG and 2nd generation LBG vary in their perspectives on "diversity?"
3. How do 1st generation OBG, 2nd generation OBG and 2nd generation LBG vary in their perspectives on "individual identity?"
4. How do 1st generation OBG, 2nd generation OBG and 2nd generation LBG vary in their perspectives on "gospel receptivity?"

Chapter 5
LEADERSHIP AND DISCIPLESHIP IN USGPCs

INTRODUCTION

A Christian visionary leader is the one who moves the people who are led along the untreaded way. Lack of leadership training is tantamount to lack of mobilization for mission. Christian leaders should be proactive, leading to complex physical and spiritual growth. Development of a congregation is the internal spiritual growth of the members of that congregation. Similarly, discipleship is the core of the spiritual formation of the church. In addition, the GPCs as social institutions need to step in to help the nurturing and socialization of Ghanaian young generations. Christian education within the USA GPCs is, thus, inevitable. While some Ghanaians have immigrated with their children, others are immigrants giving birth to younger generation citizens of the USA.

The priority of the church should be to intervene and help nurture its young generations without taking over parental responsibility. First, the development in Chapter 5 consists of equipping the leaders who will equip others for growth. This is one of the urgently needed intra-developmental distinctive of the GPCs. This chapter covers a theological description of meaningful Christian leadership, addresses the theoretical framework of leadership, and concludes with the development ministry as leadership training. Second, development also includes a combination of discipleship, nurturing, and socialization of younger generations. Here, the chapter continues with the scriptural and theological foundations of discipleship, the general developmental marker in the church. In addition, another developmental issue in the chapter will be the exploration of the nurturing of younger generations. The final section will discuss the socialization of young people by the GPCs in the USA.

THEOLOGICAL DESCRIPTION OF MEANINGFUL CHRISTIAN LEADERSHIP

Biblical texts exist for the foundations of leadership. Meaningful Christian leadership is needed for the promotion of the faith. This kind of leadership is strongly Holy Spirit inspired and is what the 21st century Church needs. When development is practical in the body of Christ, it exhibits discipleship, leadership maturity, and regenerated believers who are transformational to the context in which they are found.

Theological Framework of 21st Century Christ-like Leadership

The Bible offers believers the model of Christ for Christian leadership. Contemporary Christians need such Christ-like leaders. The leaders that Christ wants in the 21st century include:

Righteous Holy Spirit-filled Leaders: The church of Christ needs Holy Spirit-filled leaders to sustain growth and development. Leadership that is not empowered by the Holy Spirit invariably results in sterility, moral degeneration, nominal membership, formalism, and corruption. The first disciples who qualified for leadership were those who were full of the Holy Spirit and wisdom (Acts 6:3). Among the deacons chosen was Stephen, described as a man full of God's grace and power (Acts 6:8). At the inception of Saul's conversion, Ananias told him, "Brother Saul, the Lord— Jesus…has sent me so that you may see again and be filled with the Holy Spirit" (Acts 9:17). This promise prevailed when the Holy Spirit instructed the believers in Antioch to separate Paul and Barnabas for the Gentile mission. Again, for Paul, the three basic character traits required of Holy Spirit-filled Christian leaders are to be approved of God, to be a workman who is not ashamed of Christ, and to handle the Word of God correctly (2 Timothy 2:15). Such character traits are Holy Spirit-inspired.

Servant Leaders: The central idea of appointments for high office in Scripture is the choice of God-dependent leaders. In the OT, whether kings, priests, or prophets, leaders are those who were close to God and servant leaders. For instance, Daniel was close to God because he had a marvelous prayer life (Daniel 6:10). Nehemiah was also close to God because he prayed (Nehemiah 2:4). The NT also illustrates and teaches servant leadership. Disciples are to follow Christ in their leadership style by imitating their Lord and Master. Christ told the disciples and admonished believers that whoever wants to be great must be a servant and whoever wants to be first must be a slave (Matthew 20:25-27). Christian leadership should be servant leadership manifesting the gifts of the Holy Spirit. There is dignity in humble service. However, it is tough to be a servant leader because success and achievements can lead to pride, self-confidence, and self-dependence. Every Christian leader must stay close to God in order to exhibit humble servant leadership.

Sacrificial Leaders: The Bible makes it clear that Christ wants us to offer ourselves as living sacrifices (Romans 12:1, 2). Sacrificial leaders should lay aside selfish desires to follow Christ, putting all energy and resources at Christ's disposal, and trusting Him for guidance. The church needs sacrificial leadership modeled on the life of Christ that exhibits a life of self-sacrifice and absolute commitment.

Ministry of Coordination: Coaching Amid Diversity

The role of leadership is to coordinate the diverse ministries and gifts necessary to unify and strengthen the Body of Christ (Ephesians 4:1-16). Equipping others for ministry is a tough job. Nevertheless, leaders should create an enabling environment for Christ's ministries to operate by facilitating, coaching, and equipping. Leaders should think of themselves as coaches building teams in which other members are given certain responsibilities by delegation and helping them realize their gifted potential. Metaphorically, a coach is a leader who establishes a special relationship with a team through team building. "The Christian tradition is team-work obsessed. The doctrine of creation trumpets a God who shares creative power with us…collaborators in our emergence" (Leonard Sweet 1999: 191; <http://www.AquaChurch.com> February 21, 2012). Teams should be built for vocation in God's Kingdom. In such team building for mission, the leader or coach is enabled to train others for the mission field.

Three principles are the basis for team building. First, team building is based on the "homing" principle. "Home and family are universal experiences…They reflect the practical realities of everyday economic and social necessity…achieving a place of belonging" (Robert Kysar 1999: 67, 68). The team-building ministry of a church is belonging that is metaphorically expressed in homing. Second, Christian team ministry is a community of believers who have communed together and are in fellowship under the banner of our Lord Jesus Christ. Discussing the biblical principles of a team, E. Stanley Ott stressed the "with-me" principle by stating, "Mark 3:14…embodies what ministry team is about — with Jesus — with one another…having passion for vision, being alert to new ideas, energized by the new ideas, having a bias for action, being learning organizations, and having permission to act" (2004: 42). Team building as the basis of community building (Romans 15:5, 6) is found among diaspora Ghanaian Christians. Third, closely related to team building is coaching. Christian coaching is a tripod based on Christ-centered focus, relationships, and sustained growth and action. "Christian coaching is a focused Christ-centered relationship that cultivates a person's sustained growth and action" (Linda Miller and Chad Hall 2007: 10). Suggesting a special relationship in an equation for Christian coaching Jane Creswell stated, "Coaching is relationship that involves Christ's presence and truths...This equation must be viewed like a mathematical formula: Christ's vision and mission + Scriptural principles + Christ's presence + High standard of excellence as a trained coach = Christian Coaching" (Jane Creswell 2005; Linda Miller and Chad Hall 2007: 10).

Shepherding in Promoting the Faith

It is Christian leaders' responsibility to give pastoral care to protect the flock and to feed the sheep by teaching God's Word (Acts 20:28). Pastoral leaders should always keep in mind that the flock under their care is no other than believers as sheep purchased for God with His Son's precious blood. The true pastor (shepherd) should diligently protect the sheep from their enemies (Acts 20:25-31). All along Satan has been raising internal false teachers and persistently and viciously works by infiltrating God's flock from outside with imposters. These imposters adhere to unbiblical and humanistic doctrines, worldly thought, and pagan ideas; ideas which possess the potential ability to draw members away from Christ's teachings toward themselves and their distorted teachings. A solemn obligation of all leaders is to guard the church from these attackers.

Declaration of the whole will of God is the duty of Christian leaders to promote the faith. Further, Paul admonished and encouraged the leaders of Ephesus to guard themselves and the faith and he presents leadership as the 4-fold pastoral teaching ministry: preaching, correcting, rebuking, and encouraging (2 Timothy 4:2, 3). In these shepherding ministries the faith is strongly promoted and guarded. It is the clergy's responsibility to equip the laity to participate in leadership in order to promote and guard the faith. Ministers should empower members through working on their strengths and weaknesses by communicating effectively, training them for ministry, and giving them recognition and delegated responsibilities. This gives members ownership of Christ's ministry. Christian leaders are to oppose all who would distort the fundamental revelation to protect the flock from spiritual wolves and false teaching. They must discipline in love, correct, and firmly refute all within the church who distort the truth because they should always remember their accountability for the flock (Acts 20:26, 27).

FRAMEWORKS OF SECULAR AND CHRISTIAN RELATIONAL LEADERSHIP

Theoretically, there is a disconnection between the secular linear and Christian relational leadership. A comparative analysis of the leadership of high and low context cultures as well as secular and Christian leadership is relevant. Such analysis is unavoidable because Christian OBG leaders have emigrated from high- to low-context cultures with different leadership styles. The application of such leadership styles in a different context is the challenge for such immigrants.

Secular Linear Versus Christian Relational Leadership

Unlike worldly secular management, the pattern and process by which a godly leader influences others is outworking of "vision sharing/goal setting, team-building, member-mobilization, and progress assessment/practical accomplishment" (Wan 2010). Such a pattern and process lead to disciple making at the micro level, kingdom building at the macro level, and seeks to be God-honoring. It is such godly leaders who are redeemed, reconciled, regenerated, and empowered by the Holy Spirit. Western linear leadership is disconnected from such Christian relational leadership. While linear leadership is dictatorial, Christian leadership is based on a servant model, which gets its significance from a vertical relationship with God. Figure 5.1 illustrates (Wan 2010).

Figure 5.1: The Pattern and Process of a Relational Leader

Secular Management of the World	Leadership of the Christian Faith
The focus is on the system and structure	The focus is on people
Operation is based on control of the process	Based on the constraint of God's love, therefore we build people up in love
Tendency is to be very near sighted—short-term	Long-term with the Kingdom perspective, with the ultimate goal of honoring God and blessing others
Frequent question is, "How and what to do"	The focus is more on "for whom I am doing it" and "what reason should be the motivation" and that tendency should be relational more than programmatic
Achieving goal and changing where we are in order to get things done	Gazing our eyes on Jesus, asking what He wants us to do, and we will do things right in His sight rather than our own

The GPCs are in multi-cultural context, but the leadership mindset of the Ghanaian is different from the Western conception of leadership. Servant leadership is the model for both the diaspora Ghanaian and American Christian citizenry in the USA culture (Wan 2010). The character of a godly leader should be marked by the fact that the leader's personality is called and commissioned by the Father, redeemed, and reconciled by the Son, and regenerated and empowered by the Holy Spirit. Christians may have a different task or assignment, but the ultimate task is making disciples and building God's Kingdom.

An additional quality of servant leadership is its focus on serving the Lord out of which grows the willingness to serve others. Jesus demonstrated this pattern and all Christian leaders are expected to follow this unique principle. By focusing on the vertical relationship with God, the motive, mode, and ultimate goal of leadership should all be God-oriented. In other words, Christian leaders should be Christ-dependent or inspired by the Holy Spirit. This is more than the Western task-oriented (getting things done in order to have the program completed) leadership. It is also more than the others-oriented in the African traditional leadership. While there are some Americans who see Western leadership as similar to biblical leadership, relatively, African leadership orientation seems more similar to the biblical leadership. Figure 5.2 compares the characteristics of Western linear and servant Christian leadership (Wan 2010).

Figure 5.2: Comparison of Western Linear and Christian Leadership

Leadership Characteristic	Power Leadership of the World	Christian Servant Leadership
Trademark	I want to be the boss	I am the servant of all
Foundation	Power	Love for God and Obedience
Process	Achieve success (success is measured by quantifiable outcome)	Matter of faithfulness to God, truthfulness to the calling, willing to fail and suffer personally so that the overall task could be accomplished
Operational Process	Exercise our authority and acquire power to ourselves	Willing to share leadership and exercise the power along with others
Eventual Goal	Personal accomplishment	Ultimate goal is to please the Lord and bring honor to His name by serving others
Profile	Leader should have self-confidence and exercise his influence on others	A leader should be one who has faith in the Lord and desire to please and seek His will for guidance in His leadership
Eventual Outcome	Leader is ambitious with strong drive toward accomplishment	Humble spirit seeking God's guidance and requiring others to partner to bring honor to God's Name
Overall Perspective	Based on self-motivation and the utilization of others to accomplish a certain goal	This orientation is willing to be obedient to the Lord, to love others and eventually bring honor to God's Name

High and Low Context Cultures Leadership

In both high and low contexts, Christian leaders should be proactive, leading to complex physical and spiritual growth. One of the complexities of diaspora leadership is that GPC OBG Christians are from a high-context culture with different leadership styles who live in a low-context culture. In fact, a Western or low-context culture leadership style (business-oriented management style) might not be effective in the USA GPCs. Similarly, traditional leadership styles from a high context culture might equally be useless in the USA GPCs. Striking a balance is the complex challenge. James Plueddemann differentiated between leadership in high and low context cultures as illustrated in Figure 5.3 (James Pluedemann 2009: 88) on page 121.

DEVELOPMENT MINISTRY IN LEADERSHIP TRAINING OF USA GPCs

Training takes several forms in GPCs' ministry. There is the formal training for the ministers, pastors, evangelists, and catechists. There is also the informal training that the lay leadership such as caretakers, presiding elders, stewards, and the like should go through. In all these cases, adult learning methods should be employed.

Theological Basis for Training in Relational Leadership

The obvious Christian example is taking Christ Jesus as our model. Christ is the Master Teacher. Jesus' training model is from the trainer's viewpoint. It includes, firstly, obedience and holding on to the teachings of Christ, our Lord (listening to the instructor and obeying what is taught). Secondly, there is discipleship, that is, the learning process of apprenticeship (knowledge: the quest of searching to know the truth that sets us free). Thirdly, an important learning process is listening to the Counselor about what is said by the Lord (Holy Spirit endowment and empowerment to learn to do what Christ says) (Galen Currah and George Patterson 2010). These training and learning themes are models that the Christ-like leadership needs in the 21st century Church today. They are summarized in Figure 5.4 (Galen Currah and George Patterson 2010) on page 121.

These themes are derived for Galen Currah and George Patterson's suggested six training themes drawn from Jesus' model in biblical texts. John's narrative illustrates a special process from the learner's viewpoint. These are indicated in Figure 5.5 (Galen Currah and George Patterson 2010) on page 122.

Figure 5.3: High Context and Low Context Leadership

Content	High Context Leadership	Low Context Leadership
Time	Many things can happen at the same time. It may be difficult to begin and end a meeting on time, or to isolate one activity at a time	Meetings begin and end on time and should be scheduled in an orderly sequence. People want to stick to the agenda
Communication Style	Communication is indirect, with emphasis on nonverbal messages. Tone of voice, posture and facial features have group meaning	Communication is direct—either spoken or written. The idea being discussed is more important than the feelings behind the statement
Authority	Prestige is given by the group and becomes almost permanent. Others will be expected to respect rank. Formal credentials are important and need to be evident. Age is often a criterion for respect	Authority is earned by individual effort and accomplishment. It is temporary and dependent on continued successful performance. Formal credentials are not as important as performance
Leadership Style	Leader is usually controlling in order to maintain group harmony and conformity. The leader often has a charismatic personality. Followers appreciate strong leaders	Leaders allow others to have significant input into decision making. Followers are more likely to question the ideas and decisions of the leader. Leaders respect individual initiative from the group members
Conflict Resolution Style	Indirect resolution is sought through mutual friends. Displeasure is shown through nonverbal, subtle communication. Direct conflict resolution may be avoided for as long as possible. Preserving harmony is emphasized	Resolution is sought through direct confrontation. People will meet face-to-face and articulate difficulties verbally. Speaking the truth is emphasized and appreciated
Goals	The highest goal is to build interpersonal relationships and making friends. Group harmony is highly valued	Goals are task-oriented. The leader will want to accomplish a precise, predetermined job within a prescribed time frame

Figure 5.4: Summary of Jesus' Training Methods

Type	Method	Action
Calling	Appointment of Co-Workers	Call and appoint co-workers; make training a serious preparation for immediate implementation
Authorization	Trainee Oriented	Authorize co-workers to do all the activities of ministry; do not reserve privileges for yourself
Instruction	Firm Strategic Plans	Firm planning strategy; instruct co-workers in where they are to go, which communicates where they will penetrate, how they are to make contacts, what they are to do, and what will be their message
On the Job Training	Trainees' Implementation	Continue to train only those who implement their plans; send workers immediately to implement their training on-the-job, in the field, with their host population
Feed-back	Evaluation	Have co-workers report back on what they did, what they said, and what were the immediate results; base further instruction on new learning needs
Rest	Recuperation	Provide rest for recuperation; spend some time together

Figure 5.5: Jesus' Training Method Illustrated from Four Texts

Matthew 9:37- 10:1, 5	Mark 6:6-8, 30	Luke 9:1-6, 10	Luke 9:62 – 10: 1, 17, 19	John 8: 31, 32 John 14:23-26;
9:37 Then He said to his disciples, "The harvest is plentiful but the workers are few. 38 **Ask** the Lord of the harvest, therefore, to send out workers into his harvest field. 10:1 He **called** the twelve disciples to him and gave them **authority** to drive out evil spirits and to heal every disease and sickness. 5 these twelve, Jesus **sent** out with the following **instructions**	6:6 Then Jesus went round **teaching** from village to village. 7 **Calling** the twelve to him, he **sent** them out, two by two, and **gave** them **authority** over evil spirits. 8 These were his **instructions**... 30 The apostles **gathered** around Jesus and **reported** to him all they had done and **taught**. 31 Then because so many people were coming and going that they did not even have a chance to eat, he said to them, "**Come with me by yourselves** to a quiet place and get some **rest**"	9:1 When Jesus had **called** the twelve, he gave them **power and authority** to drive out all demons and to cure diseases, 2 and he **sent** them out to preach the kingdom of God and to heal the sick. 3 And he **told** them...6 So they set out and went from village to village, preaching the gospel and healing people everywhere. 10 When the apostles returned they **reported** to Jesus what they had done. Then he took them with him and they **withdrew by themselves** to a town called Bethsaida	9:62 Jesus replied. "No one who puts his hand to the plow and looks back is fit for service in the kingdom of God. 10:1 After this the Lord **appointed** seventy-two others and **sent** them two by two ahead of him to every town and place where he was about to go. 17 The seventy-two **returned with joy and said,** "Lord, even the demons submit to us in your name." 19 "I have given you authority	8:31 To the Jews who had believed him Jesus said, "If you **hold** to my **teaching**, you are really my disciples. 32 Then you will know the truth, and the truth will set you free. 14:23 "If anyone loves me, he will **obey** my **teaching**...24 He who does not love me will not **obey** my **teaching.** These words you hear are not my own; they belong to the Father who sent me...but the **Counselor**, the Holy Spirit who the Father will **send** in my name, will **teach** you all things and will **remind** you of everything I have **said** to you"

OBG High Context Traditional Learning Styles

With a different mindset in leadership styles, traditional Ghanaian learning styles differ greatly from the learning styles in the USA pop-culture. The challenge is how the traditional learning style would apply effectively to persons who may have gone through American formal schooling. Sometimes it becomes challenging with regard to continuity (continuing Ghanaian traditional learning styles and disregarding those of the USA) or discontinuity (discontinuing the Ghanaian traditional learning styles and adopting the American ones). This is especially true with the second and third generations who have different leadership concepts. Figure 5.6 represents OBG traditional learning styles.

Figure 5.6: Learning Styles of Ethnic Akan People Group

Learning Styles	Description	Spiritual Dimension
Apprenticeship	On the job attachment	Vertical and horizontal relationship with God and persons
Directional Listening	Encoding-processing-decoding-decision and action	
Participatory Repetition	Learning by doing	
Role Playing	Skits; acting; roles taken up by learners	
Elderly Mentoring	Learning through role models	
Group Mentoring (Community)	Community ("Pressure"): learning by observation and copying	
Group; Peer; Team	Group; peer pressure: always a leader emerges; e.g., formally in puberty rites	
'Discipleship'	Christian: Christ's "follow me" training style	

The styles represent preference for participant learning among the Akan. An important addition is in connection with the vertical and horizontal relationship with God and human beings. This is useful for the leadership training of diaspora OBG Christians. The last learning style discipleship while similar to the Akan learning style, is not strictly Akan but scriptural.

Christian Visionary Relational Leadership Training

A Christian leader is one who knows, treads, and shows the way. Christian relational leaders should be visionary. A visionary leader is the one who turns his/her vision into a mission and inspires those led in motion along the treaded way towards a goal. Christian relational leaders should be authoritative, reflecting almighty God's glory and authority and power of the Holy Spirit. Christian leaders must be authoritative in the sense that people love to be led by a leader who inspires confidence. Members of the Body of Christ would follow

LEADERSHIP AND DISCIPLESHIP IN USGPCS

willingly and without any question leaders who show themselves wise and strong in Christ and who adhere to what they believe in Him. James Plueddemann stated, "In practice, leaders must do three things: collect and focus on the vision, make sure that every strategy in the organization contributes to the vision; connect strategies to the needs and opportunities of the current situation" (2009: 191, 192). Plueddemann suggested that the primary focus of a Christian leader is to make sure that the strategy fits the situation and contributes to the vision. Figure 5.7 suggests the relationship between the leadership components in both high and low contexts (Plueddemann 2009: 201).

Figure 5.7: Relationship Between Vision, Situation, and Strategy

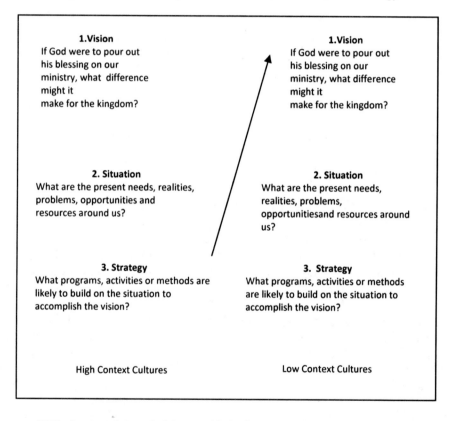

With the situation and vision established, strategy describes the activities or methods of achievement of the vision. For training in whatever context, leaders should formulate a balance between vision, situation, and strategy. "Vision describes qualities in people that bring glory to God...Vision challenges the leader to think big...The situation is the current needs, realities, challenges, opportunities, and resources around us...assessing the situation forces leaders to be realistic" (Plueddemann 2009: 192-195). In Figure 5.7, the placements of vision, situation, and strategy are done differently than Plueddemann's for better understanding. The positions of situation and strategy are exchanged because it is after the needs, challenges, and opportunities are thought through before strategies are formulated by leadership for action. Figure 5.8 is a summary of the comparison of the relationship found between vision, situation, and strategy of both high and low contexts (Plueddemann 2009: 201).

Figure 5.8: High and Low Contexts Vision, Situation, and Strategy

Activity	High-Context Culture	Low-Context Culture
Vision	Is intuitive with a general sense of direction.	Is precise with predictable and quantifiable objectives.
Situation	Comes from an instinctive reading of the environment.	Is analytically and logically analyzed.
Strategy	Often arises from unexpected opportunities and spontaneously changes when the situation changes.	Is planned far in advance and is tightly evaluated in light of measurable objectives.

With diaspora Ghanaians, the awareness and comparison between the vision, situation, and strategy is expedient since they are from high-context cultures who find themselves in low-context multi-cultural USA.

GPCs Diaspora Ministerial Training: Formulating Formal Practice Design

Leadership development cannot be done without some form of formal instruction. Based on the vision and situation, the current strategy by the GPCs should be to train potential pastors in the USA. Suggested designs for the training of USA GPCs' ministers could be formulated for this important but long overdue pastoral training. Here, the learning units of meaningful formal pastoral leadership training competencies based on the curriculum developed by the Institute for International Christian Communication (IICC) are suggested in the appendices D.II and D.III. These figures are a continuous six-week course for the special tent ministerial training comprising learning units, related topics, and description of the course content.

THEMATIC RESEARCH ON USA GPCs LEADERHIP AND LEADERHIP TRAINING

One of the greatest requirements or urgent necessities for the USA GPCs is the ministry of pastoral care. The congregations, societies, and assemblies need ministerial leadership. Both the clergy and laity freely expressed their leadership models, styles, and roles in the ethnographic research interviews.

Pastoral Insights on Leadership Styles, Roles, and Models

The ministers shared their views on leadership styles, roles, and models. Gyang-Duah, commenting on these leadership markers said,

> My model of leadership is Jesus Christ. I always strive to answer the question, "What will Jesus do?" My leadership role is team oriented. Delegation is valuable in such leadership. I appreciate reorientation of leadership style to functional leadership that is welcoming to all kinds of people; not only those one knows and relate to. Listening is helpful. Ministers ought to be listeners. Decisions taken by consensus are always the best. It is quite frustrating and disappointing to find cliques of session members arrogate to themselves undeserved and unqualified authority of decision making outside the sessions (Interview, November 3, 2010).

Yaw Asiedu also talked about his leadership by stating,

> I consider leadership to mean several things. For me, leadership in the Christian faith is God's calling. Therefore, leaders should be God-dependent and God controlled. I cannot be a do-it-all leader. I should partner with the laity to preach, lead worship services, conduct counseling, officiate customary and Christian marriages, lead naming ceremonies, and attend funerals, and the like (Interview, March 19, 2011).

Similarly, Joyce described her leadership as a calling when she said, "To be a pastor is a ministerial calling. It is more of God-dependence. Though I am a female, God has used me to take the congregation to the current high level. As a leader, I am only able to give what I have; what I have is Jesus Christ. Currently I am satisfied with my leadership model, style, and role (Interview, April 9, 2011).

Like Joyce, Stephen Kwaku Owusu also considered leadership as a calling. He said, "Christ calls believers to be disciples first. This is the foremost leadership calling. It is the duty of the pastor to train both those who are Methodists and those who are not about the doctrines of the church. In humility, my model is Christ-like leadership" (Interview, November 19, 2011).

Carroll said,

Before one handles any responsibility, one has to know what leadership role that one is in. I am still learning, man of God, what is at stake here in PIC or any other place in America. With regard to style, I am relational. I like one-on-one interaction with people. In addition, I like to embrace the idea of motivation of people to do things on their own in their faith. I am saying it again, I like leading from behind. I am not the type of push-forward where I do-it-all (Interview, March 11, 2012).

Untrained Leadership Insights on Leadership Styles, Roles, and Models

Dwomo Sarpong expressed, "I believe in all embracing leadership. For me, such leadership style will lead to mobilization for evangelism and demographic growth" (Interview, November 23, 2010). Paul Asiama just said, "I do not have the right personnel to work with" (Interview, October 18, 2010). That is all that he could say. Unlike Asiama, Ansah Ntow stated, "My style is servant leadership. But as a leader, it is my responsibility to mobilize the people to move forward. I have the gift of being very observant. I thus learn by participating and observing the pastors. I believe in on the job self-training" (Interview, April 10, 2011).

Opanyin Fosu, another untrained caretaker perceived pastors as having the responsibility of leadership of the church. He suggested,

> At certain point I held the leadership of the society for four years. At that time Rev. Dr. Arthur was attached to this society for our pastoral oversight. We then needed a resident pastor. When we heard that Rev. Nathan was studying for his masters, we accepted him as our resident pastor. This arrangement did not work when the church eventually broke up. When Rev. Nathan left us, by God's grace, we got in touch with Rev. Edu-Bekoe, a Presbyterian minister who offered pastoral care despite denominational differences. He was commuting from Princeton to help us. Currently, the Very Rev. Owusu is the minister-in-charge. It was Rev. Edu-Bekoe who linked us with Rev. Owusu who returned home after his studies at Princeton. We then requested the Methodist headquarters in Ghana to post him to us since 2008. With our experiences with these ministers, I suggest that the clergy should offer the needed leadership; untrained lay leaders are mere helpers (Interview, November 19, 2011).

Pastoral Insights on Leadership Training

Again, some of the ministerial leaders commented on the limited leadership training in the GPC. Gyang-Dauh said,

As the chairperson of the OMF, it is my direct responsibility to organize training. Tentatively, I drew the following training activities for PCG OMF district.

Month/Date	Activity	Congregations
December 10, 2010	Leadership Training	PCGNY, Manhattan, NY Ebenezer PCG, Bronx, NY Newark PCG, Irvington, NJ
January 14-16, 2011	Leadership Training	Emmanuel PCG, Norton, VA Adom PCG, Adelphi, MA

Similar leadership training is ongoing. We believe it is through training that the administration and development of the congregations will improve (Interview, November 23, 2010).

With a sigh, Yaw Asiedu confirmed the acceptance of the clerical responsibility for training and the absence of leadership training. He started by asking,

Leadership training? This is one of the challenging areas of the USA PCG ministry. When I was commissioned, I had to go back to Ghana for short-term special ministerial training (SMT). Nothing has happened since then in PCGNY. With regard to the laity leadership training programs have been discussed. Something is in the pipeline (Interview, March 19, 2010).

Joyce responded, "The USA PCG congregations need more ministers. I join the advocacy group who are calling on the PCG to expedited action on the local training of pastors. This will improve our leadership development" (Interview, April 9, 2010). Stephen Kwaku Owusu said, "My style is that of training others to delegate roles to them to uplift the society" (Interview, November 19, 2011). Carroll simply said, "As I said earlier, I like creating an enabling environment for training others to perform while I lead from behind. Such attitude would motivate others to mature in their faith and deliver in leadership roles" (Interview, March 11, 2011).

Untrained Leadership Insights on Leadership Training

All the caretakers interviewed also saw the need for training. Paul Asiama commented,

Training of the leadership is important and very urgent. On one hand, we need trained and more seasoned ministers from Ghana but due to the stringent visa requirements it is difficult to get them here. On the other hand, training here in the USA is not easy for fear of losing jobs. In addition, some Presbyters have positional but not functional leadership. Therefore, training here in the USA should be expedited. Leadership training is long overdue (Interview, October 18, 2010).

Dwomo Sarpong responded, "Leadership training is needed urgently in the USA PCG. Most of the lay leaders do not know much about the denomination. Back home members were more committed to the church. Lack of commitment is the problem" (Interview, November 23, 2010). Ansah Ntow, who believes in taking initiatives, said,

> I have had no formal training as a leader. But I do learn much from observation. It is my gift to interpret, initiate, and do it. First, I selected some key people to learn how to preach. Second, I trained service leaders. I then asked them to observe me while I did everything for one month. Thereafter, the others trained started to see themselves as partners in development and open to delegation (Interview, April 10, 2012).

Opanyin Fosu repeated his idea of the pastoral responsibility to lead and train the laity. He insisted, "The pastors are to lead and offer pastoral care for the church. However, there is dire need for trained laity. We offer our services to the church but the lack of training may make us falter. I know so much about Methodism from my background. In matters of spirituality, however, the clergy are far ahead of some of us. It is the duty of the pastors to train us" (Interview, November 19, 2011)

DISCIPLESHIP IN THE USA GPCs

Discipleship is the basic intra-developmental ministry that has the purpose of bringing believers to spiritual maturity. Discipleship involves what happens during the weekdays. If diaspora GPCs' development and missions are not resulting in character forming relationship habits of members who relate the Word of God to their private lives, then there is a missing link in discipleship.

Responsible Discipleship (Endowment)—*Didache*

Discipleship is a process that takes place within a life-long accountable relationship with Christ. The Greek word for discipleship is didache which means apprenticeship or learning. Unlike the disciples of the rabbis who sought masters, it is Christ Himself who calls "'Follow Me!'(Matthew 8:19ff). Following Jesus…and sharing His mission thus belong together" (David Bosch 2005: 38; Moreau and Snodderly 2011: 56). For success in Christian ministry, believers should turn back to the NT method of discipleship as exhibited by the master teacher Jesus. James Dunn posed the question, "Does the church which came out match the expectation of the reign of God? ... missionary work was quite naturally understood as an attempt to extend God's Kingdom in the world" (1992: 93). Thus, Christians are reminded to study and implement the Scriptural method of discipleship.

Generational Identity Formulation: Social Mobility Through Education

Every society influences and shapes a person's identity formulation. Ultimately, this influences the acceptance and reception of migrant second generation children. "Immigrants who possess skills that the host country is looking for are able to achieve higher economic success and see that their children are more accepted in the host society" (W. Haller and P. Landolt 2005: 1182-1214). Normally, discrimination and marginalization have a serious impact on individual identity formulation. "If the economic status of immigrants makes their children to become part of the society, it takes less time...This helps them to explore all the opportunities the society offers. If the children are perceived as 'other' because of their parents' economic status they are stigmatized and relegated to the background" (Suarez-Orozco and Suarez-Orozco: 91-98). The Lausanne document for evangelization aptly described the perception of immigrants. It stated, "The host community...might feel uncomfortable about the 'newcomers,' or even see them as threat...They might be seen as economic threat – affecting jobs and housing...they might be seen as cultural threat...they might be seen as a religious and ethical threat" (Tom Houston et al. 2010: 11).

LBGs are no different from their OBG parents in terms of marginalization.

Marginalization of the "other" happens because many indigenous people think immigrants deprive them of their jobs, education, and financial benefits. It is thus the question of "us" against "them" — the "we" versus the "others." One major means that second generation diaspora Ghanaians use for gradual assimilation and social mobility is through education in the host cultures. For instance, there is the perception that without an American education, job marketability is negligible in the USA. Therefore, parents, church elders, and children's advocates, do advise the children and the youth to take advantage of the enormous opportunities and potentialities available to them in the USA. However, the ever-increasing categorization, stereotyping, and discrimination of immigrant children have the potential to impact them to form socioeconomic groups. Most Ghanaian younger generations would rather use the opportunities available positively, to improve their social status through education.

Widening Generational Gap

The existence of the generational gap of diaspora Ghanaians is dependent on the dominant adult culture and the creation of youth cultures. The dominant culture is a serious challenge to Ghanaian youth. Mueller suggested that in the American dominant culture, the "'perfect storm, forces, and trends affecting' the youth include the 'rapidly changing, free fall families'" (2007: 39-76). Youthful independence creates its own protective sub-culture. In the creation of their own

NURTURING YOUNG GENERATIONS IN THE USA GPCs

One fact consistently stressed is the relatively woeful failure of the family, as a social institution, to nurture and socialize young people in the Ghanaian diaspora. To answer this issue, the church could offer cultural and moral values. This is an advocacy for the complementary responsibilities of the family and the church. Generational differences within the USA population are exemplified by "baby boomers," a generation born between the late 1940s and early 1960s after the Second World War in addition to Generations-X and Y. The nomenclature used to describe younger generations is varied. As Lisa La George stated, "Students born between the years 1985 and 2000 have been called the 'Net Generation'..."Mosaics'...and 'Emerging Adults'....Another descriptor assigned to this current generation is 'Millennials'" (2011; Moreau and Snodderly 2011: 91-102). Walt Mueller, describing Generation-Y and its digital attachment stated,

> Generation Y...The cries rising out of their deep hunger and thirst are loud, very loud...in their music, books and films. We observe it in their choices and behaviors. They long to be meaningfully connected to life. But the complexities of their world have made it difficult for them to hear the good news—at least in the way the church is now spreading it
> (Mueller 2006: 18, 19).

The reason for Generation-Y's attachment to the computer is reception of "acceptance, understanding, community, meaning, and guidance" (Mueller 2006: 17), in addition to individual satisfaction from their online friends.

Ghanaian Diaspora Younger Generations

Ghanaian immigrant generations vary in the preservation of traditional Ghanaian culture and adaptation of the USA popular culture. For Suarez-Orozco and Suarez-Orozco, immigrant younger generations go through a "process of varied experiences depending on socioeconomic status of their parents" (2001; Yeboah 2001: 91-98). It is expedient to add to their categorization the third generation. This is because out of socio-economic expediency, emigrants into the USA stay so long that their children grow to become adults who in turn give birth to the third generation. Ian Yeboah recognized three major categories of younger generations in the USA: "Children with at least one immigrant parent (hybrids); Children born in the United States whose parents are immigrants; and Children who were born in the homeland of parents and brought to the United States (2009: 91-98). These are referred to as the second-generation (1.5) immigrants."

followers to be salt and light is, at best, truncated mission" (2004: 88, 89; Wan and Edu-Bekoe 2010: 23). Figure 5.9 describes Patterson's seven essentials for discipleship and mission practice.

The seven mission practices in Figure 5.9 on page 132 could only be implemented successfully by discipleship essentials. Ghanaian Christians are very religious and many of them in the diaspora have gone through mission schools, professed Christianity, or are prone to the Christian faith.

Figure 5.9: George Patterson's Essentials for Mission

Mission Essential	Congregational Mission Activities (Missions)
Church Government	Make disciples the way our King said, teaching them to obey His commands (Matthew 28:18-20)
	Obey God-given human leaders (Hebrew 13:7).
Growth	Let small churches and cell groups multiply (Acts 2:46).
	Meet in larger assemblies, or gather cells in larger congregations (Acts 2:46)
Training	Practice the NT 'one another' commands (Colossians 3:12-16)
	Use mentoring chains to train new leaders (2 Timothy 2:2)
Education	Academic training (Acts 22:3)
	Training children in age-segregated groups (Proverbs 22:6)
Support	Mobilize 'tent-makers,' gear non-budgeted projects to time limitations (2 Thessalonians 3:6-12; Acts 20:32-38)
	Support elders when church is able and they are doing their job worthily (1 Timothy 5:17, 18)
Evangelism	Seeker (Acts 19:1-10), Seeder (Acts 10), and Feeder (Acts 16:31), groups
	Let the gospel flow in the normal biblical way in existing social networks (Acts 16:31)
	Use media and large meetings to supplement the more common NT practice (Mark 4:1, 2)
	Avoid trying to push lots of camels through the needle's eye, but a few are 'possible' (Luke 18:25-27)
Organization	Organize Body, as Scripture requires (1 Corinthians 12)
	Use for special, temporary projects (Acts 6: 1-7)
Know Jesus, Pray	Meet the risen Christ, experience His powerful Presence, and pray in His name (John 14:18; 16:24)
	Learn facts about Jesus (Hebrews 5:12-14)

However, in order to fulfill this kind of mission, such Christians should obey their God-given mandate to reach out and embrace their non-Christian counterparts in love and humility. Christian mission should go beyond simply not condemning non-Christians, but by actively reaching out to them. Prayer is the master key for success. The usefulness of the innovation of telephone prayer makes up for the lack of time for corporate prayer due to work schedules and dispersed living locations of congregational members. Actually, the prayer line activities exhibit a composition of all the discipleship essentials, the Word of God, prayer, fellowship, and witness for the 21st century diaspora church as illustrated in Appendix D.I.

John Stroman recommended three basic principles for successful discipleship. He stated, "Successful Christian discipleship is mastering the basics...a small group meeting that followed three basic principles: prayer, study of scriptures, and witnessing" (1999: 69). Discipleship as character-forming habits is difficult but establishment of its model will result in a spiritual revolution of the church—awakening, regeneration, and revival. Five out of the seven principles suggested by Jack Stewart for which discipleship exists are "Being relational before instructional...promoting practices that become character-forming habits...greater maturity that is measured in Christ, requiring the continual presence of the Holy Spirit, and...often cross bearing" (2005 PTS Church Mobilization course). Some believers hunger for leaders who will lead them—people who can say our faith is leading us into doing what our calling enjoins us to do both in our character and charisma. Leaders should help members to discover the gifts the Holy Spirit has given them. With such discovery they cannot rest until they have made disciples and mentored others to do same. "Discipling is an intentional relationship in which we walk alongside other disciples in order to encourage, equip and challenge one another in love to grow toward maturity in Christ. This includes equipping the disciples to teach others as well" (Greg Ogden 2003: 129). In such transformational development, discipleship then becomes following Christ in His steps (1 Peter 2:21).

Discipleship Essentials: God's Word, Prayer, Fellowship, and Witness

For the successful functional discipleship, the inevitable practical markers include the Word of God, prayer, fellowship in an environment conducive for Christian education, and witnessing. George Patterson suggested that congregations should strategize on "how to implement missiologists' lists of essentials...seven areas of church activity, each of which contains two or more pairs of ways of doing the activity, which must be kept in proper ratio or alignment, varying from time to time and field to field" (2010 DIS Evangelism and Church Planting course). In a completely new way of discipleship, Jesus instilled a change of missionary consciousness in the disciples by sending the twelve and the seventy-two (Matthew 10:1-16, Luke 9:1-6, and Luke 10:1-20). The two missions, as well as the post-Easter experiences, initiated this change of consciousness.

James Dunn stated, "Jesus' discipleship...of God's New Covenant had its soul in evangelization...the character of discipleship from the beginning was community organized to support missionaries reaching out...'to maintain a witness by the very quality of their community life'" (1992; Wan and Edu-Bekoe 2010: 23). Diaspora GPCs mission practice should apply the recommendation from Moreau et al. They stated, "Mission that does not include incorporating those led to Christ...teaching them to obey all that Christ commanded his youth culture "outside influences are shaping teenage values; and changing values are leading to new trends" (Mueller 2007: 39-76). Mueller wrote that some forces and trends affecting teenagers include:

- Families Are Changing: Increase and acceptance of divorce, rise in cohabitation and out-of-wedlock births, crisis of fatherlessness...mothers who work outside the home, and decreasing amount of time parents are spending with their kids.

- Outside Influences Are Shaping Teenage Values: Music, advertizing, and other media, digital revolution, peer group, globalization, and postmodern worldview.

- Changing Influences Are Leading to New Trends: Sex...prevalence of substance abuse... epidemic of teenage depression and suicide... Our teenagers live in sex-saturated society. The dominant message they hear from the media is that sex is an appetite to be indulged and enjoyed whenever, wherever, however, and with whomever they like.

- Principles That Bridge the Cultural-Generational Gap:

- Understanding the World of Kids is Primarily a Parent's Calling.

- It's Never Too Early; It's Never Too Late.

- It Won't be Easy; Pain is a Blessing.

- Understanding Youth Culture Equips Parents to Pass on the Torch of Faith.

- Understanding Youth Culture Fosters Relational Closeness (2007: 39-76).

All these are cross-cultural. A summary of the differences in values of OBGs and LBGs is illustrated in Figure 5.10 (Wan and Edu-Bekoe 2011; Moreau and Snodderly 2011: 46, 47).

Figure 5.10: OBG and LBG Morality and Values Differences

OBG	LBG
Cognition and Emotion	
Happiness is paramount! Enjoy life Humility: Gentle; peaceful; modest Honor: Honor wise elders Shame: Frown on sin; evil Pain: show no pain—glad to make sacrifices	Success: Involving status, wealth, and proficiency. Competitive: self-believing—"Toot your own horn; no one will?" Future for youth Honor: Behave, speak, and dress American Shame: Not of any moral grounds but identifying with the Ghanaian culture Do not be tortured—no kind of a masochistic nut
Interpersonal Relationships	
Community: commonality before self Sharing: Everything belongs to others Elderly Respect: no criticism for elders Universal acceptance: Good from all others; despise and chastise the bad Children: Gifts from God; shared with others	"Self as number one!" syndrome Ownership: Preference for outhouse; rather than sharing mansion Critics as good analysts Persuade, convince, and proselytize—be an evangelist/missionary "I'll discipline my own children; Don't tell me how to"
Learning	
Knowledge learning through legends: great past stories Sankofa: "Return to take"; old traditional ways and values, the best, been proven Mother-tongue aspirations: Cherish own language; speak it	Learning is schooling; get all schooling; cannot be taken from you Look to the future for things new: "Tie your wagon to a star; keep climbing up, up" You are American; speak English
Religion	
Religion, supreme; relevant; transcends all life's aspects	Individualistic religion
Socio-Economic-Cultural	
Diligence: hard work is sacred Leave things natural Medicinal herbs; God's gifts from mother earth Land is precious: Orient self to the land	Live with your mind: think intelligently. Show teacher how well you know the answers. Good at books "You should see land when God had it all alone" Synthetic medicines: "Today's laboratories can do anything" Orient yourself to a house, a job

LBGs are in a different world from their parents. Several factors make the nurturing of Ghanaian children in the USA challenging. First, host culture impact, particularly from the school and peer pressure, seems overwhelming to LBGs. Exposed to the American way of liberal life, mostly outside the home, they find it difficult to accept adult "conservative" views. As USA citizens, LBGs are more inclined to emulate American culture than Ghanaian culture. For instance, "African children in public schools are under pressure to belong and are bullied by fellow black children and calling them 'African' because of their accent" (http://www.americanabroadusa.net; Funmi Adepitan 2011: 26). Second, differences in the generational morality values are problematic. Honor for them is to speak, put on clothing, learn, and behave like African-American citizens. Shame is not going against any moral values of the society but not speaking and living like their African-American counterparts. Third, the lack of meaningful parenting has overwhelming influence on Ghanaian children. The absence of the father and the father figure create a huge psychological trauma for some Ghanaian children. Fourth, the absence of discipline is another challenge. In Ghana, parents relatively spank their children when they go wayward. In America, that will be child abuse. Adepitan cited an African school teacher, "There are many wild…children out there who have no parental control and terrorize the teacher and everybody…So when the African children see this power held…they begin to have ideas on how to 'liberate' themselves from parental care" and control (2011: 26).

These and other differences of morality and values between the OBGs and LBGs indicate that expectation of a strictly Ghanaian cultural attachment by a different generation seems too much. Such behavioral expectation from LBGs, born, socialized, and acculturated in the USA seems difficult, paternalistic, and overbearing. Urging them to learn the culture of the motherland is also problematic. They question the desirability and values of such "outdated normative traditions." Here is the basis for OBG-LBG conflict. Despite their acculturation and assimilation they are neither Ghanaian nor American, though. Relatively, some LBGs are disjointed and disoriented in terms of their Ghanaian roots.

Loss of LBGs' Identity

LBGs' assimilation is problematic. Therefore, the perceived loss of identity of LBGs is another challenge in the USA, as suggested in Case Story 4.2. While Christian OBGs are comfortable with their cultural identity their LBG children are not. Coupled with other challenges such as hurting cognitive dispositions, lack of parental time and care, and paternalistic adults, the magnitude of LBG identity loss is enormous. This enormity is linked to split personality or cognitive dissonance. Summary of the challenges and opportunities of "ministering to the diaspora" Ghanaians in the GPCs are presented in Figure 5.11 (Wan and Edu-Bekoe 2011; Moreau and Snodderly 2011: 44-45).

Correspondingly, the challenges and opportunities of "missions/ ministering through" the diaspora GPCs are also presented in Figure 5.12 (Wan and Edu-Bekoe 2011; Moreau and Snodderly 2011: 44-45).

Figure 5.11: "Ministering to the Diaspora" Ghanaians in the USA GPCs

Challenges	Opportunities
Communities	
Diverse cultures; worldviews. Ethnic churches. Similar mainline denominations. Pastoral care and counseling. Lack of trained leadership. Pluralistic environment.	Formation and Nurturing congregations. "Home" from home. Operation as community. Family values ecclesiology. Using cultural values: stories, proverbs, wise sayings, etc.
Generations	
OBGs Widening generational gap. Dominant Multi-culturalism. Cultural Dislocation: Challenging Cross-cultural Ministry. Delineating Polychromic-Monochromic Time. Cosmological Warfare. **LBGs** Linguistic diversity. Cultural identity loss. Peer pressure. Pop-culture assimilation	**OBGs** Mother-tongue gospel; monolingual congregations. Meaningful engagement. LBGs' care Responsible discipleship. **LBGs** LBGs hunger for God. Generational-gap as positive evangelization vehicle. Youth worship: Different times? Different congregations?

Figure 5.12: "Ministering through the Diaspora" Ghanaians in the USA GPCs

Challenges	Opportunities
Congregations	
"Colonization": Local mainline Paternalistic church oversight. Challenging employment schedules. Long-distant congregational locations. Spiritual warfare.	Practice: authentic Christians; Africans. Functional: satisfying felt-needs. Self-help; communal support. Support for transnational overseas churches. Rites of passage Cclebration. Meaningful engagement; toleration and cooperation. Responsible discipleship. Countering cosmological evil spirits; healing and deliverance. Attractive worship for all races; all generations. Building bridges among races
Generations	
OBGs LBGs' socialization. Caring for LBGs. **LBGs** Peer Pressures in Ministry. Difficulties in operating as current members. Mother-tongue challenges.	**OBGs** Socializing LBGs through worship Training for LBGs. **LBGs** Teaching mother-tongue through LBG 2 Action Ministry: drama, poetry, dancing, etc. Deliverance from "modern day demons."

Just as there are challenges, there are also opportunities as indicated in both Figures 5.11 and 5.12. This is positive. While these challenges should be faced and solutions found, the opportunities should be taken up with regard to the formation, development, and mobilization for diaspora missions for both OBGs and LBGs. Socialization is the means to do this.

SOCIALIZATION OF YOUNG GENERATIONS IN THE USA GPCs

Socialization is the totality of the processes and methods through which a people's group educates its younger generations formally or informally. The informal is the process of education through parents, peer groups, and social institutions such as the church. Through its children and youth ministries, nurturing and socialization of young people (children and junior youth or teenagers) could be meaningfully offered by the GPCs. In this way, cultural and moral values could be offered.

Complexities of Socialization of Young Generations

Experiences of the younger generations in the USA are complex. The complexities occur because of the multi-cultural or "salad bowl" nature of the host society. As the Lausanne document for evangelization stated,

> The American ideal of society was the Melting Pot where everything is assimilated in the whole. For some time that has been replaced by the Salad Bowl idea in which each part contributes to the whole whilst maintaining its distinctive form and favor. Some prioritize Integration while others emphasize Multi-culturalism. Many want contact but fear assimilation while others desire total Separation. Whatever form the interaction may take, the result will still inevitably be change and the changes have to be coped with (Tom Houston et al. 2010: 11).

Within such complexities, OBG parents initially have a lot of influence on their children's behavior, thus affecting their cultural identity. However, there are other institutions that also impact their children's cultural behavior. Here is the complexity.

Identity Negotiation of Young Diaspora Ghanaians

Most Ghanaians do not categorically consider their children as totally assimilated African-Americans. Nevertheless, there is the perception that in the

USA, some OBGs speak of their LBG children as not Ghanaian. This attitude is typical for the hybrids with Ghanaian parents in mixed marriages. "The USA adult generation has failed to understand the real worldview of today's youth" (Mueller 2006: 18, 19). In the Ghanaian diaspora, LBGs feel they are not being heard since their parents covertly or overtly refuse to listen to them. Their usual cry is "nobody wants to listen to me." Some overwhelmed LBGs then become victims of USA pop-culture. OBGs should help them negotiate their identity formulation in the American multi-cultural context.

Diaspora GPCs can train and disciple the younger generations, which will help develop a new age group capable of reaching the unreached in the USA. As enablers, GPCs diaspora leaders should mentor the young generations for life-long connections between faith and vocations. Leaders should help members to discover their spiritual gifts. Galen Currah stated, "Practical mentoring focuses on apprentices' churches and cell groups, meeting their urgent needs" (Currah <http://MentorNet.ws> September 5, 2011). Through this church role in the USA GPCs, socialization of the younger generations will be achievable.

Training of the Younger Generations in the GPCs

While the school uses pedagogy to formally educate children, the environment for training them in the church is different from the school. Training children is also obviously different from that of adults. For both adults and children in the church, informal and non-formal education should be used. While Table IV in Appendix D illustrates the similarities and differences between formal and informal training, that of Table V represents the differences between the training of adults from that of children. These tables are adaptations from the Corporation of Public Broadcasting (2002: 1, 2). In Figure 5.13 are suggested methods of training the church may use to help socialize the younger generations.

These plans and materials are also adaptation from Russel Robinson (1994) as well as Robert Kohls and Herbert Brussow (1994: 63). In addition, some of the materials used to formulate these training activities are also from Luis Bush (2009), The Presbyterian Church of Ghana Bible Study and Prayer Group (BSPG) discipleship material (2001), and James Heimbeger (2003). "Although socialization is often associated with ethnicity, there are very few empirical studies that focus on it as independent variable in ethnic identity retention" (Isajiw and Makabe 1982: 2). C. Nanlai suggested that socialization is not the prerogative of parents and family alone. He posited, "Yet parents are only one possible source of cultural transmission. Peers and larger social networks, churches, temples, playgrounds, and schools are also significant in child socialization" (1993: 183-200).

Figure 5.13: Suggested Plans and Materials for Socialization in USA GPCs

Children's Ministry (CM)			
Generation	Plans	Materials	CM Trainers
CM's Service (CMS)	Annual CS Schedule	Bible, Bible stories books, hymn books, audio-visual aids, etc.	Children's ministry service teachers, the agents, and other children loving adults
	Christian films and videos for children	Television set, DVD & CD player, DVDs and CDs	Children's ministry service teachers
	Drama & role playing	Short skits for children	Same as above
	Child peer mission & evangelism	Luis Bush, *The 4/14 Window*	Children's ministry service teachers, the agents, and other children loving adults
Junior Youth (JY) Ministry			
Generation	Program	Needed Materials	JY Leaders
Junior Youth Ministry Service (JYMS)	Annual JY schedule	Bible, Bible stories books, hymn books, audio-visual aids, etc.	JY service leaders, the agents, and other junior youth loving adults
	Christian films and videos for youth	Television set, DVD & CD player, DVDs and CDs	JY ministry service leaders
	Drama & role playing	Short skits for adolescents; Short Christian plays	Same as above
	Discipleship training	Selections from PCG BSPG discipleship training materials	Same as above
	Youth Bible study	Selections from PCG Basic Bible Study materials	Same as above
	Youth peer mission & evangelism	Luis Bush, *The 4/14 Window* "Your Church Can Change the World"	Same as above

THEMATIC RESEARCH ON USA GPCs' DISCIPLESHIP AND SOCIALIZATION

Five of the ministers, three caretakers, three second-generation (1.5) OBGs, and two LBGs responded to the issues of the development of the younger generations. There was the recognition of the need for discipleship, nurturing, socialization, and mentoring.

Pastoral Insights on Discipleship and Socialization

Gyang-Duah stated,

> Centralized well developed materials for Bible studies in discipleship, and mentoring should be provided from the OMF head office. The "prayer line" concept should be embraced by all the PCG congregations. Members should be encouraged to fellowship in revivals, healing, and deliverance, among others (Interview, November 23, 2010).

Gyang-Duah also continued to express his views on the issue of parental responsibility and GPCs' role of nurturing children when he said,

> Even when parents are together, some children become neglected. Parents work on two or three jobs to survive without enough time and supervision of their children. Most Christian parents should rather be encouraged to train the children instead of leaving everything on the school. It is their Christian duty. In the PCG, the children's services help the training of children through biblical stories, singing of hymns and choruses, role-play, and recitation. Greater responsibility, however, is on the parents (Interview, November 23, 2010).

With regard to socialization and nurturing of children Yaw Asiedu stated,

> I believe in "Train a child in the way he should go, and when he is old he will not turn from it" (Proverbs 22:6). Parents, therefore, have better responsibility to nurture their children. There seems to be a breakdown of the Ghanaian diaspora family because divorce rate is so high. This has resulted in the breakdown of moral and cultural values (Interview, May 30, 2010).

The response of Asiedu on the generational gap and the mother tongue aspirations was different from the other ministers,

> Experience helps me to recognize the reality of generational gap. Most Ghanaian children become assimilated because they go to school, communicate with their peers, and play with other children in their neighborhoods. I disagree with the call to communicate only in the mother tongue in PCG congregations. Some LBGs even find speaking in the mother tongue unattractive (Interview May 30, 2010).

Joyce who has two active children in the church recognized the responsibility of all stakeholders. She stated,

> In some homes, children are virtually hooked to social networks such as Facebook, Twitter, LinkedIn, and the like. Nonetheless, most children accompany their parents to church. That is good because parents have the responsibility to train their children in the home. The reality is that LBGs are

nurtured in different environments from their OBG parents. All stake holders: parents, the church, and EAs should come together to help the LBGs (Interview, April 9, 2010).

Stephen Kwaku Owusu's comments on parental responsibility and the generational gap were interesting. He said,

> The question of the gap between the OBGs and our children depends on who is involved. There are those born overseas and brought into America. They do better in school and are morally better than those born in the USA. In addition, their relationship with their parents and work ethics are better. Those who were born here look upon themselves as African-Americans but they are not. They sometimes understand their parents' languages but they do not accept and speak those languages. They are influenced by others in the system such as the school, peers, and neighborhoods. Those called the "Ghanamade" are those children who are brought here and lose parental control. They are the sorest of all. Apparently, some of the parents did not really know those children before they were brought here. They may be having hidden characters which the parents did not know before they brought them (Interview, November 19, 2011).

Carroll started her ideas about parenting, nurturing, and socialization of the African diaspora children by saying,

> One single word for answering your question, man of God, is need. Need might not be immediate satisfaction but might come with time. In nurturing and socialization of children, I will say the importance of straightening the marriage institution is the first option. Seminars for couples should start. I mean fathers and mothers should come together for discussions and brainstorming. From there we can start to train the children. Remember, parents trained will culminate in children trained too. Whatever level of development the parents have will reach and reflect on the training of their children (Interview, March 11, 2012).

Prompted to elaborate, Carroll continued,

> The Bible says that children are like arrows; they are to be sharp, they have to be strong, and they have to go far. Look at the Indians. Many Indian women have PhDs but they stay in the home to train their children first before looking for jobs. That is why Indian women are strong and their homes are also strong while their children are trained to accept their Hindu faith. Christian parents should set their priorities right. Christian children should be trained according to God's principles, values, and standards (Interview, March 11, 2012).

Kwaku Boakye responded,

> The youth is the potential for the church. Children face many challenges in the school. The church should find ways to keep the youth and use them. Youth services help to keep the youth away from temptation. They also help to teach the youth more about Christ. And they help them to develop their talents: playing of musical instruments, preaching, leading services, and singing, among others. Honestly, I don't enjoy the adult services because I don't get much from them. I just observe what is going on. Bible studies, retreats, camping, conferences, and workshops, among others, will bring the needed impact on the youth (Telephone Conference Interview, October 3, 2010).

Tiwaa, who strongly defended the LBGs against their OBG parents, contended,

> OBGs dwell too much on the negatives: their children are disrespectful, disobedient, badly mannered, and the like. The OBGs should rather think positive about their children. Raised back home, OBGs have different cultural and moral values from those of the LBGs, which they claim are better. That is problematic. The generational gap is existent because OBGs always have wrong perceptions about their children. The problem is in the way the parents themselves behave. In the NY metropolis, do you see the environment in which their children are raised? They are always in the poor neighborhoods. That is the problem (Interview, November 12, 2010).

Second Generation LBG Insights on Generational Gap and Youth Nurturing

Adjoa Debrah-Dwamena's views disagreed with those of Tiwaa. She defended their OBG parents when she said,

> The way some children behave these days is not good. For me, home is more than the immediate family. Here in America, the parents have to work leaving the children home. Much has to do with the society too. In the traditional societies there is much respect for the elderly. It also has to do with discipline. Discipline that our parents knew back home has been thrown overboard. Though I was born here in the USA, I was disciplined. The parents may be trying their best. The church should involve the youth now. If we are not involved now, the future of the church is bleak (Telephone Conference October 3, 2010).

Effe in Portland, OR said, "Youth services are important for us. The message will relate to the conditions of the youth. For instance, purity, abstinence, and obedience could be preached" (Interview, February 2, 2010).

SUMMARY

This chapter began with scriptural and theological foundations for Christian leadership, followed by discussions on "relational leadership," "Christian servant leadership," and "high context leadership." Insights from the above discussions were applied to the presentation on USA Ghanaian discipleship and USA GPCs leadership and leadership training.

QUESTIONS FOR DISCUSSION

1. How is the relational leadership of Christian faith different from secular leadership?
2. How is Christian servant-leadership different from the power leadership of the world?
3. What is the difference between high context leadership in comparison to low context leadership?
4. Can you give a summary of Jesus' training method in discipleship?
5. Are there differences between the OBG and LBG in terms of morality and values?
6. What are the challenges and opportunities in "ministering to the diaspora" and "ministering through the diaspora" Ghanaians in the USA GPCs?
7. What are the suggested plans and materials for socialization in the USA GPCs?
8. If you are serving any diaspora community in USA, are there transferable principles from the Ghanaian diaspora to your ministry context of a different diaspora group?

Part III

CASE STUDIES

'To God's elect, strangers in the world, scattered throughout...who have been chosen according to the foreknowledge of God the Father, through the sanctifying work of the Spirit, for obedience to Jesus Christ and sprinkling by His Blood" (1 Peter 1:1, 2).

Part Three comprises missiological case studies of the diaspora GPCs in the USA, conclusion and recommendation.

Chapter 6
CASE STUDIES IN EUROPE AND THE USA

INTRODUCTION

Post-independent Africa has witnessed a massive immigration of Africans into the Euro-American milieu. This has impacted the whole globe because Africans are working around the globe to seek for greener pastures. "Some of the African nations which have taken advantage of exporting their nationals...attracted by the 'bright nation developed life,' include Ghana" (Moses Biney 2005: 67). Since the Africans are inseparable from their religion they carry their Christianity wherever they are scattered. Therefore, Africans plant churches of their various denominations in the diaspora. Chapter 7 discusses case studies of such planted congregations. The chapter begins with examples of African diaspora churches in Europe. It continues with instances of Presbyterian Church of Ghana (PCG) congregations in the USA exemplified by the PCGNY. It is then completed with four other case studies of GPCs.

AFRICAN DIASPORA CHURCHES IN EUROPE

Instances abound in the formation of African diaspora churches all over the globe. Europe and North America have the bulk of such African churches. Two of such examples are the Kingsway International Church in London, UK and the Embassy of God Church in Kiev, Ukraine. Both of these diaspora churches were formed by Nigerians. The basis of the formation of these foreign churches is provided by Jehu Hanciles.

Overview of African Diaspora in Europe

To be able to understand the complex context of African diaspora, arguments between two female Western scholars about African Christians in Europe are relevant. On one hand, Roswith Gerlof argues that Africans in Europe see themselves as Africans before being Christians; she argues they are Africans and must be taken as such before taken as Christians. Her point is that their particularity and identity must be recognized. Africans should not be labeled as Christians so they lose their identity. This contention is from anthropological and sociological level of explanation.

On the other hand, Gerrie ter Haar discusses the question of identity and self-perception as the term "diaspora" is applied to African immigrant. She argues that "the long-used term of African diaspora for African Americans has found a generic use for all Africans living outside the continent" (Ter Haar 2001: 5). In addition, there are the "notions of ethnicity and fundamentalism that make the conclusion that there is an ideology embedded in these concepts which contributes to the segregation of African immigrants in Western society" (Ter Haar 2001: 6). Consequently, she argues that Africans in Europe see themselves first as Christians before being Africans. Ter Haar feels that by referring to them as Africans in Europe demeans them and denies these diaspora Christians the universality of the faith.

Formation of African Churches in the Diaspora

Jehu Hanciles provided an important missiological reflection in his five missionary functions of African immigrant churches in *Beyond Christendom*. These include:

- Links between migration and religious commitment: African immigrants represent the face of Christianity to a good proportion of the nation's disadvantaged and marginalized populations.

- Witness and with-ness: African immigrant Christians and their descendants have a striking record when it comes to winning converts among immigrants.

- Perception of Euro-America as mission field: African immigrants encounter societies in which Christianity is experiencing decline in numbers and influence making them "mission field."

- Familiarity of religious plurality: African immigrant Christians are far more attuned than American Christians to religious plurality, an area of increasing challenge for American Christianity. This contention points to the fact that African immigrants typically come from a context of religious plurality.

- Transnationalism: African Christian immigrants have strong linkages with their Christian roots in their home nations (2008: 379, 380).

"African immigrant churches are among the fastest growing in American cities, where they increasingly exhibit a strong missionary consciousness" (Hanciles 2008: 381). Ter Harr affirmed Hanciles's "strong missionary consciousness" of the leaders as well as members of immigrant churches in the West. "God is bringing the refugee missionaries...they may not be documented, but God has a divine purpose for them. God has brought the whole world to one place, just as on the day of Pentecost" (Tom Marfo 2004; Bediako, et al. 2004: 157). With Hanciles's functions in mind, the formation of the two Nigerian diaspora churches formed Europe is discussed.

Case Study 1 (In Europe): Kingsway International Christian Centre (KICC)

The KICC (2011) was formed under the leadership of Matthew Ashimolowo in 1992. He and 300 members rented a hall at Holloway Boys School, North London. Eighteen years later, KICC has up to 12,000 in attendance every Sunday. They describe themselves as "the largest growing church in Western Europe." In addition to the mother church in London, they have seven other branches around the UK. KICC Sunday morning chapels are small churches within the KICC network with up to 100 adults. These fellowships meet on Sundays and also hold special events at other times throughout the year. Each chapel is headed by a minister. When chapels grow beyond 100 adults, they become branches. There are currently 13 chapels.

Internationally, KICC has affiliated branches (i.e. they are a part of the KICC group of churches and share the same values and mission statement) with eight branch churches in Nigeria, five in Ghana, one in Dublin, one in Namibia, and one in South Africa. KICC is definitely growing, reaching many local residents through their branch churches and chapels. Not only are they reaching people locally; and internationally beyond them to reach others. For example, planting churches in Ghana by starting in 2002, there are five branches in Ghana (KICC Dominion Centre (Ghana), KICC Gloryland Hotel (Ghana), KICC Teshie-Nungua (Ghana), KICC Cape Coast (Ghana) and KICC Achimota <www.kiccghana.com, 08/22/11>. They exemplify the diaspora mission strategy of ministering through the diaspora and beyond them geographically and racially reaching others.

Here, in the influx of diaspora population in the UK, diaspora congregations are to be mobilized for the Great Commission when individual Christians are motivated and empowered to carry out their missionary duties to reach their fellow kinsmen in the homeland and elsewhere. This is what is meant by "ministering through the diaspora." This is aptly illustrated by the case study of KICC.

Case Study 2 (In Europe): Embassy of the Blessed Kingdom of God Church (EBKGC)

The Embassy of the Blessed Kingdom of God Church (EBKGC) for all Nations is the new name of the church started in Kiev, Ukraine by another Nigerian, Sunday Adelaja. It was formerly started as the Word of Faith Church. On February 6, 1994, seven people met in an apartment in Kiev to worship their God and to know His word. Little did they suspect that this small genesis was the tiny mustard seed that will grow into a big oak tree—the largest global African diaspora church. Just after ten years this church grew to about 20,000 members strong. The unique thing about this assembly is that unlike many of the African immigrant congregations, the majority is native Ukrainian.

The website of the church indicates that one million people received Jesus Christ as their Lord and Savior through this church. On September 12, 1994, the church was officially registered at Kiev City Administration. One mayor of Kiev had since his election become a committed member. God has a big vision for his church from growing a strong church with thousands of members out of a handful of people who will take the gospel into all the world (primarily into China and Arab countries) and will make all nations disciples of Jesus Christ establishing His Kingdom on earth.

God found a man with the potential for making this church's vision a reality. He called Sunday Adelaja from Nigeria to serve Him in Ukraine. At the moment Sunday has an international apostolic ministry helping plant Christian churches in Ukraine and other nations. Some other branches are the Embassy of God English Church, Kiev and the Embassy of God Church, Berlin (Adelaja, 2011). Focusing now on the Ghanaian diaspora, several factors are the causes.

CASE STUDIES OF PRESBYTERIAN CHURCH OF GHANA IN THE USA

When Ghanaians are dispersed in the USA, three main social institutions that exhibit the subsequent gathering of the diaspora are the family, ethnic associations (EAs), and the churches. For the mere reason that Ghanaians carry their Christianity to wherever they are globally, the community congregations they form is a means to exhibit their demographic distribution.

CASE STUDIES IN EUROPE AND THE USA

Ghanaian Protestant Congregations in the USA

Almost all the Ghanaian denominations, including the Catholics and Anglicans, exist in the USA. Accordingly, Ghanaian Protestant churches (GPCs) are scattered all over the USA. Few of the GPCs in the USA are listed in Figure 6.1.

Figure 6.1: Some Ghanaian Protestant Churches in the USA

Denomination	Location	Type
Presbyterian	Presbyterian Church of Ghana in New York, (PCGNY) New York, NY	Mainline
	New Jersey PCG, Irvington, NJ	Mainline
	Ebenezer PCG, Bronx, NY	
	Calvary PCG, Columbus, OH	Mainline
Methodist	Ghana Emmanuel Methodist Church, Newark, NJ	Mainline
	Methodist Church Ghana, Queens, NY	Mainline
	Methodist Church Ghana, Brooklyn, NY	Mainline
Church of Pentecost	Church of Pentecost (CoP), Bronx, NY	Pentecostal
	Church of Pentecost (CoP), Philadelphia, PA	Pentecostal
	Church of Pentecost (CoP), Houston, TX	Pentecostal
Apostolic Church	Ghana Apostolic Church, Bronx, NY	Pentecostal
Victory Bible Church	Victory Bible Church, Irvington, NJ	Charismatic

The list may not be exhaustive. The causes for the formation of these "alien" churches are both similar and varied. Contextualization is universally an invaluable theme. Therefore, back home in Ghana or in the diaspora contextualization is an inevitable practice of the Christian faith. The historical connections of Ghanaian churches in the USA include the Presbyterian reformed pietism, the Methodist awakening and holiness revival, and the Pentecostal and Charismatic spirituality.

Classification of USA Presbyterian Church of Ghana Congregations

Two groups of Ghanaian Presbyterian churches are in the USA. They are PCG members who are in the diaspora from Ghana or those PCUSA affiliated who are also from Ghana. Diaspora missions and CP are challenging because the two classifications belong to two different supervisory bodies in the USA. While those affiliated with the PCUSA belong to the Conference of Ghanaian Presbyterian Churches in North America (CGPCNA), those affiliated with the PCG belong to the Overseas Mission Field (OMF) district (proposed presbytery). Figure 6.2 classifies the Ghanaian Presbyterian churches in the USA. Part of the statistics in this table is extracted from the PCG OMF report on proposed overseas presbytery submitted to the 2010 9th General Assembly

Figure 6.2: Classification of Ghanaian Presbyterian Congregations in the USA

Congregations Affiliated to the PCUSA & PCC			PCG Congregations		Members (2009)	Members (2010)
Congregation (Church)	Presbytery	Location	Congregation	Location		
Bethel Presbyterian Reformed	NY City	Brooklyn, NY	PCGNY, Manhattan	Harlem, NY	330	450
Christ The King Presbyterian	New Capital	Langley Park, MD	Ebenezer PCG	Bronx, NY	260	310
Ebenezer Presbyterian	New Capital	Woodbridge, VA	Worcester PCG	Worcester, MS	184	249
Emmanuel Presbyterian Reformed	NY City	Bronx, NY	Bethel PCG	Chicago, IL	44	70
Trinity Presbyterian	NY City	Bronx, NY	*Adom* PCG	Adelphi, MD	95	130
United Ghanaian Community	Philadelphia	Philadelphia, PA	Houston PCG	Houston, TX	44	70
United Ghanaian Presbyterian	New Covenant	Houston, TX	Calvary PCG	Columbus, OH	133	128 (-)
Ramseyer Presbyterian	Scioto Valley	Columbus, OH	Newark PCG	Irvington, NJ	208	247
PCG Fellowship	Cherokee	Atlanta, GA	Emmanuel PCG	Norton, VA	137	215
			Nursery Congregations			
Ghanaian Presbyterian Fellowship	New Castle	Wilmington, DE	Cincinnati	Cincinnati, OH	25	42
Ghanaian Presbyterian	Quebec	Montreal, CAN	Atlantic City	Atlantic City, NJ	23	19 (-)
Ghanaian Presbyterian	Toronto	Toronto, CAN	Queens	Queens, NY	22	40
			Trinity PCG	Chicago, IL	39	30 (-)
Total		12	13		1,544	2,000

(GA) that was held at the Takoradi Polytechnic in the Western Presbytery, August 6th-11th, 2010 and the report to 2011 GA at Abetifi Ramseyer Lay Training Center in the Kwahu Presbytery, August 19th -24th, 2011.

The existence of two separate Presbyterians congregations affiliated to two different entities has its own challenging ramifications. The classification of PCG congregations in Figure 6.2 illustrates the parallel existence of two Ghanaian Presbyterian congregations in the USA. Three observations need reflecting on. First, the researcher has had connections with three of the congregations affiliated to the PCUSA before and is thus informed of their operation. These include United Ghana Community Church (UGCC), Presbytery of Philadelphia, Philadelphia, PA, Bethel Presbyterian Reformed Church (BPRC), Presbytery of New York, Brooklyn, NY, and Christ the King Presbyterian Church (CKPC), Langley Park, MD. Second, the complexity is that the CGPCNA includes two Ghanaian congregations in Canada. They belong to the Toronto and Quebec presbyteries of PCC, respectively. This is the much talked about Canadian model. This model is a "partnership" arrangement in which PCG ministers are, paradoxically, posted to serve as attaché ministers for a period of five years before they are re-posted back to Ghana. In effect the Canadian model is total assimilation or integration of the diaspora Ghanaian Presbyterian congregations. There is total loss of congregational identity. Third, from the statistics, it is noted that three (congregations) Calvary PCG, Columbus, OH, Atlantic City PCG, Atlantic City, NJ, and Trinity PCG, Chicago, IL recorded reduction in membership. The causes for this negative growth should be identified and solutions found by the OMF district leadership.

Case Study 3:
Presbyterian Church of Ghana in New York (PCGNY), NY

PCG has triple heritage that has influenced its polity, ethos, and practice globally. This triple heritage is composed of the Basel evangelicalism, Scottish Presbyterianism, and African dexterity and charismatic influences. From the Basel Evangelical Missionary Movement (BEMS) had been the pietism inherited from Calvinistic and reformed theology. The second heritage came from the Scottish United Presbyterian Free Church (SUPFC) missionaries who were invited to replace the BEMS during the 1917 First World War (WW1). In fact, the reformed Presbyterian polity that has been the hallmark of PCG was inherited from the Scottish. The third heritage is from the African independent charismatic and Pentecostalism. "Each of these influences—the pietism of the Baselers, the polity of the Scottish Presbyterians, and the new charismatic emphasis—moved to New York City and is potentially evident in any given worship service and in different parts of the church's life" (Mark Gornick 2011: 94). The general vision, core values, and mission statements of the PCG are as follows:

> Vision: To be Christ-Centered, Self-Sustaining, and Growing Church.
> Core Values: Centrality of the Word of God, Discipline, and Hard work.
> Mission Statement: To uphold the Centrality of the Word of God and through the enablement of the Holy Spirit, pursue a holistic ministry so as to bring all creation to glorify God; mobilizing the entire Church for prayer; improving growth through evangelism and nurture; attaining self-sufficiency through effective resource mobilization ...and cherishing partnership with worldwide body of Christ" <http://pcgonline.org; http://pcgfacebook@gmail.com>. (February 7, 2012).

PCGNY as a global Ghanaian pioneer congregation was formed in 1985. As suggested earlier in Chapter 3, in the nucleus formation of a church, a group of community people will initially gather to form a nucleus of the congregation, society, or assembly. Most of the GPCs were formed in this way. Asked about the formation of the OMF district of the PCG, Gyang-Duah responded,

> Initial core members organize themselves together and then invited the PCG to come in to offer pastoral care and supervise them. PCGNY and the OMF were formed in this way. Credit should be given where credit is due. Factually, the genesis of PCG congregations depended heavily on the efforts of our retired senior minister Rev. Dr. Kumi-Dwamena. His efforts were supported by others such as the late Mrs. Ohemeng in whose living room PCGNY as a congregation started (Interview, November 28, 2010).

Moses Biney stated, "Three conditions had led to its founding...the settlement of Ghanaians in New York state and adjourning states, Connecticut and New Jersey, between 1970s and 1980s...the mysterious deaths of a number of Ghanaians in the early 1980s...need for a community of faith that would cater to the needs of the Ghanaian families, especially in times of bereavement" (2011: 68, 69). In his interview with the founding mother, Mrs. Ohemeng, two more subsidiary reasons accounted for the formation of the congregation. "Many children born to Ghanaian parents could neither understand nor speak their parents' indigenous languages...Ghanaian immigrants felt unwelcome in American churches and either refused to join them, or showed a lack of commitment even when they joined" (Biney 2011: 69); <http://pcgny.org> (February 5, 2012).

Based on the mission of the PCG, the PCGNY has the following vision and mission statements:

> Vision: To lead people to deeper commitment of faith in God and fellowship with one another, through Jesus Christ.

Mission: The empowerment of the Holy Spirit to broaden the use of our God-given talents, time and resources to advance the mission outreach of the congregation and the works of the large church.

Purposes: PCGNY endeavors to be a Christ-centered church with the following purposes:

- To lead men, women and children into a saving faith in Jesus Christ.
- To provide spirituality energized preaching based upon scripture, and related to everyday life.
- To promote spiritual, moral and social welfare of our youth.
- To develop and strengthen lay leaders to serve the spiritual needs of the church.
- To offer a varied music program that is enjoyable and spiritually uplifting.
- To actively evangelize and win souls for Christ.
- To deploy ourselves in servant ministry, both here and throughout the world <http://pcgny.org> (February 5, 2012).

One inherited practice is when the original group began monthly prayer meetings. At one of such prayer meetings the core members decided to continue the monthly meetings during the summer of 1985 in the apartment of one member at the Covenant Avenue, NY. Those nucleus members who carried this Presbyterian trait in PCGNY included, "Francis Kumi-Dwamena (now retired reverend), Eugene Adum Kwapong, Bediako Yirenkyi, Yaw Asiedu (also now retired reverend), Seth Ossei-Asare, Frank Sakyiama, Joseph Boateng, Mrs. Margaret Ohemeng (late), and Thelma Annan...Sunday November 24, 1985 marked a significant point...On that day, over a hundred worshippers congregated at Broadway Presbyterian Church to form the nucleus of the Ghana Presbyterian Church in New York City" (Biney 2011: 70). The congregation was formally inaugurated on May 28, 1998.

Basic Doctrinal Principles—Pietistic and Reformed Presbyterianism:

The PCG as a denomination based on the pietistic and Calvinistic reformed Presbyterianism has the following as its tenets or basic doctrinal principles:

- Absolute sovereignty of God
- Total depravity of the person
- Christ-centric salvation

- Empowerment and endowment of the Holy Spirit
- Pietistic and victorious righteous Christian life
- Four-fold indispensable solas
  - Sola gratia—grace alone
  - Sola fidei—faith alone
  - Sola Kristi—Christ alone
  - Sola Scriptula—Scripture alone
- Priesthood of all believers
- Ecclesia reformata semper reformanda—the church reformed, always reforming.
- Five-fold practice of the Christian faith:
  - Best in prayer
  - Orderliness
  - Neatness
  - Discipline
  - Sharing the Life of Christ (Spread of the Good News)—Asempatrew

CASE STUDIES OF OTHER USA GHANAIAN PROTESTANT CHURCHES

An overview of the formation of five main examples of the planted GPCs from different denominations is provided here to help understand the CP by diaspora Ghanaians. This is helpful to understand the ethos, polity, and operational practice of these GPCs. All the five started as home group prayer cells but have grown to be planted churches. Apart from the Ghana Emmanuel Methodist Church (GEMC), the other four had their historical leadership connections with the PCG in one way or another. The specific churches selected to represent the other denominations are Ghana Emmanuel Methodist Church, Newark, NJ, the Church of Pentecost International, Philadelphia, PA, the Victory Bible Church International, Irvington, NJ, and Portland International Church, Portland, OR. They are made up of two mainline, one Pentecostal, and two charismatic churches. The PIC is not strictly, Ghanaian. Though Ghanaian-led, it is composed of a mixture of several international members with the majority currently Ghanaian.

Case Study 4:
Ghana Emmanuel Methodist Church (GEMC), Newark, NJ

The holiness movement, the root of Pentecostalism, started with John Wesley's teachings, ethos, doctrine, and practice in England. "Our religion is Christianity or it is nothing...Wesley also emphasized holiness. For Wesley, 'Salvation had to include an element of imparted holiness as well as imputed holiness'...there is a natural linkage of holy living and social reform" (Casely Essamuah 2010: xxxiii-xxxv). Since its genesis, holiness, exhibited in the discipleship essentials, has been the cynosure of global Methodism.

The formation of GEMC, Newark, NJ was based on such holiness doctrine. Some members of the Ghana Methodist Church had been commuting to worship with the United Church in Bronx, NY from Newark, NJ. On their second visit they considered the idea of forming a Methodist society in Newark with one Rev. Ebenezer Aduku. As it is normal with Ghanaian migrant churches, it also started with families in a home prayer cell. The Ababio family offered their home to start. Michael Gyamfi stated, "The Friday meetings started on May 15, 1998...Later Kate Matilda Appiah joined them...At the very first divine service as a society on November 28, 1998, the members present in Nana Kyei Ababio's home at the Washington Street, were Very Rev. Ansah Arkoful, Rev. Ebenezer Aduku, Nana Kyei Ababio, Mrs. Elizabeth Ababio, Bridget Ababio, Doris Ababio, Richmond Ababio, Evelyn Ababio, Nat Boateng, Joseph Brenyah, Agnes Brenyah, Comfort Dapaah, and Regina Boakye" (10th Anniversary Brochure 2011: 19). In effect, the bulk of the original members were from the Ababio and Brenyah families.

After the first two services, membership had already outgrown the Ababios' living room. The society was therefore, moved to the Recreational Hall Facility on the same 440 Washington St. in Newark. With the Very Rev. Kwaku Owusu posted as the resident pastor after his master's program at the Princeton Theological Seminary in 2007, the society acquired its own facility at the Broad St. in Newark. Like some GPCs, the growing of GEMC has not been without its crises and conflicts. For instance, its naming was even reached after much conflicts and arguments. Michael Gyamfi again stated,

> The church existed for over five months without a name. The name Ghana Evangelical Methodist Church was suggested, but was rejected because of the word Evangelical. Members preferred to be identified as Ghana Methodist. After much deliberation...Emmanuel came up...it was unanimously agreed by all members to use that name. The reason was that in spite of all the problems and hardships the Lord had been with His church. The church from that moment became known as Ghana Emmanuel Methodist Church" (10th Anniversary Brochure 2011: 20).

Basic Doctrinal Principles—Holiness Movement in Methodism:

- The Methodist Church, Ghana claims and cherishes its place in the Holy Catholic Church, which is the Body of Christ.

- Doctrines of the Evangelical Faith, which the Methodism has held from the beginning and holds, are based upon the divine revelation recorded in the Holy Scriptures. The Methodist Church acknowledges this revelation as the supreme rule of faith and practice.

- These Evangelical Doctrines to which the Preachers of the Methodist Church, both ministers and Laypersons pledged are contained in Wesley's Notes on the New Testament and the first four volumes of Sermons.

- The Notes on the new Testament and forty-four sermons are…to set up standards of preaching and belief which should ensure loyalty to the fundamental truths of the Gospel of Redemption and secure the continued witness of the Church to the realities of the Christian experience of salvation.

- The conference shall be the authority within The Methodist Church, Ghana for interpretation of the doctrinal standards of the Church.

- Every individual has particular ministry to carry out in the church.

- Ministry is not the exclusive preserve of the ordained (Casely Essamuah 2010: 179-199).

Case Study 5:
Church of Pentecost International (CoP-I), Philadelphia, PA

The Church of Pentecost (CoP) has its roots in the PCG. Its founder Peter Anim was compelled to exit the PCG to form the Christ Apostolic Church (CAC) because of his charisma of speaking in tongues, intensive charismatic prayer, and faith healing. Anim operated as African prophetic leader initially. In the beginning CAC's operation was based on the doctrine of Faith Tabernacle Church in Philadelphia. Later, with the arrival of the invited British Apostolic missionary, James McKeon, the church split over the issue of faith healing. The faction led by McKeon became the CoP, one of the classical Pentecostal churches of Ghana. It "[t]races its roots…when God made a covenant with a group of worshippers through a prophecy that HE would raise a nation out of Africa that would be separated and light to the world, heralding the 2nd Coming of Christ; and that the Gold Coast (now Ghana) had been

chosen to fulfill this eternal Will and purpose of God"
<http://www.ghurchofpentecostusa.org> (March 16, 2012).

Demographics from another denomination used for this book is the Church of Pentecost International (CoP-I). Figure 6.3 is an overview of the regional distribution of the assemblies of the CoP-I in the USA (The Church of Pentecost U.S.A. Inc., 2010a).

Figure 6.3: Regional Distribution of the CoP Membership in the USA

Region	Number of Members	% of Membership
New York Region	6, 095	37.4
Washington Region	4, 692	28.8
Chicago Region	3,024	18.5
Western Region	2, 480	15.3

Stated at the website of the CoP-I is the mission of the denomination,

The Church of Pentecost is a worldwide, non-profit making Pentecostal church…to bring all people everywhere to the saving knowledge of our Lord Jesus Christ through the proclamation of the gospel, the planting of churches and the equipping of believers for every God-glorifying services. It demonstrates the love of God through the provision of social services in partnership with governments, communities and other like-minded organizations < http://thecophq.org/mission.html> (March 16, 2012).

Statistics indicate that between 2004 and 2010, the CoP assemblies identified as "'international missions' had increased from within 55 to 78 countries" globally (Baidoo 2005; Amegah 2010; Herppich 2011). In the USA, it has about 105 assemblies planted all over major American cities. With the bold global focus of bringing the world to the saving knowledge of Christ, the CoP has a calling of God's first covenant with the church. Discussing Ghanaian churches in North America and their horizontal integration, Wisdom Tettey stated about the CoP, "Its primary purpose is to practice and propagate what our Lord Jesus Christ commanded in Mark 16:15-16…Church members believe that God had a covenant with the founders of the church to use missionaries from the Gold Coast (now Ghana) to win souls for Christ throughout the world in order to fulfill His divine purpose (2001; Olupona and Gemignani, 2001: 247).

Beliefs: "Our beliefs (Tenets) are solely based on biblical standards, teaching our members to live pure and holy lives at all times eschewing sin. To allow the Holy Spirit to reign in the church, bringing liberty and deliverance to all who flee into it. Prayer and teachings of sound doctrine are the vital of our service, accompanied with praises and worship"
<http://www.churchofpentecostusa.org> (March 16, 2012).

Mission: "Our ultimate mission is to win the world to Christ through propagation of the gospel to the utmost part of the earth. As such, the church launches evangelistic campaigns of various categories" <http://www.churchofpentecostusa.org> (March 16, 2012).

Vision: The vision of CoP, therefore, is stated as, "Planting and nurturing healthy churches globally…We exist to establish responsible and self-sustaining churches filled with commitment, Spirit-filled Christians of character, who will impact their communities for Christ" (Opoku Onyinah, Vision 2013).

In 1994, the Rev Omane-Yeboah, then the district pastor of the New York region scouted the Philadelphia area with the intent of planting a church. In 1995, Ofori Boamah and Ellen Odame, both of the Kofridau-Twedaase assembly of the CoP in Ghana had immigrated to the Philadelphia area. Hungry for fellowship, they temporary worshipped at the Church of God at the 41st and Chestnut Street in Philadelphia where they were warmly welcome by the pastor and the congregation. This American congregation was hopeful that through these two African brethren it could attract more Africans to join its members.

Two reasons might have made this arrangement unworkable. First, the inexpressive American worship style does not attract Africans. Africans want to clap, dance, sing, and shout to the glory of God. Second, Ofori Boamah had different plans. Okyere Asiedu stated, "At a food store on the 52nd and Walnut Street where he took a temporary job, Ofori Boamah seized every opportunity to witness to shoppers, especially Africans. Here, he met and mooted the idea of starting a prayer cell to Boakye Akyeampong of the SDA church. In turn, Boakye Akyeampong introduced Boamah to Lawrence Owusu, a long time resident of Philadelphia" (Okyere Asiedu, Mailed Hard Copy February, 2012). Okyere Asiedu looked at the formation of the assembly from another angle by stating, "Nana Adjekum, an elder of the New Jersey assembly, not knowing of anything yet about the first core founding group, sent materials to Okyere Asiedu, a recent immigrant to the Chester area near Philadelphia. This was to encourage him to use the materials as witnessing tools to gather people especially Ghanaians and to start a prayer cell" (Okyere Asiedu, February, 2012). Okyere Asiedu continued,

> As God will have it, the first person I happen to meet at a job program and speak to was Emmanuel Lartey, a roommate of Ofori Boamah. Lartey was resolute in his Catholicism but was quick to link me to Ofori Boamah who then contacted Pastor Omane Yeboah. He did not waste any time to visit the small group. He was so happy of seeing his dream come true…On two occasions, the Lord through prophesies spoke to the group about his plans for the church in the Philadelphia area and that added encouragement and enthusiasm to the group (Okyere Asiedu, February, 2012).

The tiny group was limited in its activities for fear of disturbing other residents of the West Tulpenhocken apartments where they were meeting for prayer. For instance, prayers and songs had to be hushed. Besides all night prayers, which were held almost every Friday, could be a source of discomfort and disturbance to residents. Temporarily, one pastor, Kyeremanteng of the Church of the Brethren in German Town, offered a hall for all-night prayer meetings. By December 1995, as more members joined the church it sought and found space at the multi-purpose YMCA building on Chestnut Street for Sunday services. At this point the assembly in Atlantic City worshiped with the Philadelphia assembly as an encouragement since their own services were in the afternoon. Here too the young assembly faced challenges. The location was convenient; yet, services had to be rushed through since the place was rented out to several groups. So the search for space continued.

In December 1996, the assembly moved to the Larchwood Street to worship in the old chapel of Christ of Calvary Church. Okyere Asiedu wrote, "Rev. Abner Forson, the then senior pastor of the church was so receptive and helpful in several ways. In his words, he was 'thrilled by the zeal and enthusiasm of African worshippers; the experience brings everything home and makes service to God real.' Until his death in January 2005, Rev. Forson remained a father and friend of the Church of Pentecost, Philadelphia" (Okyere Asiedu, 2012). Philadelphia CoP-I was officially inaugurated in February 1999. On this occasion, in attendance were the New York, Newark, Atlantic City, and Patterson assemblies. The Philadelphia assembly became part of the Newark district. Philadelphia became the new district capital when the Pennsylvania district was created and inaugurated on September 18, 2005.

In the formation of its local assemblies, the CoP uses several strategies. In the 2011 NAMLC, one of the EMS presenters stated,

> The Church of Pentecost has three basic ways of starting new local congregations in America. One of the most common ways new assemblies are established is when members move to a new place because of jobs, educational opportunities, business, or other reasons like family issues connections. They are likely to soon begin a prayer group in somebody's home, invite others, grow, and eventually ask for pastoral oversight from the church leadership...this is the dominant pattern of growth in Ghana and beyond (Kingsley Larbi, 2001: 252). A second pattern in the United States is beginning a new congregation with a core of members that live in one general vicinity and have been travelling some distance to attend an established assembly. Finally, the church uses a pattern of sending missionaries to pioneer new areas. The latter strategy is particularly followed for international outreach (Birgit Herppich, 2011: 12).

Despite the above attractive formation of congregations by the CoP, a caveat about the strategies is the unquestioned attraction of already professed Christians from other denominations. This pattern has been the long time *modus operandi* of the CoP. In every CoP assembly, not all members may originally be CoP members. The situation becomes worse in the Ghanaian diaspora. Not surprisingly, the information in Figure 6.4 reflects on the demographic composition of the Philadelphia CoP-I in April 2006.

Figure 6.4: 2006 Demographic Composition of Philadelphia CoP-I

Denomination	Number	Percentage (%) Number
Church of Pentecost	5	20
Presbyterian Church of Ghana	11	44
Assemblies of God	5	20
Methodist Church Ghana	2	8
Roman Catholic	2	8
Total	25	100

The above information was gathered in a brief questionnaire to answer the question, "What denomination did you belong to in Ghana before coming to America?" With regard to how they perceive themselves denominationally, only about 44% indicated that they considered themselves as members of the Church of Pentecost. Figure 6.5 is representative.

Figure 6.5: 2006 Denominational Self-Perception of Philadelphia CoP-I

Denomination	Number	Percentage (%) Number
Church of Pentecost	11	44
Presbyterian Church of Ghana	10	40
Assemblies of God	2	8
Methodist Church Ghana	1	4
Roman Catholic	1	4
Total	25	25

The implication is that there is the possibility that in the diaspora, some members may have their physical bodies in the Philadelphia CoP-I, but their hearts and souls are still attached to their denominations back home in Ghana.

Basic Doctrinal Principles—African Classical Pentecostalism:

"Based upon God's covenant with the church, the church does not solicit financial assistance from any external source…God is able to meet our needs in season to prove divine presence, blessing and glory with the church…Thus, the church operates on total dependence on God"
<http://www.churchofpentecostusa.org> (March 16, 2012).

CoP members believe in:

- Divine inspiration and authority of the Holy Scriptures. That the Bible is infallible in its declaration, final authority, comprehensive and all-sufficient in its provisions.

- Existence of the One True God, Elohim, maker of the whole universe; indefinable, but revealed as Triune God—Father, Son, and the Holy Spirit…one in nature, essence, and attribute—omnipotent …omnipresent…omniscient…

- Man's need of a Savior has been met in the person of Jesus Christ…because of His Deity…Virgin Birth…Sinless life, Atoning Death…Resurrection…and Ascension; His abiding intercession…and His Second coming to judge the living and the dead…

- Baptism of the Holy Spirit for believers with the initial evidence of speaking in tongues…and in the operation of the gifts and fruit of the Holy Spirit…

- Tithing and the giving of freewill offerings towards the cause of carrying forward the Kingdom of God. We believe that God blesses a cheerful giver…

- That the healing of sickness and diseases is provided for God's people in the atonement…However, the church is not opposed to medication by qualified medical practitioners <http://www.churchofpentecostusa.org> (March 16, 2012).

Case Study 6:
Victory Bible Church International (VBC-I), Irvington, NJ

The founder of Victory Bible Church International (VBC-I) was also a former Presbyterian who left his mother church to form his own charismatic one, out of the feeling that his charismatic gifts were not having fulfillment in the PCG. The preamble to VBC-I constitution stated, "(i) According to the Holy Scripture of the Bible it is the express purpose of God our heavenly Father, to call out of the world a saved people, who shall constitute the body or church of his son Jesus Christ, built and established upon the foundations of the Apostles and prophets, Jesus Christ Himself being the chief Cornerstone; and (ii) the members of the body, the Church of Christ, are enjoined to assemble themselves together for worship, fellowship, counsel and instruction in the Word of God contained in the whole Scriptures and for the exercise of those spiritual gifts and offices set forth in the New Testament" (VBC-I Constitution: 4).

Basic Doctrinal Principles — Gracious Existence

Purpose: We are a fellowship of believers from different nationalities, bonded together by the love of God. In our meetings, we seek the tangible manifestations of the power of the Holy Spirit as we worship and study the Bible together, obeying its truth and applying it to our lives through heartfelt prayer (Sunday Bulletin, April 15, 2012).

The PIC sums up its vision and mission practice in the acronym, GRACIOUS. One of its bulletin stated, "PIC strives, through the Grace of God, to live out the transforming Spirit of being Gracious:

Genuine Love
Reaching Out
Assurance in Jesus
Caring in Faith
Integrity and Trust
Opportunity for Growth
Uniting in Prayer, and
Searching the Scriptures" (Sunday Bulletin, April 15, 2011)

SUMMARY

Chapter 6 consisted of the description of the formation of global African diaspora churches. The chapter began with two instances of African diaspora churches in Europe. The chapter continued with the categorization of Presbyterian Church of Ghana (PCG) congregations in the USA exemplified by the case study of PCGNY. It is then completed with the exploration of four other case studies of GPCs made up of Protestant mainline, Pentecostal, and Charismatic churches. Other significant issues not well developed in the GPCs are recommended for further study in the final chapter.

QUESTIONS FOR DISCUSSION

1. According to Jehu Hanciles, what the five missionary functions of African immigrant churches?
2. Are there similarities between the two case studies of African diaspora congregations in Europe? (tips: country of origin, rapid growth, etc.)?
3. What are the three main social institutions emerged among Ghanaian diaspora?
4. What is the triple heritage of PCG? (Case study 3)
5. What are the essential tenets of African classical Pentecostalism? (Case study 5)
6. How is our knowledge of Ghanaian being enriched by the case studies of this chapter?

Chapter 7
CONCLUSION AND RECOMMENDATION

INTRODUCTION

Africa is so huge in landmass that the USA, Western and Eastern Europe, China, and India can conveniently fit into Africa with excess. For instance, Great Britain can fit into Malagasy with excess land mass. Incidentally, these countries are the recipients of the African diaspora. Currently, the largest church in Europe is African. This is amazing. The 1910 Edinburgh missionary conference had no continental African, notwithstanding the fact that Caucasians had been on the continent since 1482. In their closing remarks, some of the leading participants even predicted that by the threshold of the 21st century, Africa would totally be taken over by Islam. Such assertions seriously underestimated the actions, being, power, and operations of God the Holy Spirit as well as the sovereignty of God the Father. One hundred years after this landmark missionary conference, in Tokyo 2010, when the Swedish scholar Stefan Gustavson made the passionate appeal to the almost 2,000 delegates to "come over to Macedonia" to help Europe, the gathering included hundreds of African celebrants. Lausanne III, another commemoration of Edinburgh 1910, was held in Africa. Incredibly, Cape Town (South Africa) received over 4,000 global evangelical Christians.

Hilaire Beloc had asserted, "Europe is the Faith" (Sanneh 2003: 22). However, studies have refuted such boastful statement by Beloc. Instead, the center of gravity of world Christianity has shifted to the Southern continents (Africa, Asia, and Latin America—the majority world or two-thirds world). Such a statement reflects a "cultural captivity of the faith" (Sanneh 2003: 22); the current statement should rather be "Africa is the Faith" (Jenkins 2006: 89). The main theme of the final chapter is the composition of conclusions drawn from the research for this book. Thus, Chapter 7 covers some major challenges that USA GPCs encounter, indicates some major opportunities existing in the USA, addresses meaningful operational strategies for diaspora missions practice, and suggests recommendations for further study.

MAJOR CHALLENGES ENCOUNTERED BY DIASPORA USA GPCs

All diaspora fellowships, prayer cells, and churches are faced with cross-cultural challenges. It is more challenging for Africans from high context cultures to practice cross-cultural communication of Christ in a low context USA pop-culture. Basically, the USA Christian communities seem to ignore the existence of these churches as such in their midst. They are hardly given their due recognition. Accordingly, they face several challenges including the following ones.

Clash of Cultures and Coincidence of Double Worldviews

Having immigrated to the USA, the diaspora Africans (Ghanaians) carry their cultural orientation to America. With such cultural baggage, a clash of cultures then ensues. Closely related to this cultural baggage is their worldview. The African (Ghanaian) worldview-controlled mindset is people-oriented, conservative, and holistic. Conversely, the American scientific and technological worldview, easily adaptable to change, has little connection with that of the overseas-born traditional worldview. The overseas-born challenge is resistance, avoidance, or rejection of absolute cultural assimilation as they endeavor to eschew individualism. Maintaining, preserving, and behaving more in line with African cultural values is the challenge of the local-born in America. With differences in the mindsets of the overseas-born and local-born, the quest for outreach is complex and challenging.

The Generic Non-Acceptance of Immigrant Churches in the USA

With a few exceptions, the general non-acceptance of immigrants in the American socio-cultural context relates to the seemingly total ignoring attitude or non-acceptance of the immigrant churches within that context. Gyang-Duah enumerated some challenges of the PCG by stating,

For the PCG, first, there is the existence of parallel denomination — PCUSA. Relationship with PCUSA is based on suspicion about PCG's intentions. PCUSA does not understand why PCG has formed congregations in the USA. Nevertheless, PCG does not mean any harm. PCG's interest is to evangelize its members in the diaspora. Second, the challenge is raising enough funds to support the OMF churches. Third, acquisition of places of worship is expensive and problematic. Fourth, securing visas for ministers from Ghana to offer pastoral care is challenging (Interview, May 25, 2010).

Kwadwo Osei Ayemang of the GEMC also expressed similar challenge of non-acceptance. He said,

> In America, there are several different cultures. This is a fact that should be accepted by all. To recall, when I came to Chicago even in the eighties, you could get children who will point at you as if they had not seen a Black human being before. When you speak with adults their questions would border on "Do you have houses in Africa? Do you see the things you see here in Africa?" Sometimes they behave as if they do not even believe that there is the same God that they serve with you here. Pastor, sometimes one so marveled that one does not believe all human beings have the same God for all (Interview, December 11, 2011).

The main response and result of non-acceptance of the "other" people is to form and attend community churches where they feel accepted, loved, and understood.

Overbearing, Paternalistic, and Parallel Mainline Denominations

All the mainline Ghanaian churches have their historical counterparts in the USA. While the Presbyterians have the PCUSA, the Methodists have the United Methodist Church. At times this situation is problematic. For example, attempts at integrating Ghanaian Presbyterians by PCUSA Presbyteries are problematic. Before integrating the Ramseyer PCG congregation in Columbus, OH, the Scioto Valley Presbytery issued a declaration of intent for members to sign. It was entitled "Declaration of Intent to Become a Chartering Member of Ramseyer Presbyterian Church Columbus, OH." The form indicated, "I… (Last, Middle, First names)…of…(address)…faithfully declare my intent as a chartering member of the Ramseyer Presbyterian Church in the Presbytery of Scioto Valley, Presbyterian Church (USA)…that I will abide by the bylaws…that, I will accept the uniqueness of our church as an immigrant one which has voluntary partnership with the Presbyterian Church of Ghana"

(Declaration of Intent 2007). Some members simply broke away to form the Calvary PCG, Columbus, OH.

In God's reign coexistence and cooperation are realities. Integration or assimilation has never worked in situations of multi-cultural and ethnic diversity. As paternalistic as the situation is, a Western church may not find anything wrong with assimilation or full integration. As case in point, the Presbyterian Church of Canada (PCC) regards assimilation of migrant churches as advantageous. The churches, their properties, and finances fully belong to PCC with only indirect and loose cultural and linguistic relationship with PCG. In reality, some members of the Ghanaian Presbyterian congregations in Toronto and Montreal may still think they belong to the PCG. However, this is not the reality. Another instance is the situation in the First Presbyterian Church in New Brunswick, NJ, USA. In this congregation are about 40% Ghanaians. Consequently, any attempts to plant a PCG congregation around New Brunswick are frustrated by the leadership of this PCUSA congregation. One positive result of all this has been PCUSA's wealth, financial power, and ownership of physical infrastructure. This has positively helped the "rich in spirit but poor in resources" PCG. Positive though it may seem, this resource sharing sometimes creates challenging situations for GPCs to operate as a CPM to evangelize its ethnic groups in America.

Continuity or Discontinuity of GPCs Operational Polity

Closely related to the existence of the two parallel mainline denominations are the differences of their polity. Here, the major challenge is the USA's congregationalism vis-à-vis GPCs' relational operations. For instance, PCG's higher courts (GA and presbytery councils) have supervisory oversight of the lower ones (district councils and local sessions). Thus, each PCG congregation is semi-autonomous. Diaspora PCG congregations operate a semi-relational system. The PCG OMF operates as the USA district instead of a presbytery. However, American Presbyterianism does not have a district court. This is challenging. Recently, a "mini-Presbytery" of some delegates of global PCG congregations resolved in a communiqué to develop this OMF diaspora district system into presbyteries. The conference resolved, "Presbyteries are very important...Therefore, for us to have an effective Presbytery out of the OMF, it is being suggested that instead of one, two Presbyteries should be erected" (Draft Communiqué Committee 2010: 2). The committee suggested that the locations of the headquarters of the two presbyteries should be NY for North America and Australia and London for Europe and Asia. The challenge is whether to operate PCG's relational polity from a high context culture (continuity) or the congregational polity of the low context USA popular culture (discontinuity). This problem is not in connection with the PCG only. All the immigrant Ghanaian mainline churches have similar challenges.

CONCLUSION AND RECOMMENDATION

Disunity, Divisions, and Schisms among USA GPCs

Another factual challenge is the presence of some Ghanaian Presbyterians who are currently not members of the USA PCG. They include:

- those who are Presbyterians in heart but belong to other USA Ghanaian denominations (Edu-Bekoe 2006) and those who are totally assimilated into the PCUSA,
- those who have double membership by belonging to various American PCUSA congregations in their morning services but also retain their membership in the USA PCG congregations,
- those who belong to both USA PCG and Ghanaian PCUSA congregations, and
- those who do not belong to any of these groups and do not attend any church services at all.

The latest PCG planted congregation is the Trenton PCG, which opened in Ewing, NJ, on September 4, 2011. The New Jersey PCG, as the mother (kangaroo) church donated twenty plastic chairs to the Trenton PCG (joey). Other new congregations include the Sayreville PCG, NJ (by New Jersey PCG) and Queens PCG, NY (by PCGNY). Meanwhile, the situation is complicated by the existence of some other congregations that are not affiliated with any of these two bodies. This situation is not helpful for diaspora missions and CPMs. The classification of PCG congregations in Figure 6.2 illustrates the challenging parallel existence of two Ghanaian Presbyterian congregations in the USA.

The parallel co-existence of the two groups of Ghanaian Presbyterians in the USA has developed into a bitter rivalry, disunity, animosity, and unhealthy competition on the mission field. Over the years, this has been a disincentive for growth in both the PCG and PCUSA affiliated Ghanaian congregations. In 2010, the CGPCNA wrote a resolution to the GA of PCG in Ghana. The conference referred to "feuds and animosities...resulting in the birth of new PCG churches in Bronx, Houston, Woodbridge, and Columbus respectively, out of existing Ghanaian PCUSA churches" (Kwabena Boamah-Acheampong and Kobina Ofosu Donkor 2010: 1). Reacting to set the records straight, the leadership of the PCG OMF replied,

> We believe that the resolution has been carefully crafted to achieve an agenda—to portray the Presbyterian Church of Ghana...irresponsible...as part of the process of integration members were asked...to complete a form to commit themselves to PC(USA) totally and only have a 'Voluntary Partnership' with the Presbyterian Church of Ghana...For us partnership is not integration...The PCG is here in response to a call by Ghanaians who need pastoral care...and we cannot fail them (Edward Ansong 2010: 1-4).

Closely related is the challenging parallel existence of USA mainline churches and GPCs because schisms constitute part of the results of the historical attempts at assimilating GPCs. Other mainline churches also have this challenging situation. For instance the diaspora Methodist Church Ghana has the existence and operation of the United Methodists of the USA relatively competing for diaspora Ghanaian membership. As solution, the MCG, however, has managed to maintain a partnership with the United Methodist Church (UMC) that is based on the equality and coexistence of the two churches in the USA. In an Act of covenant between the UMC and the MCG, it is stated,

> In this Act of Covenanting, the emphasis is on our roots in the Apostolic Faith and in our contemporary experience of God's love and will.... In this covenant, The Methodist Church, Ghana and the United Methodist Church acknowledge the centrality of the Sovereignty of Jesus Christ, as basic to all relationships. Our links to the Apostolic Faith through Scripture, Tradition, Experience, and Reason lead us now solemnly affirm to each other that 'all who are baptized into Christ are members of Christ's ministry through the people of the One God, Father, Son and the Holy Spirit' (Casely Essamuah 2010: 207, 208; Commission on Christian Unity Digest: 335; Official Record, XII, 1974).

The above agreement between the UMC and the MCG indicate a huge difference with the relationship between the Methodists and that of the USA PCG and PCUSA. The GPCs should encourage its congregations, societies, and assemblies, among others, to move forward to plant more churches in their overseas mission field for the urgently expected Reign of God.

External Perception of the Proliferation of USA Ghanaian Churches

Another genuine challenge on the mission field is the perception of the external passive observers including diaspora Ghanaians. External observers keep analyzing the unfavorable fragmentation of diaspora Ghanaian churches. An anecdotal observation is that some people may have taken advantage of legal technicalities to register these churches in their personal names but using the name of their Ghanaian mother churches as cover up. Berko Owusu wrote, "The breakup...into factions could be precipitated by...personal rivalries...and materialistic inclinations...there are some...who literally went from rags to riches soon after starting their own churches" (2010: 3). Owusu's contention is that the main cause for these schisms is the hidden materialistic agenda. Rightly or wrongly, this argument constitutes an indictment of the various diaspora African (Ghanaian) churches that have mushroomed in America. Owusu may hunger for God. However, unless God intervenes, the unfortunate situation of perceived materialistic schisms may make it difficult for him to accept the good news. The hidden fact is the financial attraction in the form of dollar enticement.

Challenging Existence and Operations of Ethnic Associations

Like the churches, Ghanaian ethnic associations (EAs) aim at self-help, creation of a home away from home, and exhibition of Ghanaian cultural values in the multi-cultural American context. They also focus on shipping medical and other materials to help the poor and needy in Ghana, mobilization of funds for projects in their traditional areas, and the transmission of Ghanaian culture and morals to their diaspora children.

However, three challenges are posed by EAs for the GPCs. First, some adults initially taste life in the EAs before joining GPCs. Transfer of unacceptable influences is the challenge here. During the 2009 Christmas or end-of-year parties of the Ga-Dangme and Mfantse Associations in Houston, TX, "worldly dancing," plenty of alcoholic beverages for boozing, and "compromised fraternity" were exhibited throughout the nights. Most of the participants were professed Christians from the various GPCs. Second, EAs pose the challenge of divided attention and commitment. An example is the 22nd Ghana festival (Ghanafest) 2010 at Washington Park, Chicago, IL, on July 31, 2010. The annual festival is organized in Chicago to showcase some aspects of Ghanaian traditional culture in America by the Ghana National Council (GNC) of the Metropolitan Chicago Area. It is estimated that 6,000 participants, mostly Ghanaians, from all walks of life took part in the festival. Some aspects of Ghanaian culture displayed included chieftaincy, traditional kente clothing, and Christian, Muslim, and traditional prayers. Others were traditional dances such as adowa, kete, and borborbor. The Ghanaian ethnic affiliated groups whose customs were showcased included the Okuapeman Fekuw, Asanteman Association, Fante Benevolent Society, Brong Ahafo Association, Kwahu United, Okyeman Association, Ga-Adangme Organization, Ewe Association, and the Northern Union of the Northern, Upper West, and Upper East regions. The traditional activities such as offering of libation to the ancestors and deities might exhibit an act of syncretism on the part of the professed Christians present on the occasion. Third, having operated in the EAs, some members often make unfavorable demands on the GPCs to operate just like these social clubs. At times, finding the church uncooperative, some members backslide.

The main motive of these EAs is functional—satisfaction of needs. Some scholars such as Charles Kraft (2005: 92), employed the "need approach" and functional theories and insisted that different kinds of need have to be addressed among different people groups. However, need-satisfaction should not be the overarching framework for mission practice because it is humanistic without a strong theological foundation that reduces missiology to psychology. The various GPCs should not function as the EAs do by promoting an either/or tension between functional need-satisfaction and relational paradigms. They should rather promote the both/and relationship between the two paradigms.

Internal Developmental and Leadership Challenges

There are also internal developmental challenges. Internally, there is a lack of extensive discipleship, pastoral care and counseling, and mentorship. Untrained leadership is a major bane causing positional instead of functional leadership. For example, begun in 1985, PCGNY has created a pioneering enabling environment for diaspora Ghanaian CP. However, its demographic and spiritual growth has been too slow relative to the other newer GPCs.

OPPORTUNITIES FOR THE USA GHANAIAN PROTESTANT CHURCHES

Challenges are not insurmountable. With Christ in God's Kingdom vocation, nothing is impossible. As it strives for urgent solutions, the GPCs "will find that the above challenges could also be opportunities" (Wan and Edu-Bekoe; Moreau and Snodderly 2011:32-62) which include those suggested below.

Mutual Need for Both African and Western Christianities

Regardless of the negative perception of globalization, as neo-imperialism and American hegemony, migration has created a meeting point for both Western and African Christianities. Secularized Euro-America needs African Christianity and vice versa. The situation has encouraged mutual respect and need for each other which has resulted in the important opportunity for cross-cultural spread of the gospel and CP. Discussing Christian conversion from Western culture, Lesslie Newbigin suggested, "We need their witness to correct ours, as indeed they need ours…our need is greater…we imperatively need one another if we are to be the faithful witnesses of Christ in our many different cultures" (1986:26, 27). The call for American Christians not to ignore African Christians in their midst is an authentic call. Similarly, GPCs are offered the right atmosphere to join the CPM to spread the good news to Ghanaian and other people groups globally.

CONCLUSION AND RECOMMENDATION

Western Christianity has declined and fossilized through liberalization, humanism, secularization, and unfavorable individual and extreme religious rights. Confronting this critical situation, Western Christianity needs to learn from African Christianity. Conversely, African reverse missionaries should learn from the mistakes of their historical counterparts. On one hand, in order not to repeat the same mistakes in missionary and evangelical endeavors, Westerners should not condemn Africans and their cultures in the diaspora as European missionaries did back on the African continent in the Great (19th) century. On the other hand, African Christian missionaries in the GPCs should also not condemn the host culture as controlled by "modern-day demons" and without anything to offer. Christians in American churches and the GPCs should rather see both African and American cultures with positive lenses. Both cultures are vehicles for mission to all generations.

Huge Presence of the Unreached for Meaningful Engagement

There are many unreached local and foreign people groups in America. This is an opportunity. Meaningful engagement through toleration and cooperation is one important evangelization strategy. "Tolerance is a term defined in context...Christians are called not simply to tolerate...the missionary should recognize that cooperating with others is less likely to harm the gospel message than is an intolerant attitude that communicates posture of superiority" (Scott Moreau et al. 2004:308, 309). Some non-Christians often open up when they realize that Christians are prepared to listen to them. Instead of criticizing them, GPCs Christians should engage in meaningful dialogue and discussions without intimidating language or actions.

Another functional operation should be missions in the form of "performing acts of charity whenever appropriate, joining them in working for their benefit when they are oppressed, and demonstrating God's unconditional love for them in all circumstances" (Moreau et al. 2004:309). Brian Shipman admonished, "Don't discriminate between Christians and non-Christians when it comes to showing compassion...Your kindness will be obvious to those who don't believe in Jesus...This will give a perfect opportunity to tell them about Jesus" (1998: 328). This will culminate in the nuanced practical strategic mission to win the unreached for Christ.

Linguistic Opportunity

Most USA GPCs are mostly monolingual-homogeneous types that conduct their services mostly in Twi. Conversely, some of the assimilated monocultural but USA-church affiliated GPCs use English first before translating into Twi, making them bilingual. Lamin Sanneh stated, "In the Christian example the stress on the vernacular brought the religion into profound continuity with mother-tongue aspirations" (1989: 229). Bediako confirmed Sanneh's position by stating, "Its deeper significance is that God speaks to men and women — always in the vernacular" (1995: 60).

"These churches create a cultural refuge. They are a way for Africans to pass on to their children their African values, particularly for African immigrants who see their children quickly assimilating into African-American culture" (Daniel Wakin 2004: 33). The transmission of cultural values to LBGs is helpful for OBGs who see their children assimilating into USA popular culture. Diaspora GPCs are, therefore, seen as vehicles through which ethnic languages could be transmitted to the LBGs. The Chinese and Hispanics, for instance, have created language schools in their churches. GPCs can learn from them in their operation in the overseas mission field.

Bridge-Building Among the Races of the USA

One misconception is the quest for an easy connection between diaspora African-Africans and African-Americans. However, continental Africans and African-Americans hardly connect because they have two different cultures. In a presentation at a NW regional meeting of the Evangelical Missiological Society (EMS), Miriam Adeney affirmed,

> Africans...have wondered, "You are the richest black people on earth. Why have you taken so long to come and help us?" For their part, African-Americans have wondered, "Did your ancestors sell mine into slavery?"...Culturally...African-Americans may see "Africans as the face of poverty, disease...and backwardness." Conversely, immigrants from Africa criticize African-Americans in regard to sexual behavior, work ethic, language, and self-image (2010:7, 8).

Adeney provided one example of the many positive support ventures given to Africans by African-Americans. Citing extensively from Judith St. Clair Hull's "African American Strategies and Motivations in Short Term Missions," presentation at the EMS annual meeting, Minneapolis (2007) and Jehu Hanciles,' Beyond Christendom (Orbis Books, 2008), she illustrated her point that

> The story of Joseph is at the core of one large African-American church's mission...With many medical professionals in the church, they formed short term teams to run regular clinics in Ghana, focusing on five health issues: malaria, TB, typhoid, ringworm, and immunizations. In every six-day clinic they treat about 1,500 people and provide medicines for others (2010:8).

CONCLUSION AND RECOMMENDATION

Searching for bridge-building among the races is an opportunity. "A troubled relationship with host societies, suggesting a lack of acceptance…there is a sense of empathy and solidarity with co-ethnic members in other nations of settlement…the possibility of a distinctive creative, enriching life in host nations with a tolerance for pluralism" (Robin Cohen 1989:177-196). Diaspora GPCs members, as potential reverse missionaries, could bring their enriching lives and faith to non-Africans in the USA because they are peaceful people. Wherever they are, they live peacefully with other ethnic groups and they demonstrate an attitude of live and let live; this is pure recognition of cultural pluralism. Tiwaa asked in defense of other cultures, "Who has the better cultural and moral values? Ghanaians? Or Americans? It is neither here nor there and it's no big deal. I have White and Black friends who live in better neighborhoods with good cultural and moral values just like the OBGs" (Interview, November 27, 2010). For this youth, recognition of positive values in the other USA cultures will go a long way to improve building bridges among the races.

SIGNIFICANT STRATEGIES FOR CROSS-CULTURAL MISSIONS PRACTICE IN THE USA

New and meaningful operational strategies are needed to hasten the cross-cultural CP and communication of Christ to all the USA ethnic groups and generations. GPCs should strive to change their attitude towards CP. New and diversified strategies should be identified and implemented. The following suggested strategies are for development.

Training! Training! Training for Multiplication

Training is very essential in the GPCs in their overseas mission field. Figure 7.1 below illustrates the multiplication effect resulting from chain training.

As Paul enjoined Timothy (2 Timothy 2:2), the "Timothy multiplier effect method" of development is inevitable for church multiplication. If the leadership of these alien African churches lack leadership training they will continue to export their "thousand mile long but two feet deep" Christianity to

Figure 7.1: The Timothy Multiplier Effect Method

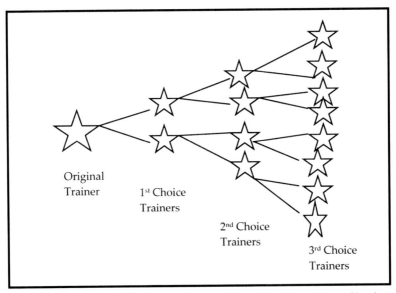

A their mission field. One method, which is "training chains of leaders who train leaders who train leaders," (Galen Currah 2011 <http://www.MentorNet.ws> May 12, 2011) could be a major biblical perspective of training for CPMs.

Meaningful Use of the Discipleship Essentials

Effective means of discipleship methods for diaspora missions might be identified and recommended for USA GPCs. The success of these discipleship methods is the implementation of meaningful prayer and fasting, Bible studies, fellowship, and witness. Fellowship is relatively implemented by all the GPCs. First, prayer and fasting constitute the key to biblical church multiplication. Monthly or quarterly fasting and prayer meetings should be organized for members' revival, healing, and deliverance. "Prayer lines" should be encouraged and opened for all the GPCs. These have been so popularized by the Ghanaian charismatic and prophetic churches that many people who do not have time for these essentials because of work schedules have taken advantage to deal with their spirituality. The mainline churches should adopt some of these methods. The focus of prayer should necessarily include church planting and multiplication. A typical example that should be embraced is the ongoing PCG OMF prayer line started by the visiting minister of the Emmanuel PCG in Norton, VA. With these, the cosmological warfare that will end in victorious Christian lives and preventive deliverance rather than curative deliverance will be emphasized. A caveat here is that some of the

Pentecostal and Charismatic GPCs for lack of time for prayer have attempted to substitute prayer for preaching in their Sunday forenoon services.

Second, every prayer meeting should be grounded on Scripture. All GPCs should incorporate Bible studies in the forenoon services on Sundays. Texts for a period of time might focus on mission and evangelization. Individual devotions and Bible study should also be encouraged. Any Christian activity that eliminates the God's Word is deficient of the presence and glory of God.

Third, diaspora GPCs' members should be mobilized for witnessing. Activities and conversation in homes and work places include one-on-one visitations, distribution of materials, "bring a friend" invitations, telephone contacts (this have been used to plant many churches in the USA. A typical example is how the Atlantic City PCG was formed through contacts with the New Jersey PCG, and home cell fellowships, among others. For instance, some of the members of Bethel PCG who reside at Bolingbrook, one of the suburbs of Chicago, IL, gather in a members' basement every Saturday between 5 and 6 pm to pray and study the Bible. Soon another PCG could be planted in Bolingbrook. This is how many of the GPCs begin. Such vibrant people are usually eager to worship God near their places of residence. These activities implemented are the necessities of holistic development for USA GPCs.

Ministry as Networking and Relational Paradigms

Networking is invaluable in diaspora mission. USA GPCs should embrace, encourage, and develop networking. Various congregations, societies, assemblies of all denominations should "let the gospel flow in the normal, biblical way in existing social networks" (George Patterson 2010). Networking which is strictly based on family and friendship has been used by the diaspora GPCs. Scripture indicates how whole families could be delivered for God's Kingdom (Acts 16:31). In addition, ethnicity is the hallmark for USA GPCs. Positive networking from the various ethnicities would benefit them.

Moreover, healing and deliverance activities continue to be a powerful means for mission as exemplified with the healing of the lame man at the Beautiful gate (Acts 4). For instance, networking with the PCGNY and Reformed Presbyterian Church in Brooklyn, the Akuapem Presbytery of PCG launched USA "Mission 2003" for healing and deliverance services in most of the Ghanaian Presbyterian congregations. Since then this team has operated in America annually. During such meetings members of other denominations join to participate. Through persistent prayer, this laudable and useful method should be reengineered, repackaged, and implemented to fit into the training programs of USA OMF PCG.

With regard to the replacement of Kraft and Hiebert's need proposals, Enoch Wan proposed a "relational paradigm" (2010: 92-100) as an alternative to the need-based functionalist approach. Ghanaian culture has a strong relational emphasis. Thus, in networking, the understanding and implementation of a relational paradigm will be practical and effective when motivating and mobilizing the GPC for mission.

Meaningful Utilization of GPCs Annual Conventions

With proper prayer, reverse engineering, and strategizing, the annual conventions of the GPCs could yield meaningful results. The CoP-I has its Christmas, Easter, Holy Ghost, and youth conventions. The Presbyterians have their annual conventions and conferences. The Methodists also call them annual camp meetings. Joint teams from both the headquarters and the local churches could be commissioned to undertake diligent feasibility studies of the major cities for church planting within the year.

Prior contacts should normally be done to select leaders under whose care the planted churches will be placed. Here, Joy Tira proposed the strategy of applying the biological "Kangaroo church birthing and reproduction model" by stating, "The mission of the church is to make healthy disciples of Jesus Christ of 'all nations' and the peoples of many nations are scattered or dispersed around the globe. The reason for this proposal is that the Church of Jesus Christ must thrive among these diaspora people of the nations" (2009; Wan and Tira 2009: 69). The idea is for a "mother" congregation (kangaroo) to plant, nurture, and support a "daughter" congregation (joey) until it becomes mature to plant another congregation. Proper planning focusing on CP will make these GPCs' annual gatherings fruitful and meaningful.

The Quest for an Equilibrium Between Institution and Movement

Another strategy is the quest for equilibrium between institution (structure) and movement (charisma). Normally, a movement is dynamic while an institution may lack initiative even though it will have all the structures. It is also argued that an institution with structures but without movement becomes stale and dormant. Conversely, a movement without order and structures becomes chaotic. The mainline GPCs have become institutions which are well structured with rules, constitutions, polity, liturgical orders, roles for the ordained and the laity, vestments, titles, and the like. Strictly formalized areas of operation had resulted in lack of planning, "old-fashioned unprogressive status, and rigidity" (Bosch 2005: 186-189).

Contemporarily, however, mainline GPCs are no longer institutions without movement. Its operational flexibility in worship experiences, prayer and deliverance camps, and alternative worship services are now relatively attractive. Such flexibility has made them receptive to everyone who opens up to the Christian faith. It is likely that not much difference may be identified in worship styles of the Pentecostal, Charismatic, and Mainline churches in Ghana today. Transfer of such vitality will make diaspora GPCs strong in the USA, seeking for an intersection between these evangelical and charismatic movements and the structures of mainline GPCs.

The Pentecostal and charismatic GPCs also have to learn proper exposition on the Word on God, orderliness, and Christian polity of church administration from the mainline churches. This will avert the "chaotic" and seemingly "shallow" practice of the Christian faith exhibited in the diaspora. This will bring depth in the diaspora African Christianity that will make the Western churches strive to have and share what these African "alien" churches have that they do not have and vice versa.

Managing Effectiveness in Planning

The first urgent and serious area for effective planning in most USA GPCs is financial management. Well-trained and qualified personnel, coupled with supervision, will culminate in healthy stewardship of the funds of the body of Christ. The second aspect of planning is the institution of development plans. In ecclesiological development, to be able to undertake any successful endeavor planning is a necessity. Tira and Santos suggest an effective planning for CP for the Greenhills Christian Fellowship (GCF) in Canada. They wrote,

> GCF Toronto Triple Vision (2007-2010): God willing, one cycle of satellite triple vision takes three to five years to fulfill…and one more year to plan and prepare the next cycle of satellite triple vision…The vision to launch GCF-Toronto in May 2007 (our Jerusalem)…The vision to birth GCF-Peel in March 2008 (our Judea and Samaria)…The vision to birth GCF-Vancouver in May 2010 (our ends on the earth) (Tira and Santos 2011; Moreau and Snodderly 2011: 63-90).

Holy Spirit inspired vision has to be turned into mission and modalities worked out to achieve goals. The GPCs can learn from and implement this "seven-year development plans" method (Tira and Santos 2011; Moreau and Snodderly 2011: 63-90) for its CP in the USA.

Reaching out to the LBGs: The 4/14 Peer Window of Hope

Reaching out to the LBG youth in America requires prayerful development of ministerial strategies. The generational gap should be seen as a positive evangelization vehicle. The concept is catching them young. For example, the historical PCG child evangelization (through the school) in Africa can be re-strategized into peer group evangelization. In the diaspora, concerned parents who recognize the reality of the generation gap will gladly come to church-sponsored parenting workshops about raising LBGs in the USA. Parents who desire their children to acquire their mother tongue will also enroll their children in church-sponsored indigenous language schools.

Worship style is another helpful means to attract LBGs. The younger generations hunger for God but from different perspectives than the OBGs. Three scholars offer suggestions with regard to the younger generations' spirituality. Cameron Strang stated, "My generation is discontent with dead religion. We don't want to show up on Sunday, sing two hymns, hear a sermon and go home" <http://www.nytimes.com/2005/05/16> 1 (October 24, 2011). Dale Wolyniak confirmed, "This Millennial generation wants a real encounter with God…that will hold them in these changing times. We create ministry outreach to the Millennial generation that is rich, deep, and meaningful" (2011; Moreau and Snodderly 2011: 278). Margaret Heffernan also suggested three areas that need attention. She stated, "I think that underneath the dazzling differences, three perennial commonalities remain: the desire for fairness, the need to be stretched, and yearning for community" <http://www.fastcompany.com/resources.talent/managing-generational-differences/052507> 2 (October 24, 2011). GPCs may have two services; the composition might be a traditional worship in the native tongue for OBGs, and a contemporary style in English for LBGs. When teenagers worship with their peers, vitality, vibrancy, and expressive worship can attract unbelieving LBGs. Even non-Ghanaian American youth may be attracted. In this is the advocacy for youth services yearned for by LBGs because they claim adult services are boring. In addition, specific issues such as holiness, abstinence, and morality relevant for the youth development could be preached to them.

Parents and adults in the GPCs should care for the LBGs both at home and within "the household of God"—the church (1Tim 3:14-16). Younger generation LBGs should not feel unwelcome; instead they are to be cared for and loved by congregational leaders who are primarily OBGs. Suggestions by three writers are relevant in dealing with this caring issue. From the secular perspective, it is suggested,

African immigrants are advised by the experts to do the following when living in the United States with school age children:

- Use denial of certain privileges (like TV, internet) to control the children.

- Don't hesitate to send your children to Africa to get a good education and the cherished African culture of hard work, self-discipline, and respect for elders.

- Send your children to private schools if you can afford it, where the indiscipline of the public school system is almost non-existent.

- Tell your children the mishaps that other undisciplined children have fallen into leading to incarceration (Funmi Adepitan 2011: 26).

From the church setting, Janice Mclean stated,

> Urban youth ministry also has...particular challenges...creating a space for...issues young people encounter in the wider community—sex, racial issues...carving out spaces where the youth are involved in the leadership...As the churches...are faithful in nurturing faith in their urban youth ministries...they will be providing their children, grand children and the generations to come with a place of belonging where they can appropriate faith in the city (2011: 13).

Mclean does not agree with the advocacy for the exclusive youth services. On the other hand, she brings an insightful contention that it will rather be beneficial for adults of the immigrant churches to fellowship with their youth where the youth will learn from the adults and vice versa for mutual understanding. Wolyniak in addition suggested how organizations can reach and then keep Millennial generations including:

- Emphasize the need for depth in teaching and community activities

- Have intentional discipleship or mentoring—challenging people rather than building a larger crowd

- Emphasize networking and technology to supplement church services

- Practice holistic spirituality—rejection of any dichotomy of spiritual and secular (2011; Moreau and Snodderly 2011: 284, 285).

The 4/14 Window is our window of hope. "It is crucial that mission efforts be reprioritized and redirected toward the 4/14 group worldwide. This requires that we become acutely aware of what is taking place in their life...will be raising up a new generation to transform the world" (Luis Bush 2009:x). GPCs should nurture their youth in their socialization process for cultural and moral values. They are their future. An indirect opportunity is offered the church by the USA generic context to use training to help nurture the LBGs. Through their training activities for the children and Junior Youth (JY) services (Figure 5.13), GPCs can help these young people to make meaningful negotiations for their identity. That will help them retain part of their positive African identity when growing up in the multi-ethnic USA. For instance, to augment the efforts to teach diaspora Ghanaian children their mother tongue, GPC congregations in the USA have the opportunity to set up language schools. Since this is operational in the Chinese and Hispanic churches, GPCs' adults should create the enabling environment for the youth to make more disciples among themselves for the church.

The Seeker, Seeder, and Feeder Cell Group Model

Seekers are persons who need Jesus. While seeders are new believers, feeders are maturing ones. George Patterson, et al. stated, "We are often asked in North America, "Why don't our small groups multiply?" To sustain multiplication, your church must form three distinct types of cells, just as New Testament churches did: seeker, seeder and feeder cells...pioneer fields include these three simultaneously" <http://www.MenotNet.com. # 70>. GPCs leadership should adopt the insights from this cell model to develop its mission vocation for rapid formation, development, and mobilization for church multiplication.

Acquisition of Property and Chapels of American Congregations

Though beginning as small home prayer cells, some African diaspora churches such as the GPCs grow up into massive congregations, societies, and assemblies. Some have succeeded in turning dilapidated warehouses, garages, and other edifices into beautiful chapels in several USA cities. Others have purchased the chapels of the "decaffeinated" American mainline churches at high financial costs. A few examples will suffice. The current sanctuary of the PCGNY was a games and sports center purchased from the metropolitan police service of Manhattan, NY. The CoP headquarters in the Bronx, NY, was also a warehouse that was purchased and developed into a very huge and beautiful worship center. The Newark GEMC also purchased their worship facility at the Broad Street from the Newark authorities.

Other examples also include the Philadelphia CoP worship center on South 206 Street, the Ebenezer PCG Chapel on 206 Bainbridge Street, Bronx, NY, and the New Jersey PCG Chapel in West Orange purchased from the Roman Catholic, Evangelical Lutheran, and the Greek Orthodox churches, respectively. Though the cost of these chapels are very expensive (some are as high as $1.6 million), these determined churches were able to negotiate to secure bank loans for their down payments after which they have been paying their monthly mortgages. The payments of these mortgages are done through members' contributions and the prudent management of the funds of these churches. African (Ghanaian) Christians believe in the providential God who is the source of the payment of these mortgages. Payment is not solely by human efforts. The providential God will pay through their efforts.

Self-Critique, Appraisal, or Evaluation

A message in the pre-2010 Tokyo consultation video clip describes some of the Southern continents' Christianity as "thousand mile long but one yard deep." To some extent, this is an apt description of African Christianity in the 21st century. Currently, John Nevius' and Henry Venn's three-selfs which are self-propagation, self-governance, and self-finance in addition to Paul Hiebert's self-theologizing are relatively all being applied. The additional proposition is self-critique to increase the depth of African Christianity. The nomenclature here includes self-assessment, self-appraisal, and self-evaluation. Diaspora Africans who are planting churches all over American cities should apply self-assessment. Africans should pause, evaluate, and criticize their practice of the Christian faith. This will help to deepen African Christianity in terms of development, mission strategies, and methodology. Here, the most important strategy is the application of the God's Word assessment. To achieve this, Africans should superimpose Scriptural absolutism in combination with cultural relativism.

RECOMMENDATIONS FOR FURTHER STUDY

Four important areas are suggested for further study, in terms of both particularities and generalities. First, in the sphere of particularities, a study into intercultural training is inevitable. Weak Christian leadership direction and training, lack of discipleship, and non-victorious Christian life are some of the problematic areas. Very few of the planted GPCs have trained and ordained ministers. These ordained ministers needed prior intercultural training for cross-cultural practice since some of them are OBG attachés to these congregations, societies, and assemblies. Some invaluable material for this training includes *Perspectives on the World Christian Movement* with its Study Guide, edited by Ralph Winter and Steven Hawthorne (2009), respectively. To help churches build up other churches in the vision for "great-granddaughter churches...they are to train believers to evangelize and train church leaders and pastors to train other pastors and leaders" (Steven Hawthorne 2009: 142-144). Such a study to implement the Timothy multiplier effect method is helpful.

Second, in another sphere of particularities, it is important to have a full study of the development of GPCs' LBGs. The reason is that diaspora Ghanaians, both documented and undocumented, have given and are giving birth to and raising citizens in the USA. For further study, mentoring these LBGs is an important area. Typical resources include *Connecting: The Mentoring Relationships you Need to Succeed in Life* by Paul Stanley and Robert Clinton. Mentoring is a means to discipleship. While the biblical motif is discipleship, the means of achieving that discipleship is mentorship, especially of younger generations (Terry Burns 2010). Regarding a definite set of assumptions about the nature of mentoring, Lois Zachary articulated, "Mentoring is a process of engagement…Mentoring…focuses on the learners, the learning process, and the learning" (2000: xviii). These, among others, in Lois Zachary's *Mentoring Guide: Facilitating Effective Learning Relationships* (2000) are invaluable materials for further study of "ministering to and through the diaspora" Ghanaian youth.

Third, in another sphere of particularities, the usefulness of a study of the financial management of the diaspora GPCs cannot be overemphasized. How are the congregations funded? How do the congregations raise their funds? Who are the signatories and how do they become signatories? Who are in charge of disbursement and how does prudent financial management impact the physical and spiritual development of these congregations? Research into this financial management in the quest to answer these questions will go a long way to validate or disprove the external perception of the motives of formation of these "alien" GPCs in the USA. Disproving such perceptions will enhance GPCs' diaspora missions practice for the rapid demographic and developmental growth.

Fourth, in the realm of generalities, a comparative study for diaspora missions and missiology is necessary. Several of the researches in diaspora studies have been nation-specific. Few writers in diaspora missiology have taken comparative studies and offered theoretical paradigms for such studies. One could read on Korean, Filipino, or Chinese, Ghanaian diaspora, and the like. Hardly ever does one read about Chinese diaspora compared with Ghanaian diaspora. It is recommended for scholars in diaspora missiology to further research in such areas to broaden the base of this relatively new area of study.

QUESTIONS FOR DISCUSSION

1. What are the major challenges encountered by diaspora USA GPCs?
2. What are the opportunities for the USA Ghanaian Protestant churches?
3. From this volume, what significant strategies can be derived for cross-cultural missions practice in the USA?
4. What recommendations are being made is this chapter for further study?
5. What ministerial principle and missiological strategy can we derive from this study on Ghanaian diaspora and congregations in the USA for other serving diaspora groups in the USA?

APPENDICES

Appendix A: Individual Ethnographic Interview Questions

I

Overseas Born Ghanaians (OBGs)

Diversity, Identity, and Receptivity of the Gospel
1. If diversity is cultural, religious, and linguistic differences, how would you describe your life in the USA multi-cultural society?
2. Could you describe your social life in the USA?
3. If identity is being physiologically, psychologically, and culturally unique, could you describe yourself and your family in the USA multi-ethnic context?
4. If receptivity of the gospel is absolute commitment to Jesus Christ as your Lord and personal Savior, could you describe how your faith is important?
5. Would you tell me your story of how you became a Christian? Could you explain how your Christian faith has helped to develop your spirituality?
6. Could you describe how your faith relates to your family, friendship, and social lives?

Formation, Development, and Mobilization for Christian Mission
1. Please, narrate your story about how you became a member of your congregation. Why do you belong to this congregation?
2. How would you describe your involvement or not in the formation of your congregation?

Appendix B: Missiological Study Research Methodology

B.I: Archival Material Resources Sourced in the Field Research

Date	Type	Archival Material	Venue
08/09	Records	Decisions of 9th PCG General Assembly	Abetifi
11/08/09	Brochure	2009 PCGNY Thanksgiving and Harvest	PCGNY
03/27/10	Records	Minutes of OMF 1st Council Meeting	Newark, NJ
05/23/10	Brochure	Ebenezer PCG 5th Anniversary	Bronx, NY
06/10	Records & Brochure	Minutes of OMF 1st Council Meeting & Inauguration of Calvary PCG, OH	Columbus, OH
06/28–07/04/10	Brochure	2nd PCG Overseas Conference and 4th OMF North America Annual Convention	Yonkers, NY
07/31/10	Brochure	22nd Ghana Festival (Ghanafest) Program	Chicago, IL
08/10	Records	Decisions of 10th PCG General Assembly	Takoradi
09/03/10	Brochure	2010 PCG OMF Youth Conference	PCGNY
09/10	Records	Minutes of OMF 3rd Council Meeting	PCGNY
11/14/10	Brochure	2010 PCGNY Thanksgiving and Harvest	PCGNY
04/08-10/11	Records	Minutes of OMF 1st Council Meeting & Inauguration of Chicago Bethel PCG	Chicago, IL
12/1-3/2010	Brochure	1st PCG OMF District Session	PCGNY
06/24-26/11	Program	2011 PCG OMF Youth Conference	Adelphi, MD
07/1-3/11	Program	2011 PCG 5th OMF National Convention	Newark, NJ
07/24/11	Program	PCGNY 25th Anniversary Celebration	PCGNY
08/12-17/11	Records	Decisions of 11th PCG General Assembly	Abetifi
09/02-03/11	Records	Minutes of OMF 3rd Council Meeting	PCGNY
09/18/11	Program	Dedication of Worcester PCG Chapel	PCGNY
12/02-04/11	Brochure	2nd PCG OMF District Conference	PCGNY

B.II: Procedural Activities for Participant Observation (2009-2011)

Date	Activity	Remarks
2009		
03 & 05/09	Visitation Fellowship with Houston PCG, TX	Various activities
05/09	Visitation Fellowship with Houston PCG, TX	Various activities
06/06–09/06/09	Return to Ghana and U.S.: Return for D. Miss. at Western Seminary in Portland, OR	Connection to PCG after 3 months break
2010		
03/10	OMF Council Meetings in PCG Newark.	Participating Minister
05/30/10	Attendance of the Youth Service, PCGNY	Worship Service
06/05/10	OMF Council Meeting & Inauguration of PCG Calvary, Columbus, OH	Participating Minister
06/28–07/4/10	2nd Overseas PCG Conference & 4th OMF North American Convention	Participating Minister
07/04–12/31/10	Visitation Fellowship with Bethel and Trinity PCGs in Chicago, IL	Various activities
08/8-22/10	Visitation Fellowship with Calvary PCG in Columbus & Cincinnati PCGs, OH	Various activities
09/3-5/10	PCG OMF Youth Conference at PCGNY	Participating Minister
12/3-5/10	1st PCG OMF District Session (Conference)	Manhattan, NY
2011		
3/1-4/8/11	Visitation Fellowship with PCG Houston, TX	Various Activities
04/10/11	OMF Council Meeting and Inauguration of Bethel PCG Chicago, IL	Participating Minister
4/11-5/8/11	Visitation Fellowship with PCG Houston, TX	Various activities
5/25–6/24/11	Visitation Fellowship with Houston PCG, TX	Various activities
06/24-26/11	PCG OMF Youth Conference, Adelphi, MD	Participating Minister
07/1-3/11	PCG OMF District Convention, Newark, NJ	Participating Minister
07/04-23/11	Visitation Fellowship with Cincinnati PCG, OH	Various Activities
07/24/11	PCGNY 25th Anniversary Celebration	Participating Minister
09/02-03/11	Minutes of OMF 3rd Council Meeting	Participating Minister
09/04/11	PCG Church Planting, Ewing, NJ	A new home church
09/18/11	Dedication of Worcester PCG Chapel	Participating Minister
12/02-04/11	2nd PCG OMF Annual Conference	Participating Minister

Appendix C: Relevant Planning Activities for Church Planting

CP Activity	Type of Relevant Activities
Scriptural Foundation (Pauline Strategies)	Paul used his fellow workers wisely in order to evangelize; Encouraged and used the churches which he had began in the task of evangelism; Withdrew from growing congregations; he engaged in evangelism, he trained others to do the same work, and left others to do the work for which they have been trained.
Formation of Master Plan	Whole church extension vocation must be bathed in prayer as believers enter a new area Basic analysis of the target area and people must be carried out; e.g. which classes are represented, their characteristics, and their distinctives; Selection of evangelistic teams on the basis of their qualifications and ability to relate to target groups; Taking cultural diversities into consideration while working on plans for making contacts in the target community; and, Reviewing and updating information gathered.
Pre-evangelistic Courtesy Contacts	Considering what people in the target culture expect newcomers to do; Classifying who are in the various segments in the target area; e.g. religious, educational, business, governmental communities, etc. Are there people who will benefit by associating with missionary-evangelistic teams? Understanding and goodwill plus other desires from the various persons upon whom believers call.
Pre-evangelistic Community Contacts	Normal everyday interaction with individuals in the community; Joining civic organizations or special-interest groups in the target area that aim at community improvement or individual growth; Taking a carefully planned area survey with carefully selected, instructed, and prepared personnel; Making use of the media in the target community.
Selective Evangelistic Contacts	Analysis of preliminary and community surveys with the view to identifying responsive individuals, families, and segments of the community; Sourcing for provision of names and addresses of newcomers in target area; Asking believers who live in the target area if they have relatives or friends in the area who might be interested; Meetings with the general public should be recorded and kept, e.g. for Bible study, evangelism, or worship)
Widespread Evangelistic Contacts	Make contacts—consider the possibilities, devise the means, motivate others—and follow through by making contacts; Keep meaningful records—whether by individuals or by teams; Ask the question, "Why will people come here?"

Appendix D: Discipleship Essentials and Leadership Training Schedules

D.I: Some Discipleship Essentials of the USA PCG Congregations

Date	Theme	Speaker	Bible Text	#
USA PCG OMF Morning Devotions				
03/21/11	To Church of Ephesus	Pastor Atakora	Rev. 2:1-7	79
03/22/11	To Smyrna & Pergamum	"	Rev. 2:8-17	87
03/23/11	To Church of Thyatira	"	Rev. 18-29	81
03/24/11	To Philadelphia & Sardis	"	Rev. 3:1-13	88
03/25/11	To Laodicea	"	Rev. 3:14-22	81
03/28/11	Who? Holy Spirit's Personhood	Rev. Edu-Bekoe	1 Cor. 12:11	83
03/29/11	Who? Holy Spirit's Divinity	"	2 Cor. 13:14	80
03/30/11	What? Holy Spirit Indwelling	"	Gal. 5:22, 23	85
03/31/11	How? Essentials of Holy Spirit	"	Eph. 5:19-21	67
04/01/11	How? Holy Spirit Temple in us	"	1 Cor. 6:19-20	80
04/11/11	Christian Living	Rev. Karikari	John 6:69	81
04/12/11	Worldly Life	Rev. Joyce	2 Tim. 3:1-5	78
04/13/11	PCG Discipline in Trust	"	Psalm 84:12	83
04/14/11	Christ in you; Hope of Glory	"	Col. 1:7	65
04/25/11	5-fold Holy Spirit Ministry Gifts 7-fold Holy Spirit Charismata & 9-fold Holy Spirit Charismata	Rev. Edu-Bekoe	Eph. 4:11-16; Romans 12:6-8; 1 Cor. 12:1-11	78
04/26/11	One Body; Many Parts	"	1 Cor. 12:12-31	60
04/27/11	Love: The Most Excellent Gift	"	1 Cor. 13:1-13	67
04/28/11	Practice Love; Desire the Gifts I	"	1Cor. 14:1-25	77
04/29/11	Practice Love; Desire the Gifts II	"	1Cor. 14:26-39	81
40-Day Lenten Weekly Fast Breaking				
03/26/11	Christian Fasting Meaning	Rev. Dr. Gyang-Duah	Matt. 6:16-18	121
04/02/11	Sin is Death to Self	Cat. Mina Kwakye Addo	Deut. 24:16	76
04/23/11	Suffering for Victory	Rev. Dr. Gyang-Duah	Isaiah 53:12	87
Passion Week Evening Devotions				
04/18/11	The Holy Communion	Rev. Dr. Gyang-Duah	Luke 22:1-23	83
04/19/11	Gethsemane and Arrest	"	John 18:1-19	65
04/20/11	The Religious Trials	"	John 18:20-27	94
04/21/11	Before Pilate & the Cross	"	John 19:1ff	76
04/22/11	Meaning of His Suffering	Each Congregation	John 18:1-19	-

D.II: Suggested Learning Units of GPCs Diaspora Pastoral Training (Wks 1-3)

Week	Learning Units (LUs) and Related Topics	Description of the Content
Week 1	**LU 001: Narrative** Knowing the Story	Abraham's journey into the diaspora Israel's Egyptian diaspora slavery Moses, Israel, and the diaspora promised land Jewish Assyrian diaspora Jewish Babylonian diaspora Post-resurrection scattering mission of the disciples
	LU 002: God Knowing God, Christ and the Power of the Holy Spirit	The role of God, Christ, and the Holy Spirit in the scriptural diaspora stories. Globalization and international migration The role of God, Christ, and the Holy Spirit in global migration
Week 2	**LU 003: Self** Knowing Yourself	The self-SWOT analysis discussions and experience Indentifying your spiritual, physiological, and psychological experiences Generational diversity in relationship to self
	LU 004: Congregants Knowing the Audience	Basic Ghanaian ethnicity and cultural diversity Reality of Ghanaian cultural and moral values Characteristics of diaspora Ghanaians Ethnic composition of the PCG congregations Reality of generational diversity Discipleship, leadership training, and mentorship Diaspora generational diversity and socialization
Week 3	**LU 005: U.S. Society** Knowing the Context	Complexity of U.S. multi-culturalism Ghanaian cultural and generational diversity in the U.S. Formation of PCG congregations in the U.S. Existence of PCUSA and the principles of partnership

D.III: Suggested Learning Units of GPCs Diaspora Pastoral Training (Wks 4-6)

Week	Learning Units (LUs) And Related Topics	Description of the Content
Week 4	LU 006: Technology Knowing the Tools	Scripture Books and textual material Use of laptops, notebooks, and computers Use of simple Powerpoint projections
Week 4	LU 007: Modification Knowing Change	Old trends of migration Former trends of Ghanaian migration Current trends of Ghanaian migration Changed and changing trends of PCG Experience and participatory learning
Week 5	LU 008: Case Studies Knowing and Developing Case Studies Methods	Developing story telling in intercultural training Compiling case studies from learning experiences Participant field research on case studies Development of case studies for leadership training
Week 5	LU 009: Assignments Knowing and Cultivating Habit of Reading and Writing Papers in U.S.	Pre-session reading and preparation: Reading about biblical biographies Reading about diaspora Israel Reading on NT scattered believers Brief reading assignments Reading the suggested assignment texts Brief course assignments taken in learning period
Week 6	LU 010: Competency Self-Evaluation	Self-evaluation of the usefulness of training Ability to recognize complexity of diversity in the U.S. Further reading assignments Short written assignments

D.IV: Similarities and Dissimilarities of Formal and Informal Training

Area	Formal Education	Informal Education
Similarities	Both formal and informal education offer relative strengths to your educational outreach project Both school and after school programs serve learners Both are relatively successful by conducive enabling learning environment Both involves younger or older learners and adult trainers	
Dissimilarities	Classrooms have same children and same teachers every day Classroom activities can last several days You can assume that classroom-based teachers have a certain level of training in educational philosophy, effective teaching strategies, classroom management, and content. Teachers need to meet educational standards and stick to a specified curriculum, which can make it more difficult for them to incorporate nontraditional content. If your project fits in a classroom, it can have a very long life; teachers will use trusted resources for years. Schools programs serve students in strictly formalized setting. Parents may be semi-passive in their connection with their children's education. Training children are the specialties of the teachers so let them do it. Teacher's profession must be performed.	After school programs are often drop-in, so attendance is inconsistent, as is leadership After school programs need to complete an activity each day because a different group of kids could be in attendance tomorrow. After school providers, by contrast, vary in experience and knowledge in teaching techniques, content expertise, and group management. Typically, materials for after-school settings need to include a lot more structure. After school programs, on the other hand, can be more flexible in content. After-school programs offer a different kind of environment, where your activities need to be as formal and where you can reach a different audience. While both schools and after-school programs serve students, many kids who feel disenfranchised at school blossom in after-school settings. Real learning can happen in a setting where kids feel less intimidated or more comfortable than they do in a formal classroom. The ultimate goal is that their success in an informal setting can lead to greater confidence in the formal classroom . An additional benefit of developing materials for informal educational settings is that they may be useful to parents at home with their kids, or to adult learners who are looking to expand their knowledge, either for their own enrichment or to increase their career options.

D.V: Pedagogy Versus Adult Learning Processes

ELEMENTS	PEDAGOGICAL Teacher Directed Learning	ADULT LEARNING PROCESS Self-Directed Learning
Climate	Formal authority-oriented Competitive Judgmental	Informal, mutually respectful Consensual Collaborative Supportive
Planning	Primarily by Teacher	By participative decision-making
Diagnosis of Needs	Primarily by Teacher	By mutual assessment
Setting Goals	Primarily by Teacher	By mutual negotiation
Designing a Learning Plan	Content units Course syllabus Logical sequence	Learning projects Learning content sequenced in terms of readiness
Learning Activities	Transmit techniques Assigned readiness	Inquiry projects, independent study, experimental techniques
Evaluation	Primarily by teacher and tests	By mutual assessment of self-collected evidence

Appendix E: List of Worshipers at PIC on April 8, 2012

#	Name	Nationality	Roll	Status	Kids
1	Kofi Nelson-Owusu	Ghanaian	Pastor	OBG	2
2	Sandra Nelson-Owusu (Mrs)	Liberian	Member	OBG	
3	Carroll	Cameroonian	Pastor	OBG	-
4	Seth Kofi Asare	Ghanaian	Elder	OBG	2
5	Sarah Asare (Mrs)	Ghanaian	Member	OBG	
6	Brando Akoto	Ghanaian	Elder	OBG	2
7	Lilly Akoto (Mrs)	African-American	Member	Citizen	
8	Yves Avignon	Togolese	Elder	OBG	-
9	Harriet Avignon (Mrs)	African-American	Member	Citizen	
10	Alex Nkansah	Ghanaian	Elder	OBG	2
11	Beatrice Nkansah (Mrs)	Ghanaian	Member	OBG	
12	Gary Huenke	White-American	Visitor	Citizen	-
13	Pat Huenke (Mrs)	White-American	Visitor	Citizen	-
14	Carlos	Haitian	Visitor	OBG	2
15	Judith (Mrs)	Haitian	Visitor	OBG	
16	Isaya Atonga	Kenyan	Member	OBG	-
17	Permor	Ghanaian	Member	OBG	-
18	Patience Permor (Mrs)	Ghanaian	Member	OBG	
19	Tom	White-American	Visitor	Citizen	-
20	Mary	White-American	Visitor	Citizen	
21	Isabel	Liberian	Member	OBG	-
22	Kwasi Agyekum	Ghanaian	Member	OBG	2
23	Pamela Agyekum (Mrs)	Ghanaian	Member	OBG	1
24	Peter Okantey	Ghanaian	Member	OBG	2
25	Sarah Okantey (Mrs)	White-American	Member	Citizen	
26	Roland Moore	Liberian-Ghanaian	Member	OBG	2
27	Charlotte Moore (Mrs)	Ghanaian	Member	OBG	
28	M. Ndembu	Congolese	Member	OBG	4
29	Y. Ndembu (Mrs)	Congolese	Member	OBG	
30	J. Ndembu	Congolese	Member	OBG	-
31	Kofi	Ghanaian	Member	OBG	
32	Derrick	White-American	Member	Citizen	-
33	James	White-American	Member	Citizen	
34	Tracy	Ghanaian	Member	1.5 OBG	-
35	Effe	Ghanaian	Member	LBG	-
36	George	Ghanaian	Member	LBG	-
37	Brian Neumann	White-American	Visitor	Citizen	2
38	Danielle Neumann (Mrs)	White-American	Visitor	Citizen	
39	Alisha Penman	Yemeni-American	Visitor	Ctizen	-
40	Seyram	Ghanaian-American	Member	LBG	-
41	Vivian	Ghanaian	Member	OBG	
42	Emmanuel Kwaku Nteh	Ghanaian	New	OBG	1
43	Tajya Peterson-Nteh (Mrs)	African-American	New	Citizen	
44	Calamo Mendes	Guinea-Bisauan	New	OBG	-
45	Angie Mendes (Mrs)	Native-American	New	Native	-

APPENDICES

Appendix F: List of Ethnographic Interviewees in the Field Research

Individual Interviews				
#	Name	Date	Status	Diaspora Congregation
1	Abena	12/2/2010	OBG	PCGNY, Manhattan, NY
2	Abigail	10/31/2010	OBG	Bethel PCG, Chicago, IL
3	Adawoo, Mary	11/27/2010	1.5 OBG	PCGNY, Manhattan, NY
4	Adi-Lamptey, Nene Billy	3/14/2011	LBG	Houston PCG, TX
5	Adomako, Kwame Afram	11/28/2010	LL; OBG	NJ PCG, Irvington, NJ
6	Adom, Sefah	8/14/2010	CL; OBG	Calvary, Columbus, OH
7	Addo-Prempeh Kwadwo	11/23/2010	OBG	PCGNY, Manhattan, NY
8	Addo-Prempeh Victoria	11/23/2010	1.5 OBG	PCGNY, Manhattan, NY
9	Afrifa, Kwame Akom	12/2/2010	OBG	PCGNY, Manhattan, NY
10	Afriyie, Collins Kwasi Asamoah	12/11/2011	OBG	GEMC, Newark, NJ
11	Agyemang, Kwadwo Osei	12/11/2012	LL; OBG	GEMC, Newark, NJ
12	Agyemang, Rex	11/28/2010	LBG	PCGNY, Manhattan, NY
13	Agyemang, Serwah	6/12/2010	1.5 OBG	Ebenezer, Bronx, NY
14	Agyare, Felicia	11/14/2010	LBG	Assemlies of God, Chicago, IL
15	Akai-Nettey	12/2/2010	OBG	PCGNY, Manhattan, NY
16	Akoto, Brando	2/12/2012	LL; OBG	PIC, Portland, OR
17	Ansah, Ntow	4/10/2011	CL; OBG	PCG, Cincinnati, OH
18	Ansah, Ntow Kofi	7/12/2011	1.5 OBG	PCG, Cincinnati, OH
19	Ansah, Ntow Afua O.	7/12/2011	1.5 OBG	PCG, Cincinnati, OH
20	Ansong, Edward	12/2/2010	LL; OBG	Ebenezer PCG, Bronx, NY
21	Anyomi, Seth (Bishop)	04/13/2012	PL; OBG	PIC, Portland, OR
22	Asah-Ntow, Eugene	6/12/2010	1.5 OBG	Ebenezer PCG, Bronx, NY
23	Asante, Mabel (Dr.)	9/4/2010	LL; OBG	PCGNY, Manhattan, NY
24	Asiama, Jane	10/10/2010	OBG	Bethel, Chicago, IL
25	Asiama, Paul	10/18/2010	CL; OBG	Bethel, Chicago, IL
26	Asiama, Sandra Ampadu	7/20/2011	OBG	Cincinnati, OH
27	Asiedu, Yaw (Rev.)	5/30/2010 & 3/19/2011	PL; OBG	PCGNY, Manhattan, NY
28	Asiedu, Okyere	12/2007	LL; OBG	CoP-I, Philadelphia, PA
29	Baah, Joyce	12/2/2010	LL, OBG	Atlantic CityPCG, NJ
30	Boadi, Miriam	7/7/2010	1.5 OBG	Adom PCG, Adelphi, MA
31	Boadi, Esther	7/7/2010	1.5 OBG	Adom PCG, Adelphi, MA
32	Boakye, Kwaku (Dr.)	9/19, 10/3 & 11/12, 2010	LL; 1.5 OBG	PCGNY, Manhattan, NY
33	Botsie-Ansah, Cynthia	6/12/2010	1.5 OBG	Ebenezer PCG, Bronx, NY
34	Boye-Doe, Stella	3/14/2010	OBG	Houston PCG, TX
35	Carroll (Pastor)	3/11/2012	PL; OBG	PIC, Portland, OR
36	Daniel	8/14/2010	OBG	Calvary PCG, Columbus, OH
37	Danso, Ernest	6/12/2010	1.5 OBG	Ebenezer PCG, Bronx, NY
38	David	3/19/2011	LBG	Houston PCG, TX

39	Debrah-Dwamena, Adjoa (Atty.)	9/19, 10/3, 11/12/2010	LL; LBG	PCGNY, Manhattan, NY
40	Edith	12/2/2010	OBG	PCGNY, Manhattan, NY
41	D. J.		OBG	Unchurhed
42	Effe	2/8/2010	LBG	PIC, Portland, OR
43	Fosu, Opanyin	11/19/2011	CL; OBG	GEMC, Newark, NJ
44	George	2/15/2010	LBG	PIC, Portland, OR
45	Georgina	10/24/2010	OBG	Bethel PCG, Chicago, IL
46	Georgina, A. N. (Mrs.)	7/8/2011	OBG	Cincinnati PCG, OH
47	Gyamerah, Foster	6/12/2010	1.5 OBG	Ebenezer PCG, Bronx, NY
48	Gyamfi, Kwame (Acct.)	9/19 & 10/3 2010	LL; OBG	PCGNY, Manhattan, NY
49	Gyamfi, Michael	12/11/2011	LL; OBG	GEMC, Newark, NJ
50	Gyan, Emmanuel Kwame	11/28/2010	LL; OBG	NJ PCG, Irvington, NJ
51	Gyang-Duah, Charles (Rev. Dr.)	5/25, 5/30 & 11/23, 2010	PL; OBG	OMF; Ebenezer PCG, Bronx, NY
52	Joyce (Rev.)	4/10/2011	PL; OBG	Worcester PCG, MS
53	Krodua-Asare, Kwaku	10/30/2010	LL; OBG	Bethel PCG, Chicago, IL
54	Kwaku	3/19/2011	LBG	Houston PCG, TX
55	Kyeremeh, Abigail	11/28/2010	1.5 OBG	Ebenezer PCG, Bronx, NY
56	Kyeremeh, Eric	11/28/2010	1.5 OBG	Ebenezer PCG, Bronx, NY
57	Kyeremeh, Mercy	6/12/2010	1.5 OBG	Ebenezer PCG, Bronx, NY
58	Lokko, Stanley	12/2/2010	OBG	PCGNY, Manhattan, NY
59	Mensah, Akwasi	6/12/2010	1.5 OBG	Ebenezer PCG, Bronx, NY
60	Mensah, Opanin	6/8/2011	OBG	PCGNY, Manhattan, NY
61	Moet	12/11/2011	LBG	VBC-I, Irvington, NJ
62	Naykene	10/24/2010	LBG	Bethel PCG, Chicago, IL
63	Naykene, Gladys	10/24/2010	OBG	Bethel PCG, Chicago, IL
64	Nelson-Owusu, Kofi	12/26/2011	PL; OBG	PIC, Portland, OR
65	Oduro-Frimpong, Abigail	6/12/2010	1.5 OBG	Ebenezer PCG, Bronx, NY
66	Okoampa-Ahoofe Kwame	7/6/2010	OBG	Ebenezer PCG, Bronx, NY
67	Okoampa-Ahoofe (Mrs.)	7/6/2010	OBG	Ebenezer PCG, Bronx, NY
68	Okobea, Afua	12/2/2010	LL; OBG	PCGNY, Manhattan, NY
69	Okpoti Sowah	11/23/1020	OBG	PCGNY, Manhattan, NY
70	Owoo, Matilda	11/28/2010	1.5 OBG	PCGNY, Manhattan, NY
71	Owusu, Ansah	12/2007	OBG	CoP-I, Philadelphia, PA
72	Owusu, Sakyiama Emmanuel	6/12/2010	1.5 OBG	Ebenezer PCG, Bronx, NY
73	Owusu, Stephen Kwaku (Very Rev.)	11/19/2011	PL; OBG	GEMC, Newark, NJ
74	Owusu, Lawrence	12/2007	LL; OBG	CoP-I, Philadelphia, PA
75	Paulina	3/19/2011	LBG	Houston PCG, TX
76	Pratt, David Ato	11/20/ & 11/27/2011	PL; OBG	VBC-I, Irvington, NJ
77	Quagrine, Josephine	7/18/2011	OBG	Cincinnati PCG, OH
78	Quarshie, Jocelyn	6/12/2010	1.5 OBG	Ebenezer PCG, Bronx, NY
79	Saka-Ntiamoah (Pastor)	12/2007	PL; OBG	CoP-I, Philadelphia, PA
80	Sarpong, Dwomo	11/23/2010	CL; OBG	PCG, NJ, Irvington, NJ
81	Sulemana, Inusah Jonas	11/28/2010	1.5 OBG	PCGNY, Manhattan, NY
82	Sylvesteer	10/31/2010	OBG	Bethel, Chicago, IL
83	Tenkorang, Helena	6/12/2010	1.5 OBG	Ebenezer, Bronx, NY

84	Teye, Dennis	8/14/2010	OBG	Calvary, Columbus, OH
85	Tiwaa	11/12/2010	1.5 OBG	PCGNY, Manhattan, NY
86	Wayoe, Gifty	10/31/2021	LL; OBG	Bethel, Chicago, IL

Target Group Interviews			
#	Group Name	Date of Interview	Status	Venue
1	Ebenezer PCG, Bronx: Target Group YPG	6/12/2010	1.5 OBGs	Youth Meeting Place, Bronx, NY
2	Survey for 1st and 2nd Generations	6/28-7/4, 2010	OBGs; LBGs	Kings Hotel, Yonkers, NY
3	*Asante* Ethnic Association (AEA), Houston, TX.	12/4/2009	Leaders: OBGs	Secretary's Home
4	Calvary PCG, Columbus, OH: Session, Adults, and YPG	8/14/2010	OBGs & LBGs	Calvary PCG Sanctuary
5	PCGNY Session	9/4/2010	OBGs	PCGNY, Harlem
6	Phone Conference Call: PCGNY Youth: Accountant, Medical Doctor, & Lawyer	9/19 & 10/3/2010	LBG, OBG, & 1.5 OBG	Telephone Call Between Portland & NY.

NOTE: During the interview, the interviewees agreed with the researcher to use their full names, first names, or pseudonyms.

CODING KEY: PL = Pastoral Leader
CL = Caretaker Leader
LL = Lay Leader

BIBLIOGRAPHY

"2000 Population and Housing Census." <http://www.ghanaweb.com > (September 9, 2009).

Achampong, Peter. *Christian Values in Adinkra Symbols*. Kumasi, Ghana: University Printing Press, 2004.

Addo, Ebenezer Obiri. *Kwame Nkrumah: A Case Study of Religion and Politics in Ghana*. Oxford: Oxford University Press of America, Inc., 1999.

Adelaja, Sunday. *Life and Death in the Power of the Tongue*. Kiev, Ukraine: Fares Publishing House, 2003.

Adeney, Miriam. "Colorful Initiatives: North American Cultures in Mission." Presentation to the 2010 Evangelical Missiological Society (EMS) North West (NW) Regional meeting at the Multnomah University and Seminary, Portland, OR on March 13, 2010

Adepitan, Funmi. "Raising African Children in America: Why is it Such a Problem?" *African Abroad-USA*, December 14, 2011: 26.

Adogame, Afe. "Betwixt Identity and Security: African New Religious Movements and the Politics of Religious Networking in Europe." *Nova Religion: The Journal of Alternative and Emergent Religions*, 7:2, November, 2003: 21-41.

_____. "The Quest for Space in the Global Spiritual Marketplace: African Religions in Europe." *International Review of Missions*, 89:354, 2000: 400-409.

_____. "Ranks and Robes: Art Symbolism and Identity in the Celestial Church of Christ in the Europian Diaspora." *Material Religion*, 5:1, 2009: 10-13.

_____. "To Be or Not to Be? Politics of Belonging and African Christian Communities in Germany." In *Religion in the Context of African*

Migration, by Afe Adogame and Cordula Weiskoppel, eds., 95-112. Bayreuth: Bayreuth African Studies, 2005.

⎯⎯⎯⎯, ed. *Who is Afraid of the Holy Ghost? Pentecostalism and Globalization in Africa and Beyond*. Trenton: Africa World Press, 2011.

Adogame, Afe, et al., eds. *Christianity in Africa and the African Diaspora: The Appropriation of a Scattered Heritage*. London: Continuum, 2008.

Adogame, Afe and Ezra Chitando. "Moving Among Those Moved by the Spirit: Conducting Fieldwork Within the New African Religious Diaspora." *Fieldwork in Religion*, 1:3, 2005: 253-270.

Adogame, Afe and Cordula Weisskoppel, eds. *Religion in the Context of African Migration*. Bayreuth: Bayreuth African Studies, 2005.

Aghamkar, Atur. "Hindu Diaspora in North America." In *Journal of the Academy for Evangelism in Theological Education*, vol. 22, 2006-2007.

Akinade, Akitunde. "Non-Western Christianity in the Western World: African Immigrant Churches in the Diaspora." In *African Immigrant Religions in America*, by Jacob Olupona and Regina Gemignani, eds. New York, NY: New York University Press, 2007.

⎯⎯⎯⎯, ed. *A New Day: Essays on World Christianity in Honor of Lamin Sanneh*. New York, NY: Peter Lang, 2010.

Alex-Asensoh, Yvette M. "African Immigrants and African-Americans: An Analysis of Voluntary African Immigration and Evolution of Black Ethnic Politics in America." *African and Asian Studies*, 8:1-2, 2009: 89-124.

Allison, Norman E. "The Contributions of Cultural Anthropology to Missiology." In *Missiology and the Social Sciences: Contributions, Cautions, and Conclusions*, by Edward Romen and Gary Corwin, eds. Pasadena, CA: William Carey Library, Evangelical Missiological Society (EMS) Series, no. 4, 1996.

Amegah, S. K. "Pentecost Chalks Successes." <http://thecophq.org/2010maynewscopchalkssuccesses.htm>. (February 13, 2012).

Ammerman, Nancy T., et al., eds. *Studying Congregations: A New Handbook*. Nashville, TN: Abingdon Press, 1998.

Anderson, Alan. *African Reformation: African Initiated Christianity in the Twentieth Century*. Trenton: Africa World Press, 2001.

_____. *An Introduction to Pentecostalism: Global Charismatic Christianity.* Cambridge: Cambridge University Press, 2004.

Ansong, Edward. "Setting the Records Straight: Reaction to the Resolution Presented to the General Assembly of PCG by the CGPCNA." August 2010.

Arthur, J. A. *The African Diaspora in the United States and Europe: The Ghanaian Experience.* Burlington, VT: Ashgate, 2008.

_____. *Invisible Sojourners: African Immigrant Diaspora in the United States.* Westport, CT: Praeger, 2000.

Asamoah, E. L. *The Preacher's Companion: Short Stories with Bibles Quotations for Sermon Preparation.* Accra: Asempa Publishers, 1987.

Asamoah-Gyadu, Kwabena. *African Charismatics: Current Development Within Independent Indigenous Pentecostalism in Ghana.* Leiden, Boston, MA: Brill, 2005.

_____. "An African Pentecostal Mission in Eastern Europe: The Church of the 'Embassy of God' in the Ukraine." *Pneuma,* 27:2, Fall 2005: 297-321.

_____. "'Get on the Internet!' Says the Lord: Religion Cyberspace and Christianity in Contemporary Africa." *Studies in World Christianity,* 13:3, 2007: 225-42.

_____. "Pentecostalism and the Missional Significance of Religious Experience: The Case of Ghana's Church of Pentecost." *Trinity Journal of Church and Theology,* vol. XII, 2002.

Ayandele, E. A. *The Missionary Impact in Modern Nigeria 1884-1914: A Political and Social Analysis.* London: Longmans, 1966.

Barret, David, et al., eds. *World Christian Encyclopedia: A Comparative Survey of Churches and Religions in the Modern World.* 2nd ed. Oxford: Oxford Univeristy Press, vols. 1 & 2, 2001.

Barth, Karl. *The Holy Spirit and the Christian Life: The Theological Basis of Ethics.* Louisville: Westminster/John Knox Press, 1993.

Bauckham, Richard. *Bible and Mission: Christian Witness in a Postmodern World.* Grand Rapids, MI: Baker Academic, 2005.

Becker, Howard S. *Writing for Social Scientists: How to Start and Finish Your Thesis, Book, or Article.* Chicago, IL: Uniiversity of Chicago Press, 2007.

Bediako, Kwame. "Africa and Christianity on the Threshold of the Third Millennium: The Religious Dimension." *African Affairs: The Journal of the Royal African Society*, vol. 99, no. 395, April 2000: 303-323.

_____. *Christianity in Africa: The Renewal of a Non-Western Religion.* Maryknoll, NY: Orbis Books, 1995.

_____. *Jesus and the Gospel: History and Experience.* New York, NY: Orbis Books, 2004.

_____. *Jesus in African Culture: Ghanaian Perspective.* Accra: Asempa Publishers, 1990.

Bediako, Kwame, et al., eds. *A New Day Dawning: African Christians Living the Gospel-Essays in Honor of Dr. J. J. (Hans) Visser.* Zoetermeer: Uitgeverij Boekencentrum, 2004.

Benedict, Ruth. *Patterns of Culture.* Boston, MA: Houghton Mifflin Company, 1989.

Beyer, Peter. *Religion in a Global Society.* London: Routledge, 2006.

Beyer, Peter and Lorie Berman, eds. *Religion, Globalization, and Culture.* Leiden: Brill, 2007.

Biney, Moses O. *From Africa to America: Religion and Adaptation Among Ghanaian Immigrants in New York.* New York, NY: New York University Press, 2011.

_____. *Singing the Lord's Song in a Foreign Land: A Socio-Ethical Study of a Ghanaian Immigrant Church in New York.* A Dissertation Submitted to the Faculty of Princeton Theological Seminary in Partial Fulfillment of the Requirements for the Degree of Doctor of Philosophy. Princeton Theological Seminary, 2005.

_____. "'Singing the Lord's Song in a Foreign Land:' Spirituality, Community, and Identity in a Ghanaian Immigrant Congregation." In *African Immigrant Religions in America*, by Jacob Olupona and Regina Gemignani, eds., 261-278. New York, NY: New York University Press, 2007.

Boamah-Acheampong, Kwabena and Kobina Ofosu-Donkor. "Resolution Presented to the General Assembly of the Presbyterian Church of Ghana by the Conference of Ghanaian Presbyterian Churches in North America." June 2010.

Bosch, David J. *Transforming Mission: Paradigm Shifts in Theology of Mission.* Maryknoll, New York, NY: Orbis Books, 2005.

Brock, Charles. *Indigenous Church Planting: A Practical Journey.* Neosho, MO: Church Growth International, 1994.

Buama, Livingstone. "The Worship Experience of the Reformed Family in Ghana, West Africa: The Cry and Quest for Liturgical Reform." In *Christian Worship in Reformed Churches Past and Present*, by Lukas Vischer, ed., 216-23. Grand Rapids, MI: Eerdmans, 2003.

Bump, Micah. "Ghana: Searching for Opportunities at Home and Abroad." Georgetown: Institute for the Study of International Migration, Georgetown University, 2006. <http/:www.migrationinformation.org> (May 21, 2012).

Burns, James. "'The West is Cold:' Experiences of Ghanaian Performers in England and the United States." In *The New African Diaspora*, by Isidore Okpewho and Nkiru Nzegwu, eds. Bloomington and Indianapolis, IN: Indiana University Press, 2009.

Bush, Luis. *The 4/14 Window: Raising Up a New Generation to Transform the World.* Colorado Springs, CO: Compassion International, 2009.

Buswell III, James O. "Contextualization: Theory, Tradition, and Method." In *Theology of Mission*, by David Hesselgrave, ed., 90. Grand Rapids, MI: Baker Books, 1978.

Caglar, Ayse. "Hometown Associations, the Recalling of State Spatiality and Migrant Grassroots Transnationalism." *Global Networks*, 2006: 1-22.

Calenberg, Rick. "Response to Diversity of the Ghanaian Diapsora in the USA: Ministering to Ghanaian Communities through Ghanaian Congregations." Presentation by Enoch Wan and Yaw Edu-Bekoe, North West Conference of the Evangleical Missiological Society. Multnomah Univeristy and Seminary, Portland, OR: Evangleical Missiological Society of America, 2010.

Cannell, Fanella, ed. *The Anthropology of Christianity.* Durham: Duke University Press, 2006.

Carroll, R., M. Daniel. *Christians at the Border: Immigration, the Church, and the Bible.* Grand Rapids, MI: Baker Academic, 2008.

Casino, Tereso. "Global Diaspora: Basic Framework for Theological Construction." In *Mission Practice in the 21st Century*, by Enoch Wan and Joy Sadiri Tira, eds., 38. Pasadena, CA: William Carey International University Press, 2009.

Chen, Lih-Chenh *Reaching the Chinese Diaspora in Africa: An Ethnography of the Chinese Diaspora in the 21st Century Africa.* Doctor of Missiology Dissertation, Western Seminary, April 2012.

Cho, Yong J. and David Taylor. *From Edinburgh 1910 to Tokyo 2010: Global Mission Consultation & Celebration*. Pasadena, CA: Tokyo 2010 Global Mission Consultation Planning Committee, 2010.

Clark, Chap. *Hurt: Inside the World of Today's Teenagers*. Grand Rapids, MI: Baker Academic, 2004.

Clarke, Clifton R. "African Epistemology and Christian Faith: Towards the Epistemic Use of Orality and Symbolism in African Christian Scholarship." *Journal of African Christian Thought*, vol. 9, no. 1, June 2006: 58.

Clayton, David. *2004 Forum Occasional Papers*, ed., 17-34. Lausanne, Switzerand: Lausanne Committee of World Evangelism, 2005.

Cohen, Robin. *Global Diaspora: An Introduction*. Los Angeles, CA: Universty of California Press, 1997.

Coleman, Simon. *The Globalization of Charismatic Christianity: Spreading the Gospel of Prosperity*. Cambridge: Cambridge University Press, 2000.

Collins, John J. *Between Athens and Jerusalem: Jewish Identity in the Hellenistic Diaspora*. Grand Rapids, MI: William Eerdmans Publishing Company, 2000.

Collins, John N. "Ordained and Other Ministries: Making a Difference." *Ecclessiology*, 3:1, 2006: 17-38.

Commission of the European Communities: Eurostat, Netherlands Interdisciplinary Demographic Institut (NIDI). "Push and Pull Factors Determinning International Migration Flows: Why and Where: Motives and Destination." <http/:www.migrationinformation.org> (May 22, 2012).

Copeland-Carson, Jacqueline. *Creating Africa in America: Translocal Identity in an Emerging World City*. Philadelphia, PA: Philadelphia University Press, 2004.

Corporation of Public Broadcasting. "Enhancing Education: Formal vs. Informal Education." Corporation of Public Broadcasting, 2002: 1, 2.

Costas, Orlando. "Christian Mission in the Americas." In *New Directions in Mission and Evangelization*, by James A. Scherer and Stephen B. Bevans. Maryknoll, NY: Orbis Books, 1994.

Cox, James. "African Identities as the Projection of Western Alterity." In *Uniquely African? African Christian Identity from Cultural and Historical Perspectives*, by James L. Cox and Gerrie ter Haar, eds., 25-37. Trenton: Africa World Press, 2003.

———. *Rational Ancestors: The Scientific Rationality & the African Indigenous Religions*. Cardiff: Cardiff Academic Press, 1998.

Cox James L. and Gerrie ter Haar, eds. *Uniquely African? African Christian Identity from Cultural and Historical Perspectives*. Trenton: Africa World Press, 2003.

Creswell, John W. *Qualitative Inquiry & Research Design: Choosing Among Five Approaches*, 2nd ed. Thousand Oaks: Sage Publications Inc, 2007.

———. *Research Design: Qualitative, Quantitative, and Mixed Methods Approaches*. Los Angeles, CA: Sage Publications Inc., 2009.

Currah, Galen. "14 Activities That Keep Disciples Reproducing and Churches Multiplying, Elements of a Pastoral Mentoring Session for Church Reproductions and 14 Reasons for the Face-to-Face Mentoring of CPM Workers." <http://www.MentorNet.com> June 2009. (August 5, 2010).

———. "Dissertation Word Software." <http://www.currah.info.com> August 2009. (August 5, 2010).

Currah, Galen and George Patterson, "Jesus' Training Methods Illustrated from the Four Gospels." DIS 744: Western Seminary, June 2010.

Danquah, J. B. *Akan Doctrine of God: A Fragment of Gold Coast Ethics and Religion*. London: Cass, 1968.

———. *Gold Coast: Akan Laws and Customs and the Akim Abuakwa Constitution*. London: George Routledge & Sons, Ltd., 1928.

Daswani, Girish. "Transformation and Migration Among Members of a Pentecostal Church in Ghana and London." *Journal of Religion in Africa*, 40:4, 2010: 442-474.

Douglas, J. D. *Let the Earth Hear His Voice*. Minneapolis: World Wide, 1975.

Dovlo, Elom. "African Culture and Emergent Church Forms in Ghana." *Exchange*, 33:1, 2004: 28-53.

Dunn, James D. G. *Jesus' Call to Discipleship*. Cambridge: Cambridge University Press, 1992.

Ebaugh, Helen Rose and Janet Saltzman Chafez, eds. *Religion Accross Borders: Transnational Immigrant Networks*. Walnut Creek: Altamira Press, 2002.

Eck, Diana L. *A New Religious America: How a "Christian Country" Has Become the World's Most Religiously Diverse Nation*. San Francisco, CA: HarperSanFrancisco, 2001.

Edu-Bekoe, Yaw Attah. *Pentecostalism: The Neo-Paradigm of Mission Strategies— Ghanaian Experience*. A thesis submitted to the Faculty of Princeton Theological Seminary for the Th. M Degree, 2006.

Edu-Bekoe, Yaw Attah. "Review of The Next Christendom: The Coming of Global Christianity by Philip Jenkins." *KOINONIA: The Princeton Theological Seminary Graduate Forum*, vol. XX 2008: 113-115.

Edu-Bekoe, Yaw Attah and Enoch Wan. "Ghanaian Diaspora: Diaspora Missions of the Presbyterian Church of Ghana in the USA." In *Diaspora Missiology: Theory, Mehtodology, and Practice*, by Enoch Wan ed., 211-230. Portland, OR: Institute of Diaspora Studies–USA, Western Seminary, 2011.

Emerson, Robert, et al. *Writing Ethnographic Fieldnotes*. Chicago, IL: University of Chicago Press, 1995.

Emerson, Michael and Christian Smith. *Divided by Faith: Evangelical Religion and the Problem of Race in America*. Oxford, NY: Oxford University Press, 2000.

Engelke, Matthew. "Discontinuity and the Discourse of Conversion." *The Journal of Christian Religion in Africa*, 34:1-2, 2004.

———. "Past Pentecostalism: Notes on Rapture, Realignment, and Everyday Life in Pentecostal and African Churches." *Africa: The Journal of the International African Institute*, 80:2, 2010: 177-199.

———. *A Problem of Presence: Beyond Scripture in an African Church*. Berkeley, CA: University of California Press, 2007.

Englund, Harri and James Leach. "Ethnography and the Meta-Narratives of Modernity." *Current Anthropology*, 41:2, 2000: 225-239.

Essamuah, Casely B. *Genuinely Ghanaian: A History of the Methodist Church Ghana, 1961-2000*. Trenton, NJ: Africa World Press, Inc., 2010.

Evangelical Lutheran Church in America (ELCA). < http://www.elca.org/Who-We-Are/Our-Three-Expressions/Churchwide-Organization/Global-Mission/Engage-in-Global-Mission/Global-Events/Glocal-Mission-Gathering.aspx> (October 1, 2010).

Featherstone, M., et al. eds. *Global Modernities*. London: Sage Publications, 1995.

Fellmann, J., et al. *Human Geography: Landscape of Human Activities*. Calgary, Alberta: Wm C. Brown Publishers, 1993.

Fernandez-Kelly, P and R. Schauffler. "Divided Fates: Immigrant Children in Restructured U.S. Economy." *International Migration Review*, 28:4, 1994: 662-689.

Fisher, Robert B. *West African Religious Traditions: Focus on the Akan of Ghana.* Maryknoll, NY: Orbis Books, 1998.

Foley, Michael and Dean R. Hoge. *Religion and the New Immigrants: How Faith Communities Form our Newest Citizens.* Oxford: Oxford University Press, 2007.

Foner, Nancy and Richard Alba. "Immigrant Religion in the U.S. and Western Europe: Bridge or Barrier?" *International Migration Review*, 42:2, 2008.

Garrett, Robert. "The Gospel and Acts: Jesus the Missionary and His Missionary Followers." In *Missiology: An Introduction to the Foundations, History, and Strategies of World Missions*, by John Mark Terry et al., 60-82. Nashville, TN: Broadman & Holman Publishers, 1998.

Garrison, David. *Church Planting Movements.* Arkadelphia, AR: WIGTake Resources, 2004.

Gemignani, Regina. "Gender, Identity, and Power in African Immigrant Evangelical Churches." In *African Immigrant Religions in America*, by Jacob K. Olupona and Regina Gemignani, eds., 133-157. New York, NY: New York University Press, 2007.

George, Lisa La. "'Kids These Days!' Generational Issues in Mission Mobilization." In *Reflecting God's Glory Together: Diversity in Evangelical Mission*, by Scott A. Moreau and Beth Snodderly, 91-102. Pasadena, CA: William Carey Library, 2011.

Gerloff, Roswith. "'Africa as Laboratory of the World:' The African Christian Diaspora in Europe as Challenge to Mission and Ecumenical Relations." In *Mission Is Crossing Frontiers: Essays in Honour of Bongani A. Mazibuko*, by Roswith Gerloff, ed., 343-381. Pietermaritzburg: Cluster Publications, 2003.

Getui, Mary. *Theological Method & Aspects of Worship in African Christianity.* Nairobi, Kenya: Acton Publishers, 1998.

Ghana News Agency (GNA). "U.S. Embassy Opens DV Lottery." <www.ghanaweb.com>. (October 21, 2009).

Gifford, Paul. "The Bible in Africa: A Novel Usage in Africa's New Churches." *Bulletin of the School of Oriental and African Studies*, 71:2, 2008: 203-259.

———. *Ghana's New Christianity: Pentecostalism in a Globalizing African Economy.* Bloomington & Indianapolis, IN: Indiana University Press, 2004.

Gill, David W. J and Conrad Gempf. *The Book of Acts in the First Century Setting, Volume 2: Graeco-Roman Setting.* Grand Rapids, MI: William B. Eerdmans Publishing Company, 1994.

Glocal Christianity. "The Theology of Multi-Ethnic Church/ Missional Theology and Glocal Christianity" <http://www.mattstone.blogs.com/Christian/glocal>. (March 5, 2012)

Glover, Ablade. "Adinkra Symbolism." Artists Alliance Gallery, Omanye House, Accra. *Adinkra Symbolism.* Accra: Artista, 1992.

Gornik, Mark R. *Word Made Global: African Christianity in the New York City.* A Thesis Submitted to the University of Edinburgh for the Degree of Doctor of Philosophy, Edinburgh: Centre for the Study of Christianity in the Non-Western World School of Divinity, New College, 2008.

_____. *Word Made Global: Stories of African Christianity in New York City.* Grand Rapids, MI: Eerdmans , 2011.

Grieco, E. M. and E. N. Trevelyan. "Place of Birth of the Foreign-Born Population: 2009." *American Community Survey Briefs* and ACS 2010 <www.http://factfinder2.census.gov>. (October 13, 2011).

Gruen, Erich S. *Diaspora: Jews Amidst Greeks and Romans.* Cambridge, MA: Harvard University, 2002.

Grunlan, Stephen A. and Marvin K. Mayers. *Cultural Anthropology: A Christian Perspective,* 2nd ed. Grand Rapids, MI: Zondervan Publishing House, 1988.

Gyekye, Kwame. *African Cultural Values: An Introduction.* Philadelphia, PA: Sankofa Publication Co., 1996.

Hagan, Jacqueline and Helen R. Ebaugh. "Calling Upon the Sacred: Migrants' Use of Religion in the Migration Process." *International Migration Review,* 37:4, 2003: 1145-1162.

Haller, W. and P. Landolt. "The Transnatinal Dimension of Identity Formulation: Adult Children of Immigrants in Miami." *Ethnic and Racial Studies,* 28:6, 2005: 1182-1214.

Hanciles, Jehu. *Beyond Christendom: Globalization, African Migration, and the Transformation of the West.* Maryknoll, NY: Orbis Books, 2008.

_____. "God's Mission Through Migration: African Initiatives in Globalizing Mission." In *Evangelical, Ecumenical, and Anabaptist Missiologies in Conversation: Essays in Honor of Wilbert R. Shenk,* by James R. Krabill, et al., eds., 58-66. Maryknoll, NY: Orbis, 2006.

_____. "Migration and Mission: Some Implications for the Twenty-first-century Church." *International Bulletin of Missionary Research*, 32:3, October 2003: 146-153.

_____. "Migration, Diaspora Communities, and the New Missionary Encounter with Western Society." *Lausanne World Pulse*, September 5, 1990. <http/www.lausannepulse.com/themedarticle> (September 25, 2009).

Hastings, Adrain. *African Christianity*. New York, NY: Seabury Press, 1976.

Hawthorne, Stephen B. *Perspectives on the World Christian Movement: A Study Guide*. Pasadena, CA: William Carey Library, 2009.

Hefferman, Margaret. *Managing Generational Differences in the Workplace*. 2005. <http://www.fastcompany.com/resources/talent/hefferman/managing-generational-differences> (October 24, 2011).

Heimbeger, James. *"Your Church Can Change the World:" A Simple, Self-Teaching Curriculum that Contains the Information, Resources, Tools and Teaching Activities to Establish an Effective Missions Program in the Cooperation of Mexico*. Mexico, COMMEX: The Department of Missions Education, the Missionary Cooperation, 2003.

Hesselgrave, David J. *Planting Churches Cross-Culturally: North America and Beyond*, 2nd ed. Grand Rapids, MI: Baker Books, 2000.

_____, ed. *Theology and Mission*. Grand Rapids, MI: Baker Books, ed., 1978.

Herppich, Birgit. "Immigration Communities in America—Objects of Mission or Missional Agents? The Case of the Church of Pentecost (Ghana) in Urban America." Presentation, 2011 NAMLC, Scottsdale, AZ, September 29-October 01, 2011

Hicks, W. Bryant. "Old Testament Foundations for Mission." In *Missiology: An Introduction to the Foundations, History, and Strategies of World Missions*, by John Mark Terry, et al., eds., 51-62. Nashville, TE: Broadman & Holman Publishers, 1998.

Hiebert, Paul G. *Missiological Implications of Epistemological Shifts: Affirming Truth in a Modern/Postmodern World*. Harrisburg, PA: Trinity Press International, 1979.

Hiebert, Paul G., et al. *Understanding Folk Religion: A Christian Response to Popular Beliefs and Practices*. Grand Rapids: Baker, 1999.

Horton, Robin. "African Conversion." *Africa*, 41:2, 1971: 85-102; 91-112.

_____. "On Rationality of Conversion, Part I." *Africa*, 45:3, 1975: 91-112.

_____. "On Rationality of Conversion, Part II." *Africa*, 45:4, 1975.

Houston, Tom, et al., eds. *Handbook: From Edinburgh 1910 to Tokyo 2010*. Tokyo: Tokyo 2010 Organizing Committee, 2010.

Houston, Tom, et al. "The New People Next Door: Lausanne Occassional Paper No. 55." In 2004 Forum Occasional Papers, by David Clayton, ed., 17-34. Lausanne, Switzerand: Lausanne Committee of World Evangelism, 2005.

Hoyt, Chris. "Going Glocal: A Conversation with Chris Hoyt, PepsiCo Talent Engagement...Leader." <http://monsterthinking.com/2010/10/28/recruitfest-glocal>. Video recording. RecruitFest, Fall 2010. (October 1, 2010).

Hunt, Stephen. "'A Church for All Nations:' The Redeemed Christian Church of God." *Pneuma*, 24:2, 2002: 185-204.

———. "'Neither Here nor There:' The Construction of Identities and Boundaries Maintenance of West African Pentecostals." *Sociology*, 36:1, 2002: 147-169.

Isajiw, W. W, and R Makabe. *Socialization as a Factor of Ethnic Identity Retention*. Toronto: Center for Urban and Community Studies, 1982.

Jenkins, Philip. *God's Continent: Christianity, Islam, and Europe's Religious Crisis*. Oxford: Oxford University Press, 2007.

———. *The New Faces of Christianity: Believing the Bible in the Global South*. Oxford: Oxford University Press, 2006.

———. *The Next Christendom: The Coming of Global Christianity*. Oxford: Oxford University Press, 2005.

———. "The Next Christianity." *Atlantic Monthly*, 290:3, October, 2002: 53-68.

Johnson, Todd M. "The Global Demographics of Pentecostal and Charismatic Renewal." *Society*, 46:6, 2009: 479-483.

Johnson, Todd and Sandra Kim. *The Changing Demographics of World Christainity, World Christian Database*. 2006. <http://www.worldchristiandatabase.org> (March 05, 2006).

Johnstone, Patrick. *Operation World*. Minneapolis, MIN: Bethany House, WEC International, 2001.

Juergensmeyer, Mark, ed. *Global Religions: An Introduction*. Oxford: Oxford University Press, 2003.

Kalu, Ogbu, ed. *African Christianity: An African Story*. Trenton, NJ: Africa World Press, 2007.

―――――. *African Pentecostalism: An Introduction.* New York, NY: Oxford University Press, 2008.

Karkkainen, Veli-Matti, ed. *The Spirit in the World: Emerging Pentecostal Theologies in Global Contexts.* Grand Rapids, MI: Eerdmans, 2009.

Kasinitz, Philip, "Identity." In *Becoming New Yorkers: Ethnographies of the Second Generation,* by Philip Kasinitz, et al., eds., 281-287. New York, NY: Russell Sage Foundation, 2004.

Kasinitz, Philip et al., eds. *Becoming New Yorkers: Ethnographies of the Second Generation.* New York, NY: Russell Sage Foundation, 2004.

―――――, et al. *Inheriting the City: The Children of Immigrants Come of Age.* New York, NY: Russell Sage Foundation: Harvard University Press, 2008.

―――――. "Worlds of Second Generation." In *Becoming New Yorkers: Ethnographies of the Second Generation,* by Philip Kasinitz et al., eds., 1-19. New York, NY: Russell Sage Foundation, 2004.

Kato, Byang. "The Gospel, Cultural Context, and Religious Syncretism." In *Let the Earth Hear His Voice,* by J. D. Douglas, 1217. Minneapolis, MN: World Wide, 1975.

Katongole, Emmanuel. *A Future for Africa: Critical Essays in Social Imagination.* Scranton, PA: Scranton University Press, 2005.

―――――. "Review of Whose Religion Is Christianity? The Gospel Beyond the West by Lamin Sanneh." *Pro Ecclesia,* 15:1, 2006: 141-145.

―――――. "A Tale of Many Stories." In *Shaping a Global Theological Mind,* by Darren C. Marks, 89-93. Aldershot: Ashgate, 2008.

Kohls, Robert L & Herbert L. Brussow. *Training Know-How for Cross-Cultural and Diversity Trainers.* Duncanville, TX: Adult Learning System, 1995.

Komolafe, Sunday Babajide. "The Changing Face of Christianity: Revising African Christianity." *Missiology: An International Review,* 32:4, 2004: 217-238.

Koning, Danielle. "Place, Space, and Authority: The Mission and Reverse Mission of the Ghanaian Seventh-Day Adventist Church in Amsterdam." *African Diaspora,* 2:2, 2009: 203-226.

Krabil, James R., ed. *Mission from the Margins: Selected Writings from the Life and Ministry of David A. Shank.* Elkhart: Institute for Mennonite Studies, 2010.

Kraft, Charles. *Christianity in Culture: A Study in Dynamic Biblical Theologizing in Cross-Cultural Perspective.* Mayknoll, NY: Orbis Books, 1979.

Krause, Kristine. "Transnational Therapy Networks Among Ghanaians in London." *Journal of Ethnic and Migration Studies*, 34:2, 2008: 235-241.

Kuffour, John Agyekum. Former President of Ghana. "Foreign Remittances to Ghana's Economy. <http://www.ghanaweb.com>. (September 15, 2007).

Kumekpor, Tom K. *Research Methods & Techniques of Social Science Research*. Accra, Ghana: SonLife & Services, 2002.

Kwast, Lloyd E. "Understanding Culture." In *Perspectives on the World Chrisitan Movement: A Reader*, by Ralph D. Winter and Steven C. Hawthorne, eds., 397-399. Pasadena, CA: William Carey Library, 2009.

Kysar, Robert. *Stumbling in the Light: New Testament Images for a Changing Church*. St. Louis, MS: Chalice Press, 1999.

Landis, Dan & Rabi S. Baghat, eds. *Handbook for Intercultural Training*. London: Sage Publication, 1996.

Larbi, Kingsley. "The Nature of Continuity and Discontinuity of Ghanaian Penetecostal Concept of Salvation in African Cosmology." *Cyber Journal of Pentecostal-Charismatic Research: African Cosmology*, 2008: 4.

_____. *Pentecostalism: Eddies of Ghanaian Christianity*. Accra: Centre for Pentecostal and Charismatic Studies, 2002.

Lausanne Committee for World Evangelization, (LCWE). *Scattered to Gather: Embracing the Global Trend of Diaspora*. Manila, Philippines: LifeChange Publishing Inc., 2010.

Lauterbach, Karen. "Becoming a Pastor: Youth and Social Aspirations in Ghana." *Young: Nordic Journal of Youth Research*, 18:3, 2010: 259-278.

Leonard, Karen, et al., eds. *Immigrant Faiths: Transforming Religious Life in America*. Lanham, MD: AltaMira, 2005.

Leviskaya, Irina. *The Book of Acts in its First Century Setting: Diaspora Setting*. Grand Rapids, MI: Eerdmans, 1996.

Levitt, Peggy. *God Needs No Passport: Immigrants and the Changing American Religious Landscape*. New York, NY: The New York Press, 2007.

_____. "Redefining Boundaries of Belonging: The Institutional Character of Transnational Religious Life." *Sociology of Religion*, 65:1, 2004: 1-18.

_____. "Roots and Routes: Understanding the Lives of Second Generation Transnationally." *Journal of Ethnic and Migration Studies*, 37:7, 2009: 1225-1242.

———. "Transnational Migration: Taking Stock and Future Directions." *Global Networks*, 1:3, 2001: 195-216.

Levitt, Peggy and Nadya B. Jarworsky. "Transnational Migration Studies: Past Developments and Future Trends." *Annual Review of Sociology*, 33, 2007: 129-156.

Lewis, Donald M. *Christianity Reborn: The Global Expansion of Evanglicalism in the Twentieth Century*. Grand Rapids, MI: Eerdmans, 2004.

Ley, David. "The Immigrant Church as an Urban Social Service Hub." *Urban Studies*, 45:10, 2008: 2057-2074.

Lingenfelter, Sherwood G. *Leading Cross-Culturally: Covenant Relationships for Effctive Christian Leadership*. Grand Rapids, MI: Baker Academic, 2008.

Lingenfelter, Sherwood G. and Marvin Mayers. *Ministering Cross-Culturally: An Incarnational Model for Personal Relationship*. Grand Rapids, MI: Baker Academic, 2003.

Loba-Mkole, Jean-Claude. "Bible Translation and Inculturation Hermeneutics." In *Biblical Texts and African Audiences*, by Ernst R.Wendland and Jean-Claude Loba-Mkole, 37-58. Nairobi, Kenya: Acton Publishers, 2004.

Lundy, David. *Borderless Church*. Authentic, 2006.

Magesa, Laurenti. *Anatomy of Inculturation: Transforming the Church in Africa*. Maryknoll, NY: Orbis Books, 2004.

Malphurs, Aubrey. *Planting Growing Churches for the 21st Century*, 3rd ed. Grand Rapids, MI: Baker Books, 2004.

Marfo, Tom. "Pastor to Migrants in Dutch Society." In *A New Day Dawning: African Christians Living the Gospel — Essays in Honor of Dr. J. J. (Hans) Visser*, by Kwame Bediako, et al., eds, 157. Zoetermeer: Uitgeverij Boekencentrum, 2004.

Marks, Darren C. *Shaping a Global Theological Mind*. Aldershot: Ashgate, 2008.

Martin, David. *Pentecostalism: The World Their Parish*. Oxford: Blackwell, 2002.

Martin, George. "Missions in the Pauline Epistles." In *Missiology: An Introduction to the Foundations, History, and Strategies of World Missions*, by John Mark Terry, et al., eds., 83-96. Nashville, TE: Broadman & Holman Pulbishers, 1998.

Mbiti, John S. *African Religions and Philosophy*. New York, NY: Praeger, 1969.

———. *Bible and Theology in African Christianity*. Oxford: Oxford University Press, 1986.

McCabe, Kristin. "African Immigrants in the United States." Migration Policy Institute (MPI), 2011. <http/:www.migrationinformation.org> (May 22, 2012).

McCurdy, David W., et al. *The Cultural Experience: Ethnography in Complex Society*. Long Grove, IL: Waveland Press Inc., 2005.

McDoughall, Debra. "Rethinking Christianity and Anthropology: A Review Article." *Anthropological Forum*, 19:2, 2009: 185-194.

McGavran, Donald A. *Understanding Church Growth*. 3rd ed., Grand Rapids, MI: William B. Eerdmans Publishing Co, 1990.

McLean, Janice A. *Living the Faith: Identity and Mission Among West Indian Immigrants in Pentecostal Churches in New York and London*. PhD Dissertation, University of Edinburgh, 2009.

Meyer, Birgit. "Christianity in Africa: From Independent to Pentecostal-Charismatic Churches." *Annual Review of Anthropology*, 33, 2004: 447-474.

⸻. "Commodities and the Power of Prayer: Pentecostalist Attitudes Towards Consumption in Contemporary Ghana." *Development and Change*, 29:4, 1988: 751-776.

⸻. "Impossible Representations: Pentecostalism, Vision, and Video Technology in Ghana." In *Religion, Media and the Public Sphere*, by Birgit Meyer and Annelies Moors, eds., 290-312. Bloomington, IN: Indiana University Press, 2006.

⸻. "'Make a Complete Break with the Past:' Memory and Post-Colonial Modernity in Ghanaian Pentecostalist Discourse." *Journal of Religion in Africa*, 28:3, 1998: 316-346.

Meyer Birgit and Annelies Moors, eds. *Media and the Public Sphere*. Bloomington, IN: Indiana University Press, 2006.

Miller, Linda J. and Chad W Hall. *Coaching for Christian Leaders: A Practical Guide*. St. Louis, MS: Chalice Press, 2007.

Moltmann, Jurgen. "Preface." In *The Spirit in the World: Emerging Pentecostal Theologies in Global Contexts*, by Veli-Mati Karkkainen, ed., viii-xii. Grand Rapids, MI: Eerdmans, 2009.

Moreau, Scott A., et al. *Introducing World Missions: A Biblical, Historical, and Practical Survey*. Grand Rapids, MI: Baker, 2004.

Moreau, Scott A. and Beth Snodderly, eds. *Reflecting God's Glory Together: Diversity of Evangelical Mission*. Pasadena, CA: William Carey Library, Evangelical Missiological Society (EMS) Series, no. 19, 2011.

Mueller, Walt. *Engaging the Soul of Youth Culture: Bridging Teen Worldviews and Christian Truth.* Downers Groove, IL: IVP Books, InterVarsity Press, 2006.

―――――. *Youth Culture 101.* Grand Rapids, MI: Zondervan, 2007.

Mugambi, J. N. K., ed. *The Church and Reconstruction of Africa: Theological Considerations.* Nairobi: All African Conference of Churches, 1977.

Murray, Stuart. *Church Planting: Laying Foundations.* London: Paternoster Press, 1998.

Mwuara, Philomena Njeri. "Integrity of Mission in the Light of the Gospel: Bearing Witness of the Spirit Among Africa's Gospel Bearers." *Exchange,* 35:2, 2006: 169-190.

Nanlai, C. "The Church as Surrogate Family for Working Class Immigrant Chinese Youth: An Ethnography of Segmented Assimilation." *Sociology of Religion,* 66:2: 183-200.

Neumann, Mikel. *Home Groups for Urban Cultures.* Pasadena, CA: William Carey Library Publishers and Distribution, 1999.

Newbigin, Lesslie. *Foolishness to the Greeks: The Gospel and Western Culture.* Grand Rapids, MI: Eerdmans, 1986.

Newell, Marvin J. *Commissioned: What Jesus Wants You to Know as You Go.* ChurchSmart Resources, 2010.

Nicholls, Bruce. *Contextualization: A Theology of Gospel and Culture.* Downers Grove, IL: InterVarsity Press, 1979.

Oduro, Thomas, et al. *Mission in an African Way: A Practical Introduction to African Instituted Churches and Their Sense of Mission.* Nairobi, Kenya: Christian Literature Fund and Bible Media, 2008.

Oduyoye, Mercy Amba. *Beads and Strands: Reflections of an African Woman on Christianity in Africa.* Maryknoll, NY: Orbis, 2004.

―――――. *Daughters of Anowa: African Women and Patriarchy.* Maryknoll, NY: Orbis Books, 1995.

Ogden, Greg. *Tranforming Discipleship: Making Disciples a Few at a Time.* Chicago, IL: Intervarsity Press, 2003.

Ojo, Matthews. "African Charismatics." In *Encyclopedia of African and African-American Religion,* by Stephen Glazier, ed., 2-6. New York, NY: Routledge, 2001.

Okorocha, Cyril C. *The Meaning of Religious Conversion: The Case of the Igbo of Nigeria.* Aldershot, Brookfield: Avebury, 1987.

Okure, Teresa. "Africa: Globalization and Loss of Cultural Identity." *Concillium*, 5, 2001: 67-74.

Olupona, Jacob K. "African Religion." In *Global Religions: An Introduction*, by Mark Juergensmeyer ed., 78-86. Oxford: Oxford University Press, 2003.

_____. "Globalization and African Immigrant Religious Communitties." In *Religion and Global Culture*, by Jennifer I. M. Reid, ed., 83-96. Lahman, MD: Lexington Books, 2003.

Olupona, Jacob and Regina Gemignani, eds. *African Immigrant Religions in America*. New York, NY: New York University Press, 2007.

Omenyo, Cephas. "Charismatic Churches in Ghana and Contextualization." *Exchange*, 2002: 253, 254.

Onyinah, Opoku. "Pentecostalism and the African Diaspora: An Examination of the Missions Activities of the Church of Pentecost." *Pneuma*, 26:2, Fall 2004: 216-241.

Operation World 2010 <www.operationworld2010.org>. (September 30, 2011).

Opoku, Kofi Asare. *West African Traditional Religion*. Accra: FEP International Private Limited, 1978.

Ott, Stanley E. *Joy of Discipling: Friend With Friend, Heart With Heart*. Grand Rapids, MI: Zondervan Publishing House, 2004.

_____. *Vital Churches Institute*. 2004.

Otto, Martin. *Church on the Oceans*. UK: Piquant, 2007.

Owusu, Berko Akoto. "Genuine Ministries or Just Money Making Ploys?" *Chicago African Spectrum*, col. 12, Issue 4, July 2010, 3.

Owusu, Thomas Y. "The Role of Ghanaian Immigrant in Toronto, Canada." *International Migration Review*, 34:4, Winter 2000.

Paige, R. Michael. *Education for the Intercultural Exeprience*. Yarmouth, ME: Intercultural Press, 1993.

Pantoja, Luis, et al. *Scattered: The Filipino Global Presence*. Manila, Philippines: LifeChange Publishing Inc, 2004.

Park, Robert E. and Ernest W. Burgess. *Introduction to the Science of Sociology*. Chicago, IL: University of Chicago Press, 1969.

Patterson, George & Richard Scoggins. *Church Multiplication Guide: Helping Churches to Reproduce Locally and Abroad*. Pasadena, CA: William Carey Library, 1993.

Patterson, George, et al., "We Started Small Groups, But They Didn't Multiply. So Now What?" <www.MentorNet.ws>, # 70. (August 25, 2010)

Payne, Jervis D. *Discovering Church Planting: An Introduction to the Whats, Whys, and Hows of Global Church Planting.* Colorado Springs, CO: Paternoster Press, 2009.

Peil, Margaret. "Ghanaians Abroad." In *African Affairs*, 34, 376: 359.

Peterson, Derek R. "Review of African Christianity: An African Story," edited by Ogbu U. Kalu. *Journal of Ecclesiastical History*, 57:1, 2006: 87-89.

Phan, Peter. "A New Christianity, But What Kind?" *Mission Studies*, 2005: 59-83.

Plueddemann, James. *Leading Across Cultures: Effective Ministry and Mission in the Global Church.* Downers Grove, IL: IVP Academic, InterVarsity Press, 2009.

Pobee, John S. *West Africa: Christ Will Be a West African Too.* Geneva: World Council of Churches Publications, 1996.

Portes, Alejandro and Ruben G. Rambaut. *Legacies: The Story of the Immigrant Second Generation.* Berkeley, CA: University of California Press, 2001.

Presbyterian Church of Ghanan Bible Study and Prayer Group. *Discipleship Training Material.* National Evangelism Committee, 2001.

Reid, Jennifer I. M., ed. *Religion and Global Culture.* Lahman, MD: Lexington Books, 2003.

Rice, Andrew. "Mission From Africa." *New York Times Magazine*, April 12, 2009: 30-37; 54-58.

Robbins, Joel. "The Globalization of Pentecostal and Charismatic Christianity." *Annual Review of Anthropology*, 33, 2004: 117-143.

_____. "Pentecostal Networks and the Spirit of Globalization: On the Social Production of Ritual Forms." *Social Analysis*, 53:1, 2009: 55-66.

Roberts Jr., Bob. "Glocal Church Ministry." In *Christianity Today*, January 2010. <http://www.christianity today.com/ct/2007/July/30.42html> (October 1, 2011)

_____. *Transformation: How Glocal Churches Transform Lives and the World.* January 17, 2006. <http://www.amazon.com/Transformation-Glocal Churches-Transform-Lives> (October 1, 2011).

Roberts, Sam. "More Africans Enter U.S. Than in the Days of Slavery." *New York Times*, February 21, 2005: A-1, B-4.

Robertson, Roland. "Glocalization: Time-Space and Homogeneity-Heterogeneity." In M. Featherstone et al. eds., *Global Modernities*. London: Sage Publications, 1995, 27-44.

Robinson, Russell D. *An Introduction to Helping Adults Learn and Change*. West Bend, WI: Omnibook Company, 1994.

Rojas, Ronald R. *Collabrative Leadership: Moving Towards Relational Paradigms in Lay Ministry Development*. Bloomington, IN: 1st Books, 2004.

Rommen, Edward and Gary Corwin, eds. *Missiology and the Social Sciences: Contributions, Cautions, and Conclusions*. Evangelical Missiological Series, No. 4. Pasadena, CA: William Carey Library, 1996.

Roof, Wade Clark. *Spiritual Market Place*. Princeton, NJ: Princeton University Press, 2001.

Rubesh, Ted. "Diaspora Distinctives: The Jewish Diaspora Experience in the Old Testament." In Enoch Wan, ed., *Diaspora Missiology: Theory, Methodology, and Practice*. Portland, OR: Institute of Diaspora Studies—USA, Western Seminary, (2011), 39-72.

Rumbaut, R. G. "Assimilation and its Discontents: Between Rhetoric and Reality." *International Migration Review*, 31:4, 1997: 923-960.

Sanneh, Lamin. *Disciples of All Nations: Pillars of World Christianity*. Oxford: Oxford University Press, 2008.

_____."The Horizontal and the Vertical in Mission: An African Perspetive." *International Bulletin of Missionary Research*, no. 4, October, 1983: 167.

_____. *Translating the Message: The Missionary Impact on Culture*. Maryknoll, NY: Orbis Books, 1989.

_____. *Whose Religion is Christianity? The Gospel Beyond the West*. Grand Rapids, MI: Eerdmans, 2003.

Sanneh, Lamin and Joel Carpenter, eds. *The Changing Face of Christianity: Africa, the West, and the World*. Oxford: Oxford University Press, 2005.

Santos, Narry F. "Survey of the Diaspora Occurrences in the Bible and of their Contexts in Christian Missions." In *Scattered: The Filipino Global Presence*, by Luis Pantoja, et al., 53-66. Manila, Philippines: LifeChange Publishing Inc, 2004.

Sarpong, Peter Akwasi. *Ghana in Retrospect: Some Aspects of Ghanaian Culture*. Tema, Ghana: Ghana Publishing Company, 1974.

Sassen, Saskia. *Globalization and Its Discontents: Essays on the New Mobility of People and Money*. New York, NY: The New Press, 1998.

———. "Regulating Immigration in a Global Age: A New Policy Landscape." *Parallax*, 11:1, 2005: 35-45.

Scharen, Christian Batalden. "'Judicious Narratives,' or Ethnography as Ecclesiology." *Scottish Journal of Theology*, 58:2, 2005: 125-142.

Scherer, James A. and Stephen B. Bevans. *New Directions in Mission and Evangelization*. Maryknoll, NY: Orbis Books, 1994.

Schwandt, Thomas A. *The Sage Dictionary of Qualitative Inquiry*. Los Angeles, CA: Sage Publications, 2007.

Scott, A. O. "Stories from a World in Motion." *New York Times*, March 16, 2008: A-1, 16.

Senior, Donald and Carroll Stuhlmueller. *The Biblical Foundations of Mission*. Maryknoll, NY: Orbis Books, 1983.

Shank, David A. "What Western Christians Can Learn From African-Initiated Churches." In *Mission from the Margins: Selected Writings from the Life and Ministry of David A. Shank*, by James R. Krabil, ed., 219-230. Elkhart: Institute for Mennonite Studies, 2010.

Shenk, Wilbert R. "New Wineskins for New Wine: Toward a Post-Christendom Ecclesiology." *International Bulletin of Missionary Research*, 29:2, 2005: 73-79.

———. "Recasting Theology of Mission: Impulses from the Non-Western World." *International Bulletin of Missionary Research*, 25:3, 2001: 98-107.

Shipman, Brian. *WWJD Today? Daily Times With Jesus: A Devotional*. Nashville, TE: Broadman & Holman Publishers, 1998.

Smith, Christian and Melinda Lundquist Denton. *Soul Searching: The Religious and Spiritual Lives of American Teenagers*. New York, NY: Oxford University Press, 2005.

Smith, Donald. *Creating Understanding: A Handbook for Christian Communication Across Cultural Landscapes*. Grand Rapids, MI: Zondervan Publishing House, 1992.

Smith, James K. A. *Desiring the Kingdom: Worship, Worldview, and Cultural Formation*. Grand Rapids, MI: Baker Books, 2009.

Smith, Noel. *Presbyterian Church of Ghana, 1835-1960: A Younger Church in a Changing Society*. Accra: Ghana Universities Press, 1966.

Snyder, Robert Charles. *Akan Rites of Passage and Their Reception Into Christianity*. New York: NY: Lang, 2003.

Soothill, Jane E. *Gender, Social Change, and Spiritual Power: Charismatic Christianity in Ghana*. Leiden: Brill, 2007.

Spradley, James P. *The Ethnographic Interview*. Belmont, CA: Wadsworth Cengage Learning, 1979.

Stamps, Donald D. *The Full Life Study Bible (New International Version-NIV)*. Colorado Springs, CO: International Bible Society, 1978.

Stanley, Paul P. and Robert Clinton. *Connecting: The Mentoring Relationships You Need to Succeed in Life*. Colorado Springs, CO: NavPress, 1992.

Stark, Rodney. *The Rise of Christianity: A Sociologist Reconsiders Christianity*. Princeton, NJ: Princeton University Press, 1996.

Stevens, W. David. "Spreading the Word: Religious Beliefs and the Evolution of Immigrant Congregations." *Sociology of Religion*, 65:2, 2004: 121-138.

_____. "'Taking the World: Evangelism and Assimilation Among Ghanaian Pentecostals in Chicago." PhD Thesis, Northwestern University, 2003.

Stinton, Diane B. *Jesus of Africa: Voices of Contemporary African Christology*. Maryknoll, NY: Orbis, 2004.

Stone, Matt. "The Theology of Multi-Ethnic Church/ Missional Theology and Glocal Christianity," June 23, 2010. <http://mattstone.blogs.com/Christian/glocal> (October 1, 2011).

_____. "What is Glocal Christianity?" June 27, 2010 <http://mattstone.blogs.com; http://www.ldoceonline.com/dictionary/glocal> (October 1, 2010).

Strang, Cameron, "Christian Cool and the New Generation Gap." *New York Times*, May 16, 2005. <http/www.nytimes.com/weekinreview> (October 24, 2011).

Strom, Adam. *Stories of Identity: Religion, Migration, and Belonging in a Changing World*. Brookline, MA: Facing History and Ourselves Foundation Inc., 2008.

Stroman, John A. *Ashes to Ascension: Second Lessons Sermons for Lent/Easter*. Lima, OH: CSS Publishing Company, Inc, 1999.

Suarez-Orozco, Carola and Marcelo Suarez-Orozco. *Children of Immigration*. Cambridge, MA: Harvard University Press, 2001.

Sundkler, Bengt. *Bantu Prophets in South Africa*. London: Lutterworth Press, 1948.

Sweet, Leonard. *Aqua Church: Essential Leadership Arts for Piloting Your Church in Today's Fluid Culture*. Loveland, CO: Colorado Group Publishers, 1999.

Taylor, Charles. *A Secular Age*. Cambridge, MA: Havard University Press, 2007.

Taylor, Mark C. *After God*. Chicago, IL: Chicago University Press, 2007.

———. *Confidence Games: Money and Markets in a World Without Redemption*. Chicago, IL: Chicago University Press, 2004.

———. *The Moment of Complexity: Emerging Network Culture*. Chicago, IL: Chicago University Press, 2001.

Taylor, Peter J. *World City Network: A Global Urban Analysis*. London: Routledge, 2004.

Ter Haar, Gerie. "African Diaspora in Europe." In *Religious Communities in the Diaspora*, by Gerie ter Haar. Nairobi: Acton Publishers, 1998.

———. *Halfway to Paradise: African Christians in Europe*. Cardiff: Cardiff Academic Press, 1998.

———. *How God Became an African: African Spirituality and Western Thought*. Philadelphia, PA: University of Pennsylvania Press, 2009.

———. *Religious Communities in the Diaspora*. Nairobi: Acton Publishers, 2001.

———. "Strangers in the Promised Land: African Christians in Europe." *Exchange*, 24:1, 1995: 1-33.

Terry, John Mark, et al. *Missiology: An Introduction to the Foundations, History, and Strategies of World Missions*. Nashville, TN: Broadman & Holman Publishers, 1998.

Tettey, Wisdom J. "Transnationalism, Religion, and the African Diaspora in Canada: An Examination of Ghanaian Churches." In *African Immigrant Religions in America*, by Jacob K. Olupona and Regina Gemignani, 231. New York, NY: New York University Press, 2007.

Theological Education Fund Staff (TEF), ed. *Ministry in Context: The Third Mandate Programme of Voice 1970-77*. Bromley: TheTheological Education Fund, World Council of Churches (WCC), 1972.

Tienou, Tite. "Evangelical Theology in African Contexts." In *The Cambridge Companion in Evangelical Theology*, by Timothy Larsen and Daniel J. Treier, eds., 213-224. Cambridge: Cambridge University Press, 2007.

Tira, Sadiri Joy. "Kangaroo Church Birthing & Reproduction Model: A Case Study of Diaspora Missiology in Action in Canada." In *Mission Practice in the 21st Century*, by Enoh Wan and Sadiri Joy Tira, eds., 69-82. Pasadena, CA: William Carey International University Press, 2009.

Tira, Sadiri Joy and Narry Santos. "Diaspora Church Planting in a Multicultural City: A Case Study of Greenhills Christian Fellowship." In *Reflecting God's Glory Gogether: Diversity in Evangelical Mission*, by Scott A.

Moreau and Beth Snodderly, eds., 63-90. Pasadena, CA: William Carey Library, Evangelical Missiological Society Series, no. 19, 2011.

Tsing, Anna Lowenhaupt. *Friction: An Ethnography of Global Connection.* Princeton, NJ: Princeton University Press, 2005.

Turner, Harold. "Problems in the Study of African Independent Churches." *Numen*, 13:1, 1966: 26-42.

Tylor, Edward. *Researches into the Early History of Mankind and the Development of Civilization.* London: J Murray, 1871.

Ukah, Asonzeh Franklin-Kennedy. "Mobilities, Migration, and Multiplication: The Expansion of Religious Field of the Redeemed Christian Church of God, Nigeria." In *Religion in the Context of African Migration*, by Afe Adogame and Cordula Weisskoppel, eds., 317-341. Bayreuth: Eckhard Breitinger, 2005.

Van der Meulen, Marten. "The Continuing Importance of the Local: African Churches and the Search for Worship Space in Amsterdam." *African Diaspora*, 2, 2009: 159-181.

Van Dijk, Rijk. "From Camp to Encompassment: Discourses of Trans-subjectivity in the Ghanaian Pentecostal Diaspora." *Journal of Religion in Africa*, 27:2, 1997: 135-159.

Vasquez, Manuel A. "Historicizing and Materializing the Study of Religion: The Contribution of Migration Studies." In *Immigrant Faiths: Transforming Religious Life in America*, by Karen I. Leonard, et al., eds., 219-242. Lanham: AltaMira, 2005.

———. "Tracking Global Evangelical Christianity." *Journal of the American Academy of Religion*, 71:1, 2003: 157-173.

Vasquez, Manuel A. and Marie Fiedmann Marquardt. *Globalizing the Sacred: Religion Across the Americas.* New Brunswick, NJ: Rutgers University Press, 2003.

Vergara, Camilo Jose. *How the Other Half Worships.* New Brunswick, NJ: Rutgers University Press, 2005.

Vertovec, Steven. "Cheap Calls: The Social Glue of Migrant Transnationalism." *Global Networks*, 4:2, 2004: 219-224.

Wahrisch-Oblau, Claudia. *The Missionary Self-Perception of Pentecostal/Charismatic Church Leaders from the Global South in Europe.* Leiden: Brill, 2009.

Wakin, Daniel. "In New York, Gospel Resounds in African Tongues." *New York Times*, April 18, 2004: A-1, 32, 33.

Waldinger, R. "Did Manufacturing Matter? The Experience of Yesterday's Second Generation: A Reassessment." *International Migration Review,* 2007: 3-39.

Waliggo, Mary John. "The African Clan as the True Model of the African Church." In *The Church and Reconstruction of Africa: Theological Considerations,* by J. N. K. Mugambi, ed., 122-124. Nairobi: All African Conference of Churches, 1977.

Walls, Andrew F. *The Cross-Cultural Process in Christian History: Studies in Transmission and Appropriation of Faith.* New York, NY: Orbis, 2002.

———. "Migration and Evangelization: The Gospel and the Movement of Peoples in Modern Times." *Covenant Quarterly,* 63:1, 2005: 3-28.

———. "Mission and Migration: The Diaspora Factor in Christian History." *Journal of African Christian Thought,* 5:2, December, 2002: 3-11.

———. *The Missionary Movement in Christian History: Studies in the Transmission of the Faith.* Maryknoll, NY: Orbis Books, 1996.

———. "World Christianity and the Early Church." In *A New Day: Essays on World Christianity in Honor of Lamin Sanneh,* by Akintunde E. Akinade, ed., 17-30. New York, NY: Peter Lang, 2010.

Wan, Enoch, ed. "Diachronic Overview of Christian Missions to Diaspora Groups." In Enoch Wan, ed., *Diaspora Missiology: Theory, Methodology, and Practice.* Portland, OR: Institute of Diaspora Studies—USA, Western Seminary, 2011, 119-130.

———. *Diaspora Missiology: Theory, Methodology, and Practice.* Portland, OR: Institute of Diaspora Studies—USA, Western Seminary, 2011.

———. "Diaspora Mission Strategy in the Context of the United Kingdom in the 21st Century." *2010 Lausanne III Commemoration of the 1910 Missionary and Ecumenical Conference.* Cape Town, South Africa: Lausanne Documents, 2010.

———. "Diaspora Mission Strategy in the Context of the United Kingdom in the 21st Century." *Occasional Bulletin,* 2011.

———. "Evangelical Theology, Postmodernity, and Promise of Interdiscplinarity." *Journal of Global Missiology,* 2009: 1.

———. "Global People and Diaspora Missiology." In *Handbook: From Edinburgh 1910 to Tokyo 2010,* by Tom Houston, et al., eds., 92-100. Tokyo: Tokyo 2010 Organizing Committee, 2010.

———. "Interdisciplinary Research Methodology for Diaspora Missiology." In *Diaspora Missiology: Theory, Methodology, and Practice.* Portland, OR: Institute of Diaspora Studies—USA, Western Seminary, 2011, 107-115.

_____. "A Missio-Relational Reading of Romans." *Occasional Bulletin, EMS*, vol. 23, Winter, 2010: 1-8.

_____. *Missions Within Reach: International Ministries in Canada*. Kowloon, Hong Kong: China Alliance Press, 1995.

_____. "The Phenomenon of Diaspora: Missiological Implications for Christian Missions." In Luis Pantoja, et al., eds., *Scattered: The Filipino Global Presence*. Manila, Philippines: LifeChange Publishing Inc., 2004.

_____. "Relational Paradigm for Practicing Diaspora Missions in the 21st Century." In Enoch Wan, ed., *Diaspora Missiology: Theory, Methodology, and Practice*. Portland, OR: Institute of Diaspora Studies — USA, Western Seminary, 2011.

143-152.

_____. "Relational Theology and Missiology." In Enoch Wan and Sadiri Joy Tira, eds., *Missions Practice in the 21st Century*. Pasadena, CA: William Carey International University Press, 2009, 10-26.

Wan, Enoch and Sadiri Joy Tira. "Diaspora Missiology." In Enoch Wan and Sadiri Joy Tira, eds., *Missions Practice in the 21st Century*. Pasadena, CA: William Carey International University Press, 2009, 27-54.

Wan, Enoch and Yaw Attah Edu-Bekoe. "Diversity of the Ghanaian Diaspora in the USA: Ministering to the Ghanaian Communities Through Ghanaian Congregations." In *Reflecting God's Glory Together: Diversity in Evangelical Mission*, by Scott Moreau and Beth Snodderly, 35-62. Pasadena, CA: William Carey Library, Evangelical Missiological Society (EMS), no. 19, 2011.

Wan, Enoch and Galen Currah. "Ethical Issues in Conducting Missiological Field Research." Presentation to the EMS/CGL Annual Conference, September 17-19, 2009, Orlando, Florida.

Wan, Enoch and Sadiri Joy Tira, eds. *Missions Practice in the 21st Century*. Pasadena, CA: William Carey International University Press, 2009.

Wang, Chin (John) T. "Mission by the Immigrant Churches: What are They Doing?" In *Reflecting God's Glory Together: Diversity in Evangelical Mission* by Scott A. Moreau and Beth Snodderly, 21-34. Psadena, CA: William Carey Library, Evangleical Missiological Society (EMS) Series, no. 19, 2011.

Ward, Peter. *Liquid Church*. Carlisle: Paternoster, 2002.

Warikoo, Natasha. "Cosmopolitan Ethnicity: Second Generation Indo-Caribbean Identities." In *Becoming New Yorkers: Ethnographies of the Second Generation*, by Philip Kasinitz, et al. eds., 361-391. New York, NY: Russell Sage Foundation, 2004.

Warner, R. Stephen and Judith W. Wittner, eds. *Gatherings in Diaspora: Religious Communities and the New Immigration*. Philadelphia, PA: Temple University Press, 1998.

Waters, Joanna L. "Transnational Family Strategies and Education in the Contemporary Chinese Diaspora." *Global Networks*, 5:4, 2005: 359-377.

Weber, Max. *The Protestant Ethic and the Spirit of Capitalism*. London: Routledge, 2002 (1930).

Wendland R. Ernst and Jean-Claude Loba-Mkole. *Biblical Texts and African Audiences*, Nairobi, Kenya: Acton Publishers, 2004.

Wijsen, Frans and Robert Schreiter, eds. *Global Christianity: Contested Claims*. Amsterdam: Rodopi, 2007.

Williamson, Sydney George. *Akan Religion and the Christian Faith*. New York, NY: Orbis Books, 1965.

Winter, Ralph. "The Process of Mobilization." In *Mission Mobilizers Handbook*. Pasadena, CA: William Carey Library Publishers, 1996.

Winter, Ralph and Stephen C. Hawthorne, et al., eds. *Perspectives on the World Christian Movement: A Reader*. Pasadena, CA: William Carey Library, 2009.

Wolyniak, Dale. "Generational Diversity and Worldviews in Missions Today: A Study of the Millennial Generation." In *Reflection of God's Glory Together: Diversity in Evangelical Mission*, by Scott A. Moreau and Beth Snodderly, eds., 272-287. Pasadena, CA: William Carey Library, 2011.

Wright, Walter. *Mentoring: The Promise of Relational Leadership*. Bletchley, Milton Keynes, Bucks, UK: Paternoster Press, 2004.

Yang, Fenggang and Rose Ebaugh. "Transformation in New Immigrant Religions and Their Global Implictions." In American Sociological Review, vol. 66, no. 2, 2001.

Yeboah, Ian E. A. *Black African Neo-Diaspora: Ghanaian Immigrant Experiences in the Greater Cincinnati, Ohio, Area*. Lanham, MD: Lexington Books, Rowman & Littlefield Publishers, Inc, 2008.

Yoder, John Howard. *As You Go: The Old Mission in a New Day*. Scottdale, AZ: Herald Press, 1961.

Yong, Amos. *The Spirit Poured Out on All Flesh: Pentecostalism and the Possibility of Global Theology.* Grand Rapids, MI: Baker Academic, 2005.

Zachary, Lois J. *The Mentor's Guide: Facilitating Effective Learning Relationships.* San Francisco: Jossey-Bass, John Wiley & Sons, Inc., 2000.

Zukin, Sharon. *Naked City: The Death and Life of Authentic Urban Places.* New York, NY: Oxford University Press, 2010.

CPSIA information can be obtained
at www.ICGtesting.com
Printed in the USA
FFOW04n1343091115
18483FF